David Earle Anderson

Merlin House - 1988

Also by Martin Green

THE TRIUMPH OF PIERROT
CHILDREN OF THE SUN
THE VON RICHTHOFEN SISTERS

New York 1913

For more than a century, New York has served as a center for international communications. The city has become not merely a theater but a production, a multimedia presentation, whose audience is the whole world.

—MARSHALL BERMAN,
All That Is Solid Melts into Air

The rebel artists displayed equal enthusiasm for two important events of 1913: the exhibition of international art held in the New York Armory and the strike of the textile workers in Paterson, New Jersey.

—DANIEL AARON, *Writers on the Left*

New York 1913

The Armory Show

and the

Paterson Strike

Pageant

martin green

Charles Scribner's Sons

■ **New York**

Charles Scribner's Sons
Macmillan Publishing Company
866 Third Avenue, New York, NY 10022
Collier Macmillan Canada, Inc.

Permissions acknowledgments appear on page 325

Library of Congress Cataloging-in-Publication Data
Green, Martin Burgess, 1927–
    New York 1913: the Armory Show and the Paterson strike pageant/Martin Green.
        p.   cm.
    Bibliography: p.
    Includes index.
    ISBN 0-684-18993-3
    1. Armory Show (1913: New York, N.Y.)—History. 2. Art, Modern—19th century—Exhibitions. 3. Art, Modern—20th century—Exhibitions. 4. Silk Workers' Strike, Paterson, N.J., 1913—History. 5. Industrial Workers of the World—History—20th century. 6. Socialism and the arts—New York (N.Y.)—History—20th century. I. Title.
N6448.A74G76   1988
709'.04'10740147—dc19   88-11595   CIP

Macmillan books are available at special discounts for bulk purchases for sales promotions, premiums, fund-raising, or educational use. For details, contact:

    Special Sales Director
    Macmillan Publishing Company
    866 Third Avenue
    New York, NY 10022

10 9 8 7 6 5 4 3 2 1

Book Design by The Sarabande Press

Printed in the United States of America

This book is dedicated to the other members of the fine arts seminar on this subject, given at Tufts University in the spring of 1987.

Grateful acknowledgment is made to Eric Homberger and Edward T. Chase, who read the manuscript and corrected various errors.

Contents

1

Definitions

*There seems a vague but real relationship be-
tween all the real workers of our day. Whether
in literature, plastic art, the labor movement . . .
we find an instinct to blow up the old forms and
traditions, to dynamite the baked and hardened
earth so that fresh flowers can grow.*
        —HUTCHINS HAPGOOD, *New York Globe*,
                                    January 27, 1913

*It is the glory of the present age that in it one
can be young. Our times give no check to the
radical tendencies of youth.*
        —RANDOLPH BOURNE, *Youth and Life*,
                                    New York, 1913

■

*O*n February 17, 1913, an International Exhibition of Modern Art was opened at the armory of the Sixty-ninth Regiment on Lexington Avenue in New York. For a month automobiles drew up outside the armory, carrying famous names, ranging from ex-President Theodore Roosevelt to the newest intelligentsia, like Mabel Dodge, John Reed, and Walter Lippmann. The latter were the enthusiasts for this new art; the former defended the old values. Also present were the painters whose works were on exhibit, like John Sloan and John Marin and Francis Picabia, and would-be painters like Bill Sanger, earning a living as a draftsman with the fashionable architects McKim, Mead, and White, but yearning to get to Paris, to the holy land of art.

Inside the Armory, for the first time as far as most Americans went, including American art lovers, were heard those epochal names Picasso and Matisse and Braque; and the ideas of cubism, futurism, expressionism began to spread their special darkness of mind. Marcel Duchamp was established by *Nude Descending a Staircase* as a master conjuror and poser of conundrums; and Gertrude Stein, an impalpable but massive presence at the Armory, portended the spread of incomprehensibility from painting to literature and all the arts.

The Armory Show was a great media event, written about in every newspaper and at every level of sympathy and understanding, but it was primarily meant for the leisure class. And while it was going on, the political radicals of the city were preoccupied with the nearby strike of the textile workers of Paterson, New Jersey, which had begun in January and was being organized by the most radical union of the day, the Industrial Workers of the World. In the middle of March, when the Armory Show came to a triumphant close with dancing and singing, a flag day was declared in Paterson by the mill owners, who hoped to break the grip of the IWW by reviving other, national, loyalties.

On June 7, twelve hundred of the striking workers crossed over from New Jersey and marched up Fifth Avenue to Madison Square Garden, then one of McKim, Mead, and White's great buildings, and only a few blocks from the Armory. There they put on a pageant in which they depicted their sufferings and announced their demands before a capacity audience of fifteen or sixteen thousand. And who were the organizers of this so different event? Mabel Dodge and John Reed and Walter Lippmann and John Sloan. It was the same people. John Sloan's wife, Dolly, had worked for the IWW strike in Lawrence, Massachusetts, the year before; so had Bill Sanger's wife, Margaret. Far apart as the Show and the Pageant stood, they spoke the same metamessage to the same people. For at that moment in history, art and politics came together, and so people's hopes and fears came together also. Irony could be transcended, because it seemed that everything one wanted stood together at the end of a single perspective and everything one hated stood together in the opposite direction. Since then, people have looked back to that moment in envy.

This book is a study of these two events, the Armory Show and the Paterson Strike Pageant. The interest of both has often been remarked, and so has the interest of their conjunction in time and in what has been called, vaguely, spirit. If no one has put the two together to discuss them analytically, it is no doubt because it is hard to find the right point of view, the set of terms which apply equally and intimately to both at the same time. It would be dissatisfying to discuss the Strike and Pageant in terms that belong to the Show and aesthetics or to subject the Show and its pictures to a strictly political analysis.

The terms I am going to employ come from two sources. First, I use the language of theater by talking fairly consistently of those who reacted to the events as their audience; but that scarcely exceeds the bounds of ordinary usage. Second, I derive some terms from Susan Sontag's essay on "The Aesthetics of Silence." She there discusses modernist art primarily, but she uses a vocabulary alien to ordinary aesthetics. Her terms belong more to religion than to anything else. She says that, "Every era has to reinvent the project of 'spirituality' for itself."[1] She defines spirituality in various ways which converge on the idea of ultimate value, or a religious transcendence of "the world," and continues, "In the modern era, one of the most active metaphors for the spiritual project is 'art'. The activities of the painter, the musician, the poet, the dancer, once they were grouped together under that generic name (a relatively recent move) have proved a particularly adaptable site on which to stage the formal dramas be-setting consciousness . . .": these are, I take it, the dramas or crises of protest which express our need to transcend the ordinary conditions of life, the limited expectations and temperate temperatures with which we ordinarily pursue even artistic and intellectual concerns. Thus she sums up the history of modernism in three anecdotes, about Rimbaud, about Wittgenstein, and about Duchamp, who turned away from poetry, philosophy, and painting to gunrunning, hospital work, and chess, respectively. She calls this their choosing silence, as far as their talents went, and she goes on to make the choice of silence characterize much of modern art, saying that that choice has become "a major standard of seriousness in contemporary aesthetics." And thus, "Modern art's chronic habit of displeasing, provoking, or frus-trating its audience can be regarded as a limited, vicarious partici-pation in the ideal of silence . . ."[2]

This idea will probably recommend itself, without my needing to add anything, as a way to approach modernist art and thought. I will note only that this paradox—not the paradox of Sontag's formula, but the facts it explains—an enthusiasm for art that expresses itself in silence, creates special problems for me as the interpreter of these events. The spirit of 1913 was an enthusiasm for communication. At least that was what the public prophets announced and what their audience thought they were getting—more and livelier exchanges of new ideas and hopes and mutual help. (Mabel Dodge recommended the Armory Show in those terms.) But some of the ideas thus welcomed turned out to be unhopeful and unhelpful, or positively sardonic about art and politics. (In the case of the Show, we shall find, Marcel Duchamp's ideas are an example.) They led quite quickly to the dissolution of the spirit of 1913. To take care of that complexity, I

5

shall try to distinguish between the spirit of the times, so generous, hopeful, and experimental, and the ideas that spirit took up, but obviously that distinction can become tricky.

However, that difficulty I can postpone. For the moment I want to return to Sontag's idea of art as a metaphor for the spiritual project. I want to suggest that another such metaphor in modern times has been politics—at least radical, populist, politics, such as those that inspired the Paterson Strike. Has it not been by participating in such politics that many people of our century have achieved, at least ideally, the experience of transcending the limits of the individual self?

Take what Mary Heaton Vorse said about her experience at an IWW strike in 1912. "There at Lawrence it seemed sometimes as though the forces of Light and of Darkness were visibly divided."[3] Or what Elizabeth Gurley Flynn said about what the IWW did at Paterson: they educated and stimulated. "Stimulation in a strike means to make that strike, and through it the class struggle, their religion; to make them forget all about the fact that it is for a few cents or a few hours, but to make them feel it is a 'religious duty' for them to win that strike."[4] And in another place, "The only people whose names are recorded in history are those who did something. The peaceful and indifferent are forgotten; they never knew the fighting joy of living."[5]

We do not ordinarily think of the writing of history as the recording of transcendence, but of course democratic political historiography is just that, and Flynn is dealing in spiritual values as much as Duchamp in this remark of his, which takes us back to Sontag: "I believe that art is the only form of activity in which man as man shows himself to be a true individual. Only in art is he capable of going beyond the animal state, because art is an outlet toward regions which are not ruled by time and space."[6] This is strikingly similar to the 1890s aestheticism of Ralph Adams Cram: "I believe only in art . . . the ultimate expression of all that is spiritual, religious and divine in the soul of man. I hate material prosperity, I refuse to justify machinery, I cannot pardon public opinion. I desire absolute individuality and the triumph of idealism."[7] Duchamp's postmodernism was in many ways a revolt against such nineties aesthetic idealism, but not, as we see, in all ways.

If we understand spirituality or transcendence in this extended sense, we can apply it to many of those involved in one or the other of our two events, and we can say that the spirit of 1913 was an aspiration to transcend what most people accepted as ordinary and so inevitable. It was the ordinariness of capitalism and liberalism and class hierarchy, in the case of the IWW strike; and in the case of the Armory Show, it was old forms of art, appreciation, and beauty. But the radicals in both cases said no to certain "facts of life." One might even suggest that what they said no to was ultimately the same in both cases—in one important sense, it was ultimately the nineteenth-century bourgeois state as it had come to be seen by its intellectuals after the middle of the century and first of all in France. Of course the revolt against academic art was often remote from the revolt against factory wages and discipline, and I don't want to melt down those differences, but I suggest nevertheless that there was a connection, and one which was strongly felt in New York in 1913.

Everyone must agree at least that modernism and revolution are both forms of nay-saying: they deny what is and has been in the name of what should be; and therefore both are forms of spirituality. More exactly, they *can* be forms of spirituality, when their partisans are intense enough in their enthusiasm and large enough in their views. It is not appropriate to use such language about artists and politicians, however modern and radical, when they are concerning themselves, as they often must, with questions of technique, or of individual prestige, or of sectarian advantage. The same is true, after all, of people of religion, when they are absorbed in credal definitions, or ecclesiastical organization, or personal ambition. Spirituality can be attributed only to *certain* phases of their lives.

Moreover, one should note that Sontag calls art only a metaphor for the spiritual project; and that is all I claim for politics. And even when one *can* call them both—metaphorically—spiritual, one certainly should not suggest that they are the same *kind* of spirituality. Looking back to the remarks of Flynn and Duchamp, one sees that the first is talking about a group and an action, the second about individuals and contemplation. In Hindu terms, the first is *karmayoga* spirituality, like Gandhi's, the second *jnanayoga*, like the hermit saints'.

7

Many such differences will appear as my narration proceeds. Nevertheless, these are the terms I am going to use because they allow me to align the two subjects in a single though complex pattern. Thus I escape the clumsiness that each one's proper language has when applied to the other, and also the aridity each point of view inflicts when adhered to rigidly; in other words, I can write a richer and more material history.

2

T H E
Show, the Pageant, and the Audience

Avant-garde has become a cliché today, but in the early years between 1908 and 1918, a shock brigade, a small group of artists, had to penetrate into unknown territory, a country full of hostile inhabitants (the bourgeoisie). Armed with nothing but their imaginations, they were fired by an immense courage.
—HERBERT READ, on dada

The Science of Revolutionary Warfare—A Marvel of Instruction in the Use and Preparation of Nitroglycerine, Dynamite, Gun-Cotton, Fulminating Mercury, Bombs, Fuses, Poisons, Etc., Etc.
—JOHANN MOST, c. 1884

Is it not much better to even die fighting for something than to have lived an uneventful life, never gotten anything, and leaving conditions the same, or worse than they were and to have future generations go through the same misery and poverty and degradation?
—ELIZABETH GURLEY FLYNN, 1917

■

*I*n New York City, then, in 1913, these two events occurred almost simultaneously and involved many of the same people. The one event belongs now to the history of art, the other to the history of labor, but they then had the same significance, of being "radical," and they were aimed at the same primary audience. That is, though they appealed ultimately to different and very large groups, one covering the whole national labor movement, the other the international art world, immediately they both appealed to the people we call Greenwich Village. This audience of intellectuals in fact applauded both events enthusiastically, and that applause marked the climax of a pre-1914 radicalism, a climate of strong hopes for a change for the better in all things. If by now they seem disparate and disconnected events, that is because we have lost touch with those hopes. Putting the two side by side again can illuminate a whole vista of history.

The decade of which 1913 was the midpoint was historically important because it saw the development (and then the defeat) of a comparable enthusiasm quite generally in America. A phrase popular at the time was "a new renaissance"; America (and Europe too) then felt itself on the brink of a renaissance like that which had begun in Italy four hundred years earlier. Walter Pach said that Paris in 1913 was like Florence then.[1] Katherine Dreier wrote about Marcel Duchamp as the modern Leonardo, already in 1919. These were aesthetes, but another man associated with the renaissance idea was Theodore Roosevelt, a name which suggests the all-American energy, the love of progress, the optimism, the bursting free from outworn bonds, which *renaissance* primarily meant. (The slogan of course suggested every good to those it convinced, but primarily it meant freedom rather than order, duty, or social justice.)

Another powerful expression of the renaissance idea was the renaissance style in architecture, particularly associated with the firm of McKim, Mead, and White. In the first decade of the twentieth century there were new and splendid buildings designed by them everywhere in New York; buildings embodying the nation's new wealth and power and explicitly associated with the original Renaissance. In an article about McKim, Mead, and White in *The Architectural Record* in 1906, Henry W. Desmond described that renaissance as marked by a renewal of faith in mankind and a celebration of man's creative power: the architecture of that time and place (Renaissance Italy) gave that society the setting it needed to renew humanism, and McKim, Mead, and White were doing the same for twentieth-century America.[2]

It has been said that in 1900 three structures dominated New York: the Statue of Liberty, the Brooklyn Bridge, and Madison Square Garden.[3] Of these, the last was the work of McKim, Mead, and White. (The bridge, being a piece of engineering, aroused the enthusiasm of modernists like Duchamp, who could not be expected to like the Garden; the statue belonged to a different genre, which we needn't discuss here.) The Garden was erected in 1887; it contained the only amphitheater in the city, and its tower—the second tallest in the city—was decorated with Spanish Renaissance motifs and fleurs-de-lys, popular in the Renaissance as emblems of the joy of life. Even the fact that White went to live in the tower and was murdered in the roof garden by a husband he was cuckolding added to the renaissance idea. For this story, the building is an important one, because it was there that the Paterson Pageant was staged.

From our point of view, the idea of an American renaissance belongs primarily to the Progressive movement, while the spirit of 1913 was radical. But then radicalism can be considered a reaction within progressivism, as well as against it. These distinctions will become clear as the story proceeds, and to begin with we can allow the two ideas to blend into each other and talk almost indifferently of either the renaissance or the 1913 idea.

A book which spread this hope at the beginning of the 1913 decade was Van Wyck Brooks's *Wine of the Puritans* (1908). This was written for intellectual readers, it did not use the slogans discussed, and it spent its energies in criticizing what existed rather than in announcing better things to come, but still it told Americans how easily they could burst their chains. It begins with Brooks in Italy debating with a friend about why they are in voluntary exile—why they find in Italy what they miss at home, which is a depth and freshness in nature, including human nature. This is not a problem important only to themselves, and soon everyone would face it, for the whole world seemed to have decided to be like America. From where the two young men sit, they see "another shipload of Italians going to take our places at home."[4]

Brooks answers his own question by describing America as a Puritan culture: which means that it was founded by full-grown, modern, self-conscious men who had uprooted themselves culturally and made themselves over, consciously and conscientiously. Despite their religious creed, the Pilgrim fathers were materialists, because they justified themselves by a work ethic. Their descendants have been enormously successful in material enterprises, but not in other forms of life; they have suspected emotion and ritual and even their own pleasures and lightheartedness.[5] They are afraid of both art and nature, so their taste in both is feeble (a similar diagnosis advanced in 1911 was given currency by Santayana's phrase, the genteel tradition). They really worship work, and their great hero is the grotesque John D. Rockefeller, a man who ought never to have lived. Italy attracts Brooks and his friend because there, whatever the poverty and backwardness, people are capable of passion and gaiety, being not yet gripped by work compulsions and love inhibitions.

This cultural analysis gives a picture of the American almost the opposite of tradition, where the American appeared as an innocent Adam, the youngest son of history, intimate with Nature, and a hero of adventures. But this new idea, based on a philosophy that made erotic values central, was to become very influential. It was to be employed by E. M. Forster, comparing Italy with England, and a little later by D. H. Lawrence (he applied it also to America, in *Studies in Classic American Literature*). At least up to the outbreak of war in 1914, this diagnosis always carried the implicit promise of

13

a cure, a renaissance; because the wrong could so easily be put right by a change of consciousness. Within it, the Puritans played the role the monks had in the other renaissance: they are the agents of fear, scruple, self-hatred—psychic darkness—which they inflict on the rest of society. Once their spell is broken, even sensitive Americans will be able to join their extrovert brothers in patriotic pride and the national expansion. Of course, it was supposed that such expansion would be unlike the old philistine, Rockefeller kind—would be a matter of idealism, not fortune building.

Brooks announces the change as imminent. "Nowadays," New England, the site of Puritan culture, can no longer impose its patterns on the rest of America. Not that he is interested in the West or the frontiersman culture; and though he praises the South for not being Puritan, he does not dare so to break with tradition as to make it a model. What he recommends is Italy and—so far as literature goes —England. Positively, Brooks's idea is potbound by the traditions of the elite institutions he belonged to. Negatively, however, it was a clear summons to a change, and in the direction of a renaissance.

Brooks was moreover allied to many forces and figures moving in the same direction. Three of these turn up later in this narrative. The first is Percy MacKaye, who founded the pageant movement in America—reopening the playhouse doors closed by the Puritans, he said. This brought political concerns together with aesthetic ones, for these pageants were designed to generate civic and national pride, and were aimed particularly at immigrants, who needed to see the national legends and symbols brought to life. MacKaye was, as we shall see, allied with leading political figures.

The second is John Collier, later federal commissioner for the Indians, but in this decade much concerned with pageants of MacKaye's kind. From 1908 Collier worked at the People's Institute at the Cooper Union, founded by Charles Sprague-Smith, for the benefit of the working class and recent immigrants. Sprague-Smith had been professor of comparative literature at Columbia University and was an enthusiast for the Icelandic sagas and William Morris's modern versions of them. He founded the institute to help the workers help themselves to acquire the independence of the saga folk. Collier worked on community values and community renewal all his life. He was a friend of Mabel Dodge, who awakened his interest in the Indians, and he brought Emma Goldman to Dodge's salon for the first time.

The third is Katherine Dreier, who founded the Cooperative Mural Workshops in 1913, "a late entry in the American Arts and Crafts movement".[6] This owed much to the art-and-culture ideas of Ruskin and Morris, transmitted via Oscar Wilde and Roger Fry (the latter's Omega Workshops in London were one of Dreier's models). Murals were a kind of visual arts equivalent of pageants: a new kind of public art, dedicated to cultural renewal. The workshops were host to Isadora Duncan in 1914, when it was hoped that she would teach the working girls of New York City how to move and dance, and Collier (who was involved in the scheme) had long been a passionate admirer of Duncan's. One of his poems compared her to Haggard's immortal Ayesha, "Bathed in a pillar of fire no tongue hath told."[7] Duncan was, as we shall see, another of the emblems of the American renaissance; and incongruous as she may seem with Theodore Roosevelt, some people admired both equally, and most enthusiasts for the renaissance admired either the one or the other.

These four people, Brooks, MacKaye, Collier, Dreier (and the other names mentioned, Roosevelt, Dodge, Hapgood) were not personally close to one another, but they belonged to the same class. This was a class to be defined in cultural terms—as those who feel themselves responsible for the quality of life of the whole society—better than in economic or political terms. Nearly everyone we shall meet in this story belonged to that class, but the two events we are concerned with aimed themselves at Greenwich Village, an audience certainly within that class but more narrowly definable and seeing itself as more radical. It is that audience we must concentrate on first.

This was Greenwich Village's heroic age; Edmund Wilson named it so in *I Thought of Daisy*; he and other latecomers looked back to the Village in 1913 with awe. It had been a place of refuge and recruitment for all those at war with the mainstream of American culture. Its inhabitants were typically rebels, against either artistic or political or sexual conventions. They included young people who had felt stifled in the small towns of their birth (conventionally located in the Midwest, but actually to be found in New England and the

South just as often). They included also refugees not from the narrow culture of the small town, but from the rich suburbs and the Ivy League colleges. (If Sherwood Anderson the novelist more famously represented the first class, Van Wyck Brooks the critic just as rightfully represented the second.) It also included immigrants from Europe, typically from Italy, who worked as maids and cooks and waiters in the Village.

In *I Thought of Daisy* the protagonist (clearly Wilson himself) looks at the Village streets and says, "There they had come, those heroes of my youth, the artists and the prophets of the Village, from the American factories and farms, from the farthest towns and prairies . . . there they had lived with their own imaginations and followed their own thought . . ."[8] It is a state of mind, indeed of the soul, which he aspires toward, and finally gains access to by an act of grace. "Now the Village was at last revealed to me; it had that day come alive about me, and I felt myself part of its life. I, like them, had turned my back on all that world of mediocre aims and prosaic compromises; and at that price—what brave spirit would not pay it?—I had been set free to follow poetry!"[9] The language is somewhat overheated and literary, but the irony is only superficial; we are in fact being offered an affirmation of faith by the next generation of American intellectuals.

This area of New York City, centered on Washington Square, had fairly recently become a residence for writers and artists. Originally a Dutch West Indies Company plantation, it was later named Greenwich by an English naval officer. By mid-century, wealthy families were building Greek Revival houses around the square and along lower Fifth Avenue. At the end of the century artists began converting their stables into studios, and writers moved there—Stephen Crane, for instance. The area had a village atmosphere, because of its quiet and crooked side streets, like Milligan Place and Minetta Lane. Rents were cheap; a room could be had for eight to twelve dollars a month.

It was the Ninth Ward of Manhattan, called the American Ward in 1875 because it then had a smaller proportion of foreign-born residents than any other. It had not been affected by the general expansion of the city, because its sets of diagonal streets blocked the through avenues.[10] But gradually tenements were erected (on the waterfront and in the black quarter) and immigrants poured in, mainly from Italy. After 1900 came a wave of southern Italians and Sicilians, who seemed to resist Americanization. The America they saw around them in their neighbors (the Irish, already established in city politics) seemed brutal and corrupt by comparison with the official rhetoric, and they kept their faith in the culture they had brought with them.

Land values fell, and for a while industry moved into the ward, but only up to about 1912. A few old families had continued to live around Washington Square (created in 1827), and they constituted a social nucleus around which a reclaimed residential district could form—as was not true on the East Side, which was in other ways similar.[11] In 1902 two settlement houses were established, which brought with them intellectuals, some of whom settled in the district after their settlement work was done.

The two social worlds, that of the immigrants and that of the artist-intellectuals—the Ninth Ward and Greenwich Village—did not mix.[12] The former seemed to the latter to care nothing for ideas or education or reform, while the Villagers seemed to their neighbors, Italian or Irish, to spend recklessly, to eat meagerly, and to live loosely—the free women of the Village turned the whole quarter into a disorderly house.

The cost of living in general was low. A meal could be bought for from sixty cents to a dollar at Polly's, Mother Bertolotti's, the Pepper Pot, or the Dutch Oven.[13] There were also the tearooms like the Mad Hatter, which had wooden tables and candlelight. (Candles were one of the Village's gentlest symbols of cultural revolt.[14]) More expensive were the Lafayette and the Hotel Brevoort; more earthy the Hell Hole at Sixth Avenue and Fourth Street, where you could see gangsters, prostitutes, longshoremen, and gamblers. Eugene O'Neill found material for his plays here, Dorothy Day for her journalism, and John Sloan and Charles Demuth drew nostalgic pictures of it.

The Hell Hole (officially the Golden Swan) has been described by Arthur and Barbara Gelb in their biography of Eugene O'Neill. "The Hell Hole was a representative Irish saloon. It had a sawdust-covered floor and rude wooden tables, and was filled with the smell of sour beer and mingled sounds of alcoholic woe and laughter. Its barroom was entered from the corner of Sixth Avenue and Fourth Street—the 'front room,' in which women were not allowed. Above the doorway swung a wooden sign decorated with a tarnished gilt swan. Farther east, on Fourth Street, was the 'family entrance,' a glass door that gave access to a small, dank, gaslit chamber known as the 'back room.' Wooden tables clustered about a smoking potbellied stove, and it was here that respectable Irish widows came to cry into their five-cent mugs of beer."[15]

There were intellectual salons, of which Mabel Dodge's deserves a fuller description, but she had rivals such as William and Marguerite Zorach's apartment on Sixth Avenue and Tenth Street, decorated in stark colors and with murals on the wall; and Bill and Margaret Sanger's; and Alyse Gregory's flat on Milligan Street, where Randolph Bourne brought his colleagues from the magazine, *Seven Arts*. These belonged more to the Village than did Mrs. Dodge's Evenings, but the latter expressed the Village's idea in extravagant or fairy-tale terms.

Of the more official institutions, I should mention the Liberal Club, which moved from Nineteenth Street to 137 MacDougal Street in 1913. It then became the famous institution that is remembered. It had been under the control of progressives and philanthropists, but under the leadership of Henrietta Rodman, spokesperson for free love, the radicals took over. Its members included many famous journalists: John Reed, Susan Glaspell, Floyd Dell, Hutchins Hapgood, Mary Heaton Vorse. There Bill Haywood talked about socialism, Horace Traubel reminisced about Whitman, Vachel Lindsay recited *The Congo*. Moreover, the club held annual fund-raising balls, called pagan routs, and there were comparable affairs given by radical magazines like *Rogue*, *The Masses*, and *Mother Earth* (this last, Emma Goldman's anarchist magazine).

Of them all, Max Eastman's *The Masses* was the quintessential Village magazine. It was politically radical and a loyal supporter of the IWW, and it blended art values with political ones. Thus one of the editors, Floyd Dell, wrote two articles on Chicago's literary shrines, in this year of 1913, in which he named the Haymarket as one of those shrines—on the grounds of the famous "riot" of 1886, the subsequent indictment of anarchists, and the agitation on behalf of the accused. This agitation undeniably involved many writers, but to cite the Haymarket itself as a literary shrine was to define literature in a very political way.[16]

Arturo Giovannitti, one of the IWW's leaders, called *The Masses* "the recording secretary of the Revolution in the making."[17] Less grandly, but just as fondly, Irving Howe has called it "a slapdash gathering of energy, youth, hope,"[18] and part of its character was to be an enterprise of privileged youth. The writers were paid, but the artists not, even though most critics, looking back, value the latter the more highly in aesthetic terms. The money to produce it was raised by Max Eastman, largely from respectable patrons like Samuel Untermeyer, a lawyer, Adolph Lewisohn, a copper king, E. W. Scripps, and Amos Pinchot. Its politics were seen as too tame by the anarchists; and its sympathies were indeed socialist, and, within socialism, owed more to Wells than to Marx.

Its literary taste was by comparison with modernism conservative. It published Sherwood Anderson and Carl Sandburg, but not T. S. Eliot or Pound or Joyce. Dell wrote to a friend, "I do not understand the new ideas about form."[19] In religious matters it was anticlerical, interpreting the Christian churches as a betrayal of the socialism of Comrade Jesus; and politically it seemed, like the editors' mentor H. G. Wells, most committed in quasi-political areas like the liberation of sexuality. The editors were feminists, but their feminism was significantly unlike that of most progressive reformers, who wanted—as a high priority—to eliminate prostitution and sanitize dance halls and end all "cheap romance."[20] The reformers were, comparatively speaking, sexual puritans. By contrast the radicals, in Dell's phrase, wanted woman to become man's Glorious Playfellow,[21] which meant, he admitted, that this form of feminism tended to express itself primarily as free love. A favorite text was Edward Carpenter's *Love's Coming of Age*.[22] This made them seem irresponsible in the eyes of some women feminists and some political radicals. Speaking from his political conscience later, Dell admitted that early twentieth-century literature had influenced them by its "unconsciously adroit emphasis upon the incidental beauty of the essentially homeless and childless and migratory life to which capitalism had largely condemned us"; he even acknowledged that Kipling was one of the chief begetters of their romanticism, shaming as it was for a group of left-wing radicals to acknowledge his influence.[23]

No doubt the magazine's most striking feature was its blending together of values, political and aesthetic. The spirit of 1913 was a glee in connecting disparate things. "For *The Masses*, beauty and the revolution were the same thing, or rather parts of the same thing. The Revolution was beautiful, and beauty was revolutionary."[24] Hence the stress on adventure, found in both Kipling and Wells, Tory and socialist: adventure eludes categories, inviting us simply to *live* more.

In literary taste this worked out to mean an enthusiasm for spirit and a distrust of form. We see this in *The Masses'* answer to the English man of letters, Edmund Gosse, who had talked of the language needing to be renewed. *The Masses* said, "We think it is not the language, but Edmund Gosse and all the other library poets that are worn out . . . [Great poetry] will be written by persons who are innocent of the smell of old books. Let Edmund Gosse . . . go down to the street, and out into the fields and quarries and among the ships and chimneys, the smoke and glory of living reality in his own time . . . Poets are the lovers of the adventure of life."[25] But it was not only traditional men of letters like Gosse who talked of the language's needing renewal. It was also modernists like Gertrude Stein. So *The Masses* was old-fashioned by avant-garde standards. The modernist enthusiasm for research and experiment in form disturbed the magazine's editors because it expressed an opposite spirit. In poetry, for instance, Eastman liked to find meter and rhyme. The magazine's artwork was more innovative: they reproduced by linecuts and used very short captions; in layout, they separated the advertisements from the reading matter and spread an illustration over two pages. But still their artists were typically New York realists like John Sloan—certainly not modernists like Marcel Duchamp, who was, as a result of the Armory Show's success, to make Sloan seem old-fashioned. The spirit of 1913 was to be subverted by some of the new ideas it on principle encouraged. Recommended generously, as forms of new life, these ideas turned out to be ungenerous themselves—suspicious, cynical, and exclusivist.

The strength and the weakness of *The Masses* is shown by Lincoln

Steffens's remark about John Reed (perhaps the magazine's most important single "discovery" in literature). "When John Reed came, big and growing, handsome outside and beautiful inside, when that boy came down from Cambridge to New York, it seemed to me that I had never seen anything so near to pure joy . . . If only we could keep him so, we might have a poet at last who would see and sing nothing but joy. Convictions were what I was afraid of."[26] We honor the honesty with which this group named their heroes and their values; but it was obviously very dangerous for any intellectual group to be so afraid of convictions, and for any aesthetic group to rely so heavily on "joy," and "singing."

At the time, however, and seen in their attacks on conservative institutions, *The Masses* and Greenwich Village seemed recklessly radical. As Arthur Wertheim says, being a Villager gave one an identity, a state of mind, and a defiant relation to society.[27] The Village lived in perpetual secession from the rest of the country. On the evening of January 23, 1917, six people climbed the Washington Square Arch and proclaimed the Village an independent republic. They held a picnic and a bonfire there, and hung Chinese lanterns and red balloons; and, accompanied by the firing of toy pistols, Gertrude Smith, a painting pupil of John Sloan's, read aloud a declaration of independence. This is a very resonant anecdote. Edmund Wilson retells it in his play about the Village and the Provincetown Players.

However, the Village is important to us perhaps less for its radical sympathies than for its intent concern with reading the signs of the times, taking the social pulse. Our two events, the Armory Show and the Paterson Pageant, offered themselves as such signs and presented themselves for such diagnoses. To some extent they were created to be read in that way, and—to that extent—they were exhausted once so read. To exaggerate the point, they were a phenomenon of daily journalism. Another way, therefore, to suggest their audience is to describe a group of journalists who were very influential at the time. In many ways, these people spoke for the Village; they were the *Village Voice* of their time; it was through them, for instance, that Mabel Dodge met the very various people she brought together.

Richard Hofstadter says, in *The Age of Reform*, "To an extraordinary degree, the work of the Progressive movement rested upon its journalism . . . It is hardly an exaggeration to say that the Progressive mind was characteristically a journalistic mind."[28] The mood of 1913 is not strictly to be called Progressive, as it was in reaction against progressivism—the Village's slogan was Radicalism; but it was recognizably a development from the earlier idea, and in the same minds. Lincoln Steffens, the supreme muckraker and Progressive, was also a central figure in 1913 radicalism.

Steffens coined that ubiquitous and multipurpose phrase "the system" during his first years as a muckraker. It originally meant a collaboration between government (at any of several levels) and business and crime. But it came to mean all that opposes the creative individual, and in that meaning the phrase belongs to 1913 radicalism. Creativity and youth were essential slogans of the Village, which thus felt itself to be traditionally American in the spirit. After all, even *Mayflower* Americans had always thought they were or had been against the system. And it is worth remembering that Mark Twain was addressed by his wife as "Youth," and Max Eastman regarded himself as one of Twain's children. Thus Steffens married a girl one third his age, and had his first child at the age of fifty-eight, and he was a friend and adviser to Theodore Roosevelt, the emblem of young manhood in politics.

Steffens more than anyone else invented the new journalism. When he joined the New York *Commercial Advertiser* in 1897, he had determined to change the paper and to create a new kind of newspaper writing. He hired new reporters and charged them to "see a murder as a tragedy rather than as a crime, a fire as a drama rather than as police news,"[29] and so on. These new journalists were mostly recent graduates from Harvard or some other Ivy League college; they aspired ultimately to write "literature"—it was one of their favorite words; and they loved the big city with a feverish passion. But their sense of privilege blended with radical sympathies. It was the Lower East Side, for instance the Yiddish theater there, which fascinated them in New York; and it was corrupt Tammany politicians, rather than moralistic reformers, who stirred their minds and warmed their hearts.

Two of them were Norman and Hutchins Hapgood. Their origins and life stories fitted the pattern for new journalists. They had grown up in a midwestern small town, Alton, Illinois, which remained the symbol of deadly dullness for them. At Harvard they, their brother, and their parents had entered the circle of William James and acquired his philosophy of change and experiment and dissent. (Max Eastman, the editor of *The Masses*, had a similar relation to the other great American pragmatist, John Dewey.) James's remark, "I cannot understand this wild swooning desire to wallow in unbridled unity," could have been a slogan for them—indeed a motto for all Greenwich Village.[30]

Of the two brothers, the more important for us was Hutchins, partly because of the way he, in the years before 1913, differed from Steffens; he therefore suggests the stress that differentiates the radicals from the progressives. He was less interested in power and politics than Steffens, more in art and eroticism. He took more interest in the Bohemian life of the unrespectable, including petty criminals. He wrote, for instance, *The Autobiography of a Thief*, transcribing for respectable readers a pickpocket's own account of his life in 1903. He had, from before 1900, two friends who inducted him into that life: "Josiah Flynt" Willard (he wrote under the name of Josiah Flynt) and Alfred Hodder. Willard was a figure of dark brooding and cynicism; he knew the world of tramps and loved it intensely, though ambivalently. Hodder was at the center of a famous sex scandal at Bryn Mawr, about which Gertrude Stein wrote an early novel. He and Willard cowrote a book called *Powers That Prey*. They fostered a complex irony in Hapgood, saying for instance that "the puritan idealist and the 'practical politician' are confederates in a game to defraud the public."[31] They taught him to prefer—as being more human—Tammany ward-heelers to WASP reformers, and he taught the reading public the same lesson. This turn of sympathy away from reform was a crucial step toward complexity as a value, and so a step toward literature and away from politics (of any practical kind).

Another mark of this 1913 kind of radicalism was its stress on spontaneity, originality, innocence. In 1892 Hutchins Hapgood delivered a commencement address at Harvard entitled "The Student as Child," claiming that childishness was a most valuable quality, and that if higher education renounced it, education would become a narrow vocationalism. Hapgood held on all his life to the childlike qualities of curiosity, enthusiasm, and eagerness for new experience, and the other Villagers believed in doing that. Art Young, cartoonist for *The Masses*, writes in his autobiography at the age of sixty, "I felt then, and still feel, that I belong with youth . . ."[32] (As a boy, he says, he found his father always solemn, and vowed himself always to take some enjoyment in life.) Hapgood described himself, complacently, as being like Melville's character Pierre: "no limitations, in a way no personality; tumultuous humanness . . . in some unspeakable way revealing the divine source from which all life springs."[33]

This group of new journalists had considerable influence at least in New York. It was closely related to the muckraker group, via Steffens. Working at the *Commercial Advertiser* were Steffens himself, who later wrote for *McClure's*, *The American*, and *Everybody's*; Norman Hapgood, who later wrote for *Collier's*; Carl Hovey, later editor of *The Metropolitan*; and Abraham Cahan, editor of *The Jewish Daily Forward*.

A similar and equally significant figure was *The Masses'* Max Eastman, ideologically most interesting, perhaps, for his feminism. The first person he names in his *Heroes I Have Known* is his mother, who was the first woman Congregationalist minister. (Later heroes included John Dewey, John Reed, and Trotsky.) One of Eastman's first acts in public life was to organize the Men's League for Women's Suffrage; and his assistant editor at *The Masses*, Floyd Dell's first book was *Women as World Builders* (1913). The causes of women's liberation and erotic liberation were always important to *The Masses*. Eastman's mother seems to have held to no Christian theology; she defined God as joy, and believed primarily in joy and growth.[34] She was ordained by a religious radical, Thomas K. Beecher, who later invited her to join him as pastor at the church in Elmira, New York, where Mark Twain and his wife's family, the Langdons, worshipped. Eastman thus knew Twain as a boy, and felt himself his heir—though he was equally the heir of Whitman. Twain and Beecher were, he says, the twin stars of his boyhood.[35] His father read the funeral services (written by Mrs. Eastman) for both Mrs. Clemens and Twain himself. It is therefore not surprising that Eastman made *The Masses* "a laughing and singing institution"—too much so, he admitted, for it to seem authentically revolutionary to a Russian Bolshevik. (The IWW too was a singing and laughing institution, and it too came to seem inauthentic next to Russian communism.) But humor was what Eastman believed in: humor is always on the side of the self against submission, he says, and of liberty against discipline.[36] It is on the side of the earth—which is of course where Eastman stands, with earth against heaven. No man ever ascended into heaven amid laughter, so laughter is a valuable spiritual prophylactic.[37]

Another 1913 radical was Margaret Sanger, remembered today as the propagandist for birth control, but then thought of as being quite generally political; her first birth control clinic was opened in 1916. As she says in her autobiography, "Radicalism in manners, art, industry, morals, politics, was effervescing, and the lid was about to blow off in the Great War . . ."[38] A religion without a name was spreading over the country . . . Almost without knowing it you became a comrade."[39] She seems to have joined the IWW in 1912, and certainly played a prominent part in both the Lawrence strike of that year and the Paterson Strike of 1913. Her husband was the draftsman at McKim, Mead, and White who yearned to go to Paris to become a modernist painter. He went again and again to see the Armory Show, and when it closed, both John Sloan and John Marin gave him pictures they had exhibited there. Thus between them the Sangers were oriented to both our events.

The relation of those events and causes to that other cause which Margaret Sanger took up was strong, but complex. It was shortly after 1913 when, sharing in a general disillusionment with that radicalism, she began to devote all her energies to free love and birth control in the name of nature. She got contributions from Mabel Dodge, among others, to a journal she began, called *Woman Rebel*. In her private journal for 1914 she wrote, "Emotion is that which urges from within, without consciousness of fear or fear of consciousness."[40] Put like that, this was a received truth, throughout the Village. But it signified a path of action down which her husband could not follow her. He wrote her, "Do you know how this last year [1913] has impressed me? That the so-called Labor Revolutionary Movement is not noble but an excuse for a Saturnalia of sex."[41]

Of all these journalists, Hutchins Hapgood was the most important to us, because of his own work and because of his close relations with Mabel Dodge. (Steffens was also a trusted adviser of hers.) A good example of Hapgood's writing is *The Spirit of the Ghetto*, a collection of essays about the Lower East Side of the city, written between 1898 and 1902 for *The Commercial Advertiser*, *The Atlantic Monthly*, and other magazines. (Until 1914, Hapgood composed three or four five-hundred-word "sketches" every week.) He was one of the first to draw public attention to the Lower East Side, which was just beginning to fascinate writers and artists. Hapgood wrote with the collaboration of Abraham Cahan, and for the first part of the book, of Jacob Epstein. Jerome Myers (one of the prime movers of the Armory Show) had discovered the East Side for painting as early as 1887, but the first exhibit of such paintings was not held until 1912. (It included several New York painters who also showed in the Armory Show.)

Irving Howe says that Hapgood was the one American writer who yielded himself imaginatively to the world of the immigrants—freely, happily, with fraternal ease.[42] An interesting contrast was Jacob Riis, a progressive journalist who brought the Lower East Side and its problems to public attention, but whose *sympathies* seemed to remain with establishment America. Moses Rischin says that Hapgood "probed the moral fabric of American society with the candor, courage, dedication, and emotional range that . . . justified his vision of himself as a social artist."[43] This was true of other new journalists in some degree, and it was they who recorded, and even inspired, the two events we are concerned with. With the cooperation of Mabel Dodge, they were able to make important things happen in New York in 1913.

It was partly coincidence that brought these lives together in this place and time; but the pattern of coincidence was too strong to be pure accident. For instance, in 1911 Steffens's wife had died, and her death was followed by that of his parents, so that a whole phase of his life (in journalism, the muckraking phase) seemed ended. He came to live in Greenwich Village, moving into the building where John Reed and his Harvard friends were already living, a building and group Reed made famous in a farcical poem, "A Day in Bohemia." As Hapgood turned from the Bowery and the bums, so did Steffens turn from Theodore Roosevelt and muckraking, and for both the new direction was emblematized by Mabel Dodge and radicalism.

This was an important new word, which defined itself in opposition to liberalism. These two men had been well known as liberals and progressives, of course; but Hapgood wrote, "It is only the radical mind . . . that sees the dangers and weaknesses of the progressive movement."[44] He had pointed out in 1907 already, in *The Spirit of Labor*, that radicalism was the word of the hour. What it meant is suggested by his criticism of Walter Lippmann, the archetypal liberal: Hapgood wrote Mabel that the bums of the Bowery were another way God manifested himself, but that he did not manifest himself in Walter Lippmann.[45] Radicals were looking for something at the root of life —in the unconscious—while liberals seemed to them wholly conscious. Radicalism also meant, of course, a sympathy with far left political groups, above all the Wobblies, but also the anarchists and others. In 1912 Hapgood wrote a preface to Alexander Berkman's *Prison Memoirs of an Anarchist*, which included the story of Berkman's attempted assassination of Henry Frick.

Their politicism was, however, literary in the bad sense as well as the good. Hapgood's wife, the journalist and novelist, Neith Boyce, declared *his* political ideas no more important in real life than "a bunch of red and blue balloons."[46] Perhaps an example of what she meant is that in 1912 he supported Theodore Roosevelt's candidacy for the presidency because he represented intuitive understanding, while Woodrow Wilson represented precise intelligence. Red and blue balloons were signs of literature and the Village, like candles.

Mabel Dodge wrote Hapgood in 1926 that he had really created her salon, because he had given her a sense of renewed life when she arrived in New York. (In 1913 her Tagore-like poem about Hapgood, "My Beloved," appeared in Emma Goldman's *Mother Earth*.) On the other hand, it was Lincoln Steffens who told her to begin her soirees. In any case, there can be no competition between the two; they were twin manifestations of the same spirit.

So much for the audience; what shall we say of the two events they were eager to discuss, to applaud, to bring about? Or rather, since describing those events is the substance of this whole book, how shall we describe in some simple preliminary way the confluence of forces that produced them? That question too could be answered in a number of ways, but the organizing idea I would like to advance is that the Show came out of the East and the Strike came out of the West. Europe (and an elite American class in touch with Europe) devised the idea of modernism and imposed it on American art, against the will of liberals as well as conservatives, while the strike-and-pageant designed by the Industrial Workers of the World came out of indigenous and partly western sources. The two had a good deal in common when they met—when one may say they married, with the blessing of Greenwich Village—but they moved along very different trajectories.

First of all, the strike-and-pageant obviously brought labor issues to public attention and demanded a class-conflict interpretation of American politics, something which the official politicians and also the leaders of the AFL avoided. It was the work of the most politically radical union on the American scene in 1913.

The IWW was unionizing two segments of the American work force which had not previously counted for much either in industrial disputes or in national politics: the immigrants from south and east Europe who in 1913 worked the mills and shops of the eastern cities; and the migrant workers of the West—loggers, lumberjacks, sailors, plus the miners (not migrant but even more militant). Both segments were distant in every way from the skilled members of the American Federation of Labor unions, the "aristocrats of labor," who showed little brotherly feeling for the immigrants and little interest in large-scale political change, concentrating on advancing the interests of their members and making secure their conditions of employment, including the differentials between their wages and those of the less skilled. The IWW's constituency came new to American politics (the immigrants often spoke and read little English, the migrants had had no vote because they had had no fixed addresses) and they were alarming to both the political and cultural establishments. But both had potentially a powerful political identity, as favorite children of the official American myth: the immigrants were those "weary and forsaken" whom the Statue of Liberty invited to these shores, while the migrants were frontiersmen, those archetypal Americans, the men of the West. Any organization which could mobilize and combine those two forces under one banner would be a powerful force in American politics.

The presence of the western idea within the IWW (in Paterson and other eastern cities) was mainly concentrated in the figure of Big Bill Haywood, with his Stetson and his western drawl and his cowboy stories. As we shall see, Haywood was born in Utah and worked in Colorado, Idaho, Nevada as a young man. He knew the life of the West in all its hardship and its violence and its glamor. He had no education but what he picked up for himself, and he did not visit New York till 1908, when he was nearly forty—he did not live there till 1912.

Despite this he was, as a westerner, familiar to the Village audience because of the immense literature about the West, at various levels of literary dignity, which flooded America and Europe. As one of Haywood's biographers says, he was as American as Bret Harte or Mark Twain.[47] Many of the anecdotes by or about Haywood are indeed close in various ways to anedotes by or about Twain (or to Stephen Crane stories, or to Davy Crockett stories). Thus in his autobiography Haywood tells of a faro table in Tuscarora composed of eight men and a woman, all of whom had killed at least one man;[48] he had often been beaten up by deputies, and was a quick hand with a gun himself. But it is even more interesting to compare him with an easterner, Theodore Roosevelt, who had won his way to the presidency, starting as a rich New York merchant's son, by means of embracing and embodying that myth of the West. Much of the action of *Ranch Life and the Hunting Trails*, Roosevelt's very popular book about his life as a western rancher, takes place just where Haywood lived—only he worked there as a miner, not as a cowboy.

This is a more interesting comparison than the one between him and Twain because Haywood actually did measure himself against Roosevelt, in various speeches, and so did other people; Debs proposed that he should run for the presidency against Roosevelt—he did in fact consider running in 1908; the May 1906 demonstrations in his favor in New York City were also anti-Roosevelt demonstrations; and he measured himself as a man against Roosevelt by sneering at the latter's cherished campaign record in Cuba.

It never came to a full-scale political clash between the two, but if certain things had happened differently—if, for instance, the Paterson Strike had ended triumphantly, and war had not broken out in 1914—they might have run against each other in 1916. They were fated rivals, because both drew on the same fund of American mythic virtues—the values of adventure and the West. American literature, from the days of Cooper on, had claimed those virtues for the gentleman class, but of course that was always paradoxical, since it was essential to that myth that one becomes an adventure hero, a true American, only by encountering nature face to face, with none of the advantages or ameliorations of birth or breeding. Roosevelt in some sense won his unique place in American politics by being more of an adventurer than anyone else in sight; but his was an invented persona, and if he had had to run against Haywood, a true son of the West, and of its proletariat, he would have been at a disadvantage. He had won his phenomenal popularity as the representative of the whole culture's youth and potency, and therefore the representative of its underprivileged. He stole the votes that might have gone to a new party, representing new Americans. It has been calculated that while Gene Debs got a million votes in 1912 when he ran as labor candidate for the presidency, he might have polled two million but for Roosevelt's Bull Moose party.[49]

It was in 1898 that Roosevelt told reporters at Montauk Point, "I feel like a bull moose. I'm ashamed to be so sound and well." This gleeful identification with an animal was a western gesture, and to turn that into a party platform, or least slogan, was characteristic of Roosevelt. Brooks, even in 1908, was scornful of such self-conscious vitality as Roosevelt's and Jack London's, and soon after 1913 such scorn was to become general among artists and intellectuals. The energy came to seem phony. And nowadays, when we read Gene Debs congratulating John Reed that "There is something that breathes and throbs in all you say," we feel embarrassed that Debs should fall for such an obvious rhetorical ploy.[50] Far from his style making Reed unique, as Debs says, it seems to us to make him typical of his times.

But such judgments come to us as inherited reaction against the spirit of 1913.

Playing the Bull Moose, Roosevelt was claiming to be a westerner by nature—not of course to be a Wobbly, but as a westerner, closer to the Wobblies than other politicians were. For the men of the IWW, at least the westerners, cultivated a style like his. They saw themselves as more original, more natural, than the people of the East. Fred Thompson, editor of their *Industrial Worker*, said later, "I believe there was a process of selection whereby those who least tolerated the ways of the east, went west. There most of them did not become settled or tied in a specific location—there weren't enough females to tie them. They were footloose . . ."[51] Roosevelt had gone west, and remained footloose—see his safaris in Africa and South America. "I think they shunned stereotype in all things. Their frontier was a psychological fact—a rather deliberate avoidance of certain conventions, a break with the bondage to the past. Yet . . . individuality and solidarity or sense of community flourished here together, and with a radical social philosophy . . ."[52]

Part of this radicalism was an anti-Christian propaganda, quoting texts by Marx and Ingersoll, and going back to Tom Paine; something quite unlike the genteel westernism of Roosevelt. Haywood tells us his wife unfortunately turned to Christian Science—"nonsense based on that profane compilation of fables called the Bible."[53] Roosevelt on the other hand quoted from *Pilgrim's Progress* and was seen by his friends as another Mr. Greatheart: his allies in the capture of the western myth for the gentleman, the writer Owen Wister and the painter Frederic Remington, always implied a Christian faith of some kind.

Haywood's West was the site of mining, not ranching, but he did try his hand at being both a cowboy and a homesteader. Even in those occupations, however, his sense of the situation was quite different from Roosevelt's—was less mythical and therefore in some sense more political. Perhaps the most striking example of the difference between the two is that Haywood, in 1905, immediately after the establishment of the IWW, proposed to found a Bronco Busters and Range Riders Union: indeed he organized one, though it did not take hold. Union meetings out on the trail of the lonesome pine! One

31

realizes how thoroughly the myth of the West has determined one's sense of the possible.

Another sign of Haywood's alienation from establishment American myths is his attitude to detectives, who have been favorite sons of the American imagination—twentieth-century knights errant—but who were, as far as he was concerned, the owners' agents against the workers. "A detective is the lowest, meanest and most contemptible thing that either creeps or crawls, a thing to loathe and despise . . . That you may know how small a thing a detective is, you can take a hair and push the pith out of it and in the hollow hair you can put the hearts of 40,000 detectives and they will still rattle. You can pour them out on the surface of your thumbnail and the skin of a gnat will make an umbrella for them."[54] This is a familiar frontier humor, but with a polemic edge unlike that it has in the American classics. Detectives are heroes for establishment writers at least by the time of Howard Pyle's *Within the Capes* (1885) and Twain's *Pudd'nhead Wilson*.

Haywood's frontier language appealed to the editor and readers of *The Masses*, among others, as an example of art still integrated into popular life—not yet specialized out to serve an elite. They had an aesthetic philosophy, though it could be called antiaesthetic. Piet Vlaag, the founder of *The Masses*, said to Louis Untermeyer in 1910, quoting William Morris, "Sure, we need art. But not art that's for the few—not art that lives in pretty ivory towers built on golden quicksands . . . Art must live with the people—in the streets, in the slums."[55]

At least sentimentally, they looked forward to a withering away of the arts. John Reed and Harriet Monroe, for instance, wanted to free art from its minority affiliations. And Hapgood, in *The Spirit of Labor*, says with obvious approval of the members of the labor movement in Chicago: "The men with temperament among them were intensely alive, so alive that 'art' seemed to them a mere trivial excrescence [which] tended to keep the proletariat enslaved . . . make man ignobly content with his bonds."[56]

But of course the crucial concerns of the IWW were not aesthetic or antiaesthetic, but political; its crucial identity was a matter of class affiliation. There was a dangerous class conflict in the air. The finance capitalist Jay Gould is supposed to have said, "I can hire one half of the working class to kill the other half."[57] And there were lots of stories of how labor leaders got seduced from their class loyalty by men of power—by for instance Theodore Roosevelt. In 1902 John Mitchell, a miners' leader, went to Washington together with some mine owners to meet President Roosevelt and was persuaded by the latter to accept the nonrecognition of his union, although Mother Jones implored him to "tell Roosevelt to go to hell." In 1906 Debs raised the cry against Haywood's imprisonment in Boise, "Arouse, ye slaves! Their only crime is loyalty to the working class."[58] He wanted to see an army raised, John Brown style, to march to Idaho to release Haywood.

The IWW was organized to lead the working class into the class war and the idea of art was incidental to that purpose—though to us, because we are going to compare this event with the Armory Show, this theme bulks large. Its idea of western adventure, on the other hand, was important to any understanding of the IWW, because that idea gave the union so much of its style and attraction. The IWW was a western union in origin. It was—or would have been, for the alliance was never quite consummated—the *joining* of the men of the West with the women (Italian and Jewish women, predominantly) who worked in the eastern mills, which might have changed American politics. But for the moment let us concentrate on the western adventurer theme; which carries us on to the Armory Show.

This American adventurer idea was a more pervasive force in American society than is sometimes realized, because the history of ideas assigns this idea to "low culture," and implies that it had no bearing on art and ideas. In fact, however, even the Buffalo Bill Wild West constituted the idea of America for intellectuals and artists. In painting, future and recent immigrants like Charles Schreyvogel and Dorothy Brett, for example, "saw" America first at a Wild West Show; and the Armory Show dramatized important Rooseveltian ideas about conquest and comradeship and racial destiny, and so on. Gifted artists like Schreyvogel, Remington, and Charles Russell devoted their talents to the western myth: the first-named won the National Academy Prize in 1900. (And the influence continued: the filmmaker John Ford kept an album of Schreyvogel prints by his bed.) Remington, who first attracted general attention for his *Century* magazine illustrations to Roosevelt's book, *Ranch Life and the Hunting Trails* in 1887, in 1889 won a silver medal at the Paris Exposition. [59]

We shall keep our eye on western art, even though it was not the only alternative to modernism, because of its unusually close connection with the "official" myths of American society—the adventure-frontier-cowboy myths. Remington claimed to paint "men with the bark on"—not men trimmed and dressed for society and not women such as aesthetes paint for; the whole cult of macho manliness is implicit in the phrase. [60] Just because of its remoteness from the actual business of Washington and Wall Street, this art was able to serve the nation and the corporations as an energizing myth. Seen from this point of view, western art is the antithesis to, and natural contrast with, the art the Armory Show introduced into America.

Thus there were severe conflicts between the laws of "highbrow" art taste and that of the West. Remington was elected to the Players Club in New York because of the interest his paintings aroused, but there he met "real" artists like Childe Hassam and was made to feel that he was only an illustrator. [61] In 1903 he got a three-year contract from *Collier's* magazine (at twelve thousand dollars a year) to do a series of centerfolds to illustrate the history of the frontier. It was an important concession in the contract that he was allowed to keep the originals himself, but in 1908 he was seen in his backyard burning those paintings, because he wanted to be known for something else —as an *artist*. Since 1902 he had been studying impressionism and was actually painting lily pads, as Monet did. [62] On the other hand, Stanton Macdonald Wright, inventor of *synchromism*, the only school known in Paris as an American rival to cubism, futurism, and so on, in later life turned to painting cowboys and lonesome pines. The tensions were strong, tugging painters (and other people) in both directions, and the issue could go either way.

Even eastern painting teachers were likely to use western language. Thus William Morris Hunt, the Boston artist with whom Remington studied at the Art Students League in the 1890s, said, "In painting as in pistol shooting, pay your whole attention to the object aimed at! Keep your finger gently on the trigger, making it close slowly, deliberately, imperceptibly . . . like fate." [63] And this was more than a verbal ploy. The *idea* of the artist was linked to the idea of the western adventurer.

The painter group who helped organize the Armory Show, the Eight, were Philadelphian in origin, and city scene painters; but allusions to the West were an important part of their mythos as artists, especially the mythos of their leader, Robert Henri, who emerged in Philadelphia, Van Wyck Brooks says, "from some Bret Harte story of the West."[64] In his case, as we shall see, the links with the West were literal as well as mythical.

Thus the idea of the West was a powerful one even among artists—indeed, among some professed modernists. Gertrude Stein, priestess of modern sensibility for those who organized the Armory Show, defined herself and her artistic projects in western terms. She distinguished American writing (her own kind, which was due to triumph in the twentieth century) from nineteenth-century English literature in largely western and frontier terms. In her *Lectures in America* of 1935, she said that English literature is all a description of "what exists and so makes the life the island life the daily island life."[65] English poetry has been about "the things they are shut in with." But in a continent, like America, the daily life is not held in within.[66] "It is something strictly American to conceive a space that is filled with moving . . ."[67] we in America have tried . . . to know that it is moving even if it is not moving against anything . . . the American's way has been not to need that generations are existing."[68] Generations, like other forms of order and hierarchy, are to be affronted by modernist writers—as they were, implicitly, by the advanced American writers of before 1900.

This may sound remote from the ordinary American cult of the West, but in fact Stein's philosophy, and even her aesthetics, were deeply involved with that idea. In the *Geographical History of America*, she says she wants to rid art of beginnings, middles, and ends, and to see the present spread out flat and endless like a prairie. She wants to transfer into aesthetics that American thrill of escaping from Europe and seeing a new land spread out before one. The straight lines on the map of America make wandering a mission—and only a big new country can give that feeling.[69] Indeed her philosophy is linked to a conventional chauvinism. The epilogue to "Brewsie and

Willie" says, "I was always patriotic, I was always in my way a Civil War veteran . . . We are there where we have to have to fight a spiritual pioneer fight or we will go poor as England . . . and don't think that communism or socialism will save you . . . and my God how I would hate to have my native land go poor . . . We are American."[70]

Then there is another western idea, different but linked, which played a part in Stein's career. Sherwood Anderson says that when he first heard of Gertrude Stein, she was being praised with genuine admiration, for having put something over on the public. The idea (which is not inappropriate to Stein, even after one has met all her intentions sympathetically) is that an artist may be an unscrupulous showman and self-publicist, while preserving a secret core of truth untainted. Duchamp as well as Stein was treated generously in this country because—though not only because—they were seen as show-men. This is quite an important factor in the history of modernism in this country after 1913.

America was the land of showmanship. For instance, between 1900 and 1913 a lot of Americans seem to have thought of P. T. Barnum as a representative American. In *The Wine of the Puritans* Van Wyck Brooks called Barnum "a colossal figure, who vividly illustrates typical American traits."[71] He is a "shrewd American casuist," like Rockefeller and Brigham Young. Theodore Roosevelt said we should take many of the pictures in the Armory Show "no more seriously than we take P. T. Barnum's mermaids." And this, though dismissive, is genial and in its way admiring. Americans cultivated the attitude of admiring anyone who prised an admission fee out of them, especially if they suspected an element of fraud; and they associated this with the West. Art Young, for instance, who wrote his autobiography as a midwesterner with a heritage of frontier tales and any-boy-can-become-president ideas, links Barnum with Twain; and apparently the two men were friends and admired each other's traits.

Thus the idea of the West has manifold uses in explaining both our two events, but above all, of course, the one designed by the IWW. The union needed to reclaim the idea from its function as upper-class propaganda, in order to associate it with working-class politics. (It is worth noting how antilabor the idea of the West could be in the popular arts as well at more respectable levels, for instance in the cowboy Westerns that Zane Grey began to write: Grey's 1919 *Deserts of Wheat* has a Wobbly for villain.)

As we turn now to the Armory Show and modernism, let us keep in mind our ultimate purpose of linking the two events, and by means of the concepts of *transcendence*. Modernism had at its roots values of a kind remote from, the reverse of, worldly or materialist values, but transferred or translated out of religious terms into those of art. A good example is Vassily Kandinsky's stress on the spiritual in *Über das Geistige in der Kunst*, published in 1912, and among our figures read at least by Dreier, Stieglitz, and O'Keeffe almost immediately. His ideas blended naturally with those of theosophy, and those of the mystical socialism of, for instance, Edward Carpenter.

Comparable ideas, differently phrased, survived in the sense of vocation of individual painters, though usually implicit and unacknowledged. Duchamp himself expressed them, and we can find other passages in Man Ray's autobiography and in Apollinaire's remarks about Braque in 1908. "He no longer owes anything to his surroundings. His spirit has deliberately challenged the twilight of reality . . . This painter is angelic. Purer than other men, he pays no attention to anything that, being alien to his art, might cause him suddenly to fall from the paradise he inhabits."[72] Hartley uses a similar language about O'Keeffe.

But religious or idealistic terms were compromised by the use made of them by the ruling class and its institutions. Beginning in France and in the middle of the nineteenth century, artists felt the need to free their art from complicity with bourgeois taste and with its origins in the bourgeois state. Responding to the same historical facts as the socialists and in some ways in step with them, the painters rebelled against their society. All the fine arts are used to beautify, dignify, enhance the ceremonial life of institutions: there are poet laureates, official painters, composers of coronation music; and these arts are housed in museums, concert halls, and theaters which have special boxes for presidents, mayors and official guests, just as there are parades and concerts for generals and bishops. And there is a special enslavement of the visual artists, who deal with patrons and palaces, presidents and millionaires, more than, say, writers do; they have to deal with all that follows from possession—from the objet d'art being an objet de virtu—which is to say, with theft, fraud, authentication, collecting, security. How to escape serving one's political masters? How to serve one's own gods and not theirs?

The artists of modernism broke free by an insurrection within the realm of art, a coup d'état that made an enemy enclave within culture. Picasso and Matisse painted pictures incomprehensible, and insulting, to the bourgeois even as connoisseur. One might almost say they confiscated his sense of sight; at least they poisoned the reassuring pleasures of visual aesthetics for him—those of landscape and sexual loveliness, as well as those of pictures. This was a guerrilla war against the bourgeois class and its hegemony, its representatives in the ateliers, its Renaissance traditions, and its Greek and Roman heritage. The great talents in a sense refused to be adults and citizens; they allied themselves to children, to primitives, to madmen, and against the dominant gender, race, and class. They denied reality via their denial of realism.

Thus Kandinsky's idealism was not harsh or revolutionary enough, and was often denied or covered up by something opposite, an apparent renunciation of all the deep, large meanings. Modernist aesthetics is just as well exemplified by this passage of Paul Valéry, quoted by J. M. Brinnin at the beginning of his book on Gertrude Stein, *The Third Rose*. "Sometimes I think there will be a place in the future for a literature the nature of which will singularly resemble that of a sport. Let us subtract, from literary possibilities, everything which today, by the direct expression of things and the direct stimulation of the sensibility by new means—motion pictures, omnipresent music, etc.—is being rendered useless or ineffective for the art of language. Let us also subtract a whole category of subjects—psychology, sociology, etc.—which the growing precision of the sciences will render it difficult to treat freely. There will remain to letters a private domain: that of symbolic expression and of imaginative values due to the free combination of the elements of language." (The application of this idea to the work of Gertrude Stein will be obvious.)

Duchamp and dada, as we shall see, went further than Valéry. Duchamp wanted to subvert painting as a whole. He was profoundly irritated by the whole art enterprise of his time. "All painting, beginning with Impressionism, is antiscientific, even Seurat. I was interested in introducing the precise and exact aspect of science."[73] Of course, this was only an aspect of science, and only a mocking version; if he wanted science to subvert nineteenth-century art, he subverted science too. And the mockery was directed as much at himself as at either activity; it was what Duchamp called metairony. Nevertheless, this was the final twist to a long tradition of dissent: a dissent on the part of art from general civilized values, in which painting had taken the lead since the 1890s. As Floyd Dell says, "Fiction itself was discovering from the painters what it itself ought to be. It was felt that writers had ceased to be artists, in a sense in which painters had remained artists." They had brilliantly refused to be in the slightest degree useful to a civilization they hated.[74]

This break of modernism with painting's past can be linked with Marcel Duchamp in particular. I have mentioned before Katherine Dreier's hailing of Duchamp as the modern Leonardo da Vinci, and a parallel between the two has occurred to lots of scholars because of Duchamp's fascination with machines and science, and his notebooks, and perhaps because of the enigmatic character of the two personalities. Leonardo's pictures have been especially the victims of modernist mockery, above all the *Mona Lisa*, so long enshrined as an icon of European art and therefore targeted by Picabia, Dali, and Duchamp himself. They drew mustaches on her, to free themselves from him, from "the eternal thief of energies"—a phrase adapted from the attack on Christianity; what Leonardo represented, like what Christ represented, was a dead prestige, an unquestionable authority which discouraged new life.

In the intensity with which Duchamp and dada worked—and simply by the fact that they continued to produce art—they subverted their own subversion, and remained the colleagues of more conventional artists. But this is of course only a partial truth, and to do justice to their deeper convictions, we ought to insist on the countertruth that they did thoroughly rebel against bourgeois culture. They were even hostile to one of the most general and generous philosophies of 1913, one of the dearest themes of the American renaissance: the love of life, the cult of life values.

Van Wyck Brooks said it was the New England character, or the clamps that New England had fixed on the American character, that did it harm. Americans were too grown-up, rational, emotionally shallow, self-conscious.[75] By contrast, Europeans had a vivid sense of the mystery in life,[76] and Italians in particular had a splendid passionate life of primitive emotions.[77] This is close to E. M. Forster and D. H. Lawrence in England and to the passion for Greece in George Cram Cook and Isadora Duncan and Gordon Craig. Given a less erotic interpretation, this idea links up, as we shall see, with the idea of an American renaissance in such bastions of the establishment as Theodore Roosevelt and Percy MacKaye. (The latter cannot of course be called radical, but these can all be seen as expressions of the spirit of 1913.)

This idea that Americans are too adult is in some ways the opposite of an older idea—to be found, however, in Henry James—that Americans are too naive and childlike. It was the adoption of erotic values which caused this reversal of images. And it was in the high culture of the eastern states that this was first found. The West still held by the older image.

Life values is a very general idea. In Max Eastman's novel about the Paterson Strike, *Venture*, the hero, based on John Reed and Eastman himself, gets a message from his dying mother, "Don't be afraid to live, Jo," given while his father is—futilely—praying. This the hero accepts, and his only problem as the novel develops is to know which form life takes today. One clue is this quotation from George Chapman, the Elizabethan playwright:

> *Give me a spirit that on life's rough seas*
> *Loves to have his sails filled with a lusty wind*
> *Even till his sail yards tremble, his masts crack,*
> *And his rapt ship runs on her side so low*
> *That she drinks water and her keels plough air.*
> *There is no danger to a man that knows*
> *What life and death is—there's not any law*
> *Exceeds his knowledge.*

This quotation is given Jo by a capitalist who turns out to be in some sense the villain of the story, and it becomes a striking demonstration of how English literature could back up and confirm quite official voices of 1913—how the Elizabethans could confirm, for instance, Kipling. But the novel suggests that such love of life has been perverted, and that by nature—as an icon of life values—the passage belongs just as much to the young radicals, to Reed and Eastman.

This is in fact one of the confusing features of the period—confusing to participants then as well as to students now. The idea of life values (vitality as the chief good) was in the process of development, and just about 1913 it began to discriminate among the forms of experience it had indiscriminately blessed before, to attach itself to certain experiences and to repudiate others. It attached itself to Woman and Nature, repudiated the City and the Machine. (To apply it more generally then become a dangerous cliché, which the keenest minds avoided.) But as late as July 1913, in *Camera Work*, John Marin said, "Shall we consider the life of a great city as confined simply to the people and animals on its streets and in its buildings? Are the buildings themselves dead? . . . You cannot create a work of art unless the things you behold respond to something within you . . . Thus the whole city is alive."[78] This is a life-values idea we associate with nineteenth-century city novels like Dickens's and Balzac's. Later Marin was to restrict the idea of life much more severely and to use it negatively.

Such an idea may seem so all-inclusive that there could be no positive dissent from it. But as we have seen, a new mode of thought came in at just this moment (under the auspices of the Armory Show) which was sharply hostile to life values, and indeed to all inclusiveness. It was associated with Cézanne in Marsden Hartley's essay contrasting the two great artist-prophets for his generation, Cézanne and Whitman. The French painter's mode of thought (and that of modernists like T. S. Eliot and Marcel Duchamp) could be called essentially critical and negative. Hartley contrasts him with Whitman as the door closed to experience versus the door open. Cézanne was the most important single influence on modern French painters. Whitman was, by general agreement, as important an influence on the American writers of 1910–1920, and of course an influence in the direction of life values. Eastman said, "We have drunk of the universe in Walt Whitman's poetry," and James Oppenheim saw him as "the ally of all those who rebelled against the New England tradition."[79] For Brooks he was of course a pagan, untainted by puritanism. Cézanne's achievement, meanwhile, was to have persevered in his lonely research until he had broken the spell of what Braque called *la fausse tradition*—that is, the great chain of European painting from 1400 to 1900. The influence of this immense negative act was strong on the French painters of the Armory Show, and via them on American painters; while Whitman's influence was strong on the American writers, and on many admirers of the IWW. (Of course, some of the writers—Eliot, for example—were closer to Cézanne, but roughly speaking the contrast holds.)

But the idea of modernism was irresistible, and its influence immense. Some of the implications of this change become clear when we look at John Reed as a poet. Eastman tells us that he and Reed "had a certain scorn of books. We wanted to live our poetry."[80] Their poetry therefore tried to be transparent to their lives, and become in fact the rhetoric of their self-presentation. It is surely fair to connect that with a recent comment by a historian of radicalism that Reed's poetic language was "wrong from the start"[81] and that *The Masses'* idea of poetry was "outdated." The historian, like everyone else, has been educated by modernism. This was also a matter of Reed's idea of being a poet, which was essentially affirmative—conveniently summed up in the phrase *a singer:* the poet affirms his side of a conflict and himself and his readers; they all line up together, with no irony running between them or aimed at them. It is not surprising that Picasso and Stein found Reed both boring and boorish when Mabel Dodge presented him to them in 1913.

The idea of the artist was to be different under modernism. One can see this in the characterization of the autobiographical hero in one of the new century's great novels, *Ulysses*. That characterization is importantly a matter of differentiating between Stephen Dedalus and his treacherous companion, Buck Mulligan. One might say that the difference between the two was a difference between the new idea of the poet and, for instance, John Reed. Mulligan (and the man from whom he was drawn, Oliver St. John Gogarty) presented himself in the same terms as Reed—as strong, brave, sexually free, sardonic about established values but essentially affirmative of nature, quint-essentially a young man. Dedalus acknowledges that he is none of these things, but asserts that of the two *he* is the poet—despite and because of his negations. This is one of the main messages of this great modernist novel, published in 1922, when Reed would have been thirty-five: verse-makers like Gogarty and Reed are fake poets. Dedalus and Joyce, on the other hand, we can associate with Duchamp—all thoroughly disillusioned and ironic minds, with no aspirations to heroism or manliness or moral beauty. (Of course, we also see an aesthetic idealism concealed at the root of that indifference.)

The freshness of experience on which Reed and Eastman prided themselves went at a discount. We can quote a witty poem by Gertrude Stein to express the modernist idea: "Long before the cuckoo sang to me I wrote a song and said the cuckoo bird is singing in a cuckoo tree, singing to me, oh singing to me But long before that very long before that I had heard a cuckoo clock."[82] The work of art begins life as a trace left in the mind by some earlier work of art, and the idea of beginning from an experience, an emotion, Nature, to proceed to create a work of art is a sentimental illusion.

If the IWW contained the spirit of the West and profited from its powers, then modernist art, as we have said, contained the spirit of the eastern states' elite and of European expatriates. At the end of the nineteenth century many American artists lived abroad, either in Paris or, like Whistler and Sargent, in London. The same was true of men of letters like Henry James and, a little later, T. S. Eliot. They it was who introduced these subversive ideas into American culture. They were in some sense in retreat from that spirit of the West, so challenging to people of refinement and sensibility, and their expatriation has often been seen as a loss for these artists and for their country. But their artistic work was also innovative and inter-nationally influential, as we see most clearly in the context of Anglo-American relations. They were creating forms of symbolism which adapted new ideas originating in Europe to traditional humanism at home, and more important, they were teaching the English artists techniques of self-defense—defense of high culture against popular attack—which had been developed in the American situation.

Symbolism and the other ideas of European modernism seem to have been developed as ways to separate the artist's audience from the contented citizen and prosperous pillar of society—the bourgeois. The artist—after 1848 and in France, especially—rejecting the bourgeoisie, refused to serve it and its representative within himself. He made his art difficult and esoteric.

The American artist was in a different situation (significantly different, not totally so). The anticultural model of the frontier exerted a pressure on American high culture from 1830 on, and the New England tradition of cultural responsibility gradually lost its self-confidence and declared itself morally bankrupt. This is what drove James and Eliot abroad. They certainly found some straightforward refuge in England, where art values were more securely tied to social ones, and so the social order protected at least some artists; but they also saw, more clearly than native Englishmen, that the same pressures would soon be felt there. They were, for instance, two of the critics who dealt most severely (though also appreciatively) with Kipling, who brought the virus of frontier culture into England—both the American frontier, where he learned the arts of the short story and the ballad, and the British frontier, on the edges of the empire. He introduced the raucous tones, and later the complex harmonies which masked those tones, which express the experience of values chaos. James and Eliot of course recognized what he was doing because it was what Twain and Harte had done before.

They taught the English-speaking world to be on guard against such ruling-class populism, however sophisticated, and to make literature esoteric in self-defense. And some of the most important gifts of the Armory Show were new techniques in that long drawn-out self-defense of high culture against popular culture.

Thus the spirituality of the modernist art of the Armory Show was the opposite, in many ways, of the spirituality of the IWW and the Paterson Strike Pageant, and both contained within them elements of the spirit of 1913, but also elements subversive of that spirit. But these conflicts and oppositions do not separate the one event from the other; rather they bring them together and show us how the Greenwich Village audience for the two events could feel them to belong to each other.

These then were two of the imaginative battles going on behind our two events—the issue of the American adventurer identity (could it be wrested from the grip of the gentleman class and invested in a proletarian political movement?) and the issue of spiritual or transcendent values in art (how to install them there without being sentimental or silly or old-fashioned). But to the intellectuals of 1913 they were equally interesting and mutually complementary.

T H E
Salons

3

Here am I, up from the sagebrush and out of the
camps, mulebreaker, worshipper of Walt Whitman, oxman, poet, rebel, brawler, dreamer,
mystic, plowman, full mongrel American—here
I presume to plant myself and write among the
works of the mighty.
— JAMES STEVENS, *Big Jim Turner*

They can't stop us. No matter what they do we
will go on and on until we—the roughnecks of
the world—will take control of all production
and work when we please and how much we
please.
— PETER CARLSON, *Roughneck*

. . . the miracle that is achieved when the surface
of a picture produces space . . . I am aware of
no paintings from the past, even the finest, that
belong to painting as clearly as his [Picasso's].
— JEAN METZINGER, *Du Cubisme*

. . . of all arts, painting now [1911] occupies
the most advanced point on the ideal curve of
evolution.
— ROGER ALLARD

In art, progress consists not in extension but in
the knowledge of its limits.
— GEORGES BRAQUE, 1917

*L*et us now look at two germinating centers of the activity we are concerned with—the Dodge salon in New York and the Stein salon in Paris—plus the nearest historical equivalent in the case of the Paterson Strike.

Mabel Dodge's Salon

In 1912 Mrs. Edwin Dodge moved back from Florence to New York and took an apartment at Number 23 Fifth Avenue, at the corner of Ninth Street. There she was to create an intellectual and radical salon, one comparable with those of Paris before the French Revolution, where the new ideas of the time could be discussed, and where events like the Armory Show and the Paterson Pageant could be shaped. Daniel Aaron has compared her with the Princess Casamassima in Henry James's novel with that title—a rich woman who amuses herself with dangerous men and ideas, a figure of the inauthentic; but in fact, of all the Americans who have aspired to play the part of intellectual muse, she played it best. Born Mabel Ganson in Buffalo, she had married and been left a widow with one son while still young. In Europe she had married a Boston architect, Edwin Dodge, and as his wife had spent nearly a decade in Florence, rebuilding and decorating a splendid villa, where she entertained Florentine nobility and artists and intellectuals from all over the world. She came back to her native country in 1912 largely because her son was then of an age to go to prep school, but also because she herself was ready for a new investment of her energies. She was finding Florence "aesthetically and emotionally bankrupt."[1]

Once settled in her new apartment, she sent her husband to live in the nearby Hotel Brevoort, the priciest of the Village hotels, frequented by Max Eastman, Charles Demuth, George Cram Cook. She had persuaded herself—and her doctor—that her husband's presence adversely affected her health. Their marriage had never satisfied her, though as was true in her other marriages, she kept the respect and the affection of her husband even while she turned away from him. He saw that she needed something more than any ordinary man could give her: she had a destiny to fulfill.

She was a carrier of ideas, a *Kulturträger*. Though not an artist or an intellectual herself, Mrs. Dodge had a gift for understanding such people's ideas and encouraging their enterprises. Personally, she was a comely and healthy-looking woman, rather round-faced and indeterminate of feature, and rather short and plump. "I was not much to look at, ever, I'm sorry to say. (Really sorry.)"[2]

The witty common sense of that remark indicates one element in her personality, and perhaps the most immediately likable, but of course there were others. Her third husband, Maurice Sterne, said that if she hadn't been born rich, she might have become a fortuneteller. "She looked like one, dressed like one, and created that kind of atmosphere."[3] That is a thrust shrewd enough to be worthy of Mabel herself, but what matters most is her genuine gifts and remarkable passion for the truth. She could make anyone talk about his or her special interest, and—this too—she could soon talk to them about it in ways that commanded their attention and respect. (This is her own claim,[4] but it was widely corroborated.)

In his autobiography, Max Eastman said, "Many famous salons have been established by women of wit and beauty; Mabel's was the only one established by pure will-power."[5] Willpower was what everyone accused her of—rightly enough, in the sphere of personal relations—but her other qualities were surely more important in the salon. In any case, the phrase sounds simpler and grimmer than Eastman means, for he goes on, "And it was no second rate salon." As he describes her, "She seems never to have learned the art of social intercourse—a rather dumb and stumpy little girl, you would say, and move on to someone who at least knew how to make conversation. You would move on just to avoid embarrassment, but before long you would be around there trying to talk to this little girl again. For there is something going on, or going around, in Mabel's head or bosom, something that creates a magnetic field in which people become polarized and pulled in and made to behave very queerly. Their passions become exacerbated, they grow argumentative . . ."[6] Once again Eastman is thumping the piano, for by general agreement people came to talk to her above all because she could make them hear themselves think. But however haphazardly, Eastman is testifying to her impressiveness.

She had several trusted advisers in organizing her salon. One was Walter Lippmann, a Harvard friend of John Reed. Born in 1889, Lippmann was the son of rich German Jewish parents in New York. He graduated from Harvard in 1910 (it took him only three years) and stayed on as Professor Santayana's assistant. Another of his teachers was the English socialist, Graham Wallas, and Lippmann learned Fabianism from him. He also wrote in admiration to Lincoln Steffens, asking for career advice, because he too wanted to be a muckraker.

He acted as Steffens's secretary, and in 1912 when local elections brought many socialists to power, Lippmann took a job as secretary to George Lunn, the new mayor of Schenectady—on the recommendation of Morris Hillquit, the New York left-winger. His first book, *Preface to Politics*, published in 1913, was "a hymn to Bull Moose progressivism phrased in the language of Greenwich Village radicalism."[7] He supplied progressivism with a philosophical basis, and declared Theodore Roosevelt with his new social vision (at this time, Roosevelt had announced a program of an eight-hour working day, child-labor laws, and directive legislation) the only complete statesman of the era. Roosevelt had been one of Lippmann's heroes from 1898 on, and his friend later. In 1935 Lippmann found it clearer than ever that 1901 through 1908, the years of Roosevelt's presidency, were the decisive period in American history. He was the first president who knew that the United States had come of age, had become a world power. (This is renaissance rhetoric.) The outward sign of that power was the Panama Canal, which Roosevelt made happen— "the vital link needed to complete the winning of the west."[8]

Lippmann's radical sympathies were strictly controlled by opposite, conservative, tendencies. He marched with the anarchists when Frank Tannenbaum was sentenced and spoke at mass meetings in Union Square with Goldman, Berkman, Haywood, Hapgood, Steffens. But as Mabel Dodge said, he had "a cool understanding and all the high humor in the world shining in his intelligent eyes," and before long it became clear that his deepest loyalties were moderate.[9]

Preface to Politics was enthusiastically reviewed by William James, and it did indeed demonstrate Lippmann's power to assimilate all sorts of new ideas—in this case, the irrationalist ideas of Bergson, Nietzsche, Sorel, and Freud—and to make them compatible with traditional moral and political values. "Men's desires are not something barbaric which the intellect must shun. Their desires are what make their lives; they are what move and govern."[10] He was thus well suited to tell Mrs. Dodge who the coming people were on the New York scene.

Her own account of 23 Fifth Avenue and its various tenants brings out the social paradox of her enterprise. It was a square, four-floor, brick house, painted brown, the front doors half glass, with knobs of darkened silver—a house out of the *Forsyte Saga*, all solid worth. The owner, General Sickles, lived on the ground floor, a one-legged veteran of the Civil War, who had a life-size portrait of himself in uniform, with his sword fixed to the wall above it, and his medals below. He was, she tells us, "perpetually indignant, and his blood was always boiling in him." He represented the past.[11] When he sent her a thank-you note, he added, "Written in the 93rd year of my life without the aid of spectacles."[12] It was the present which she represented—perhaps we should call it the promised future—which aroused his indignation.

On the top floor lived William Sulzer, the governor, and later the impeached ex-governor, of New York, married and subjugated to his ex-housekeeper. Dodge presents him to us as even more grotesque than Sickles—tall, thin, with long gray hair and long knotted fingers, a villain of melodrama, going crazy with guilt. He never went out, but turned up at one of her Evenings, where everyone else was young and ardent or idealistic. He wore wrinkled evening dress and made a political speech, full of wrinkled clichés, until his wife came and took him home. (Max Eastman describes seeing him once outside the house, looking ready to rave.)

And lastly, on the floor above hers lived a smooth young lawyer called Childs, with a wife and a neat, neutral maid. Though the reverse of Gothic, externally, Childs too emerges in Dodge's description as smoothly sinister. His legal opinions were quoted, she thinks, in the cases against the revolutionaries who came to her salon—those for whom she raised money. (On one occasion she sold her dining-room chairs to get some of them out of jail, it appears.)

In 23 Fifth Avenue, therefore, Mabel Dodge was both ensconced in the heart of respectability and actively subverting it by her activities there (and by her malicious descriptions of some years later). Below her, the army, above her, the law and politics, and both looking drab and shabby in the comparison. In her description, her slice of the building shines out—all white, against their black and gray. Her bedroom was draped in white Chinese silk and embroidered Chinese shawls, bought from smugglers on the beach at Biarritz during her second honeymoon. In the front room there was a bearskin rug in front of a white marble fireplace; there was old gray French furniture and chaises longues, old colored glass, and a Venetian chandelier in pastel shades. When, at midnight, food was served, that too seems to have been often white or pastel: turkey, ham, white Gorgonzola, with hundreds of cigarettes and bottles of kümmel in the shape of Russian bears.

Because of her money and her shrewdness, she rarely had cause to fear the police—though there was one peyote party when one participant had a bad reaction and wandered out on the streets, causing a panic—but she was always breaking important rules and defying important powers. Her salon was a place where the energies for political and spiritual and artistic change were mobilized.

The idea of her Evenings she puts thus (in a letter to the habitués, proposing that they should follow a somewhat more formal pattern henceforth): "When I came to New York to live last winter, it seemed to me that there were a great many interesting men and women, all thinking and doing different things, but there didn't seem to be any *centralization*, any place where all *sorts* of people could meet under one roof and talk freely on all subjects."[13] This she was able to provide. Lincoln Steffens spoke of her centralizing, magnetic, social faculty. "You attract, stimulate, and soothe people, and men like to sit with you and talk to themselves."[14] And what she meant by *interesting*, primarily, was radical.

Two of her main concerns were modernist art and radical politics, and so two main events of 1913 for her were the Armory Show and the Paterson Pageant. She had already collected modern paintings in Florence, and soon after arriving in New York she met the men planning the Show. Frederick J. Gregg, its publicity agent, asked her to write a piece about Gertrude Stein, to be part of the publicity. Stein was generally credited with understanding cubism, indeed with being the American cubist, and Dodge was a friend of Stein. She began her task of writing about Stein by rereading Stein's piece about her, *Portrait of Mabel Dodge at the Villa Curonia*. Both essays were published in the March 1913 issue of *Arts and Decoration*, which was dedicated to the Show. She also gave two hundred dollars and got her mother to give five hundred dollars toward the expenses. (It is worth noting how little she gave, comparatively; she was not so very rich, and she was not so very generous with money.) But she also wrote a note to Arthur B. Davies, the president of the Association of American Painters and Sculptors, a note which he had reprinted on cards, because it called the Show "the most important thing that ever happened in America, of its kind. Anything that will extend the unawakened consciousness here (or elsewhere) will have my support. Anything that will add to the racial consciousness and racial memory is worth while. [The race she refers to is the human race.] The majority are content to browse upon past achievements. What is needed is more, more, and always more consciousness, both in art and in life."[15]

She was always offering hospitality and protection to those who needed it, especially young artists. In the year we are concerned with, for instance, Robert Edmond Jones, the future theater designer, had a room in her apartment. Andrew Dasburg and Marsden Hartley received similar invitations, and Max Weber sold her pictures and came to talk to her. It was Jones she gave most to, because he needed most. She was a major support to him for several years.

Max Eastman describes Jones as having a red beard and a thin lit-up Jesus face,[16] while other observers comment on his pallor and nervousness. It seems clear that he was a highly self-doubtful personality; later Mrs. Dodge sent him to be analyzed by Carl Jung because he was afraid he was homosexual. He was sheltered from some of these stresses by a series of Harvard friends, like Reed, and by Mabel Dodge. She describes him as loving nothing but the theater, in an article she wrote, and as describing himself as "too weak to live, but strong enough to make life." He was an ardent disciple of Gordon Craig's ideas about theater as a form of religious cult—the theater as a temple.[17]

Andrew Dasburg, on the other hand, was a man romantically interesting to women, including Mrs. Dodge. Lame like Byron and handsome like Shelley, he is described by her as slender as an archangel and so fair of skin that a frosty glistening light shone over him.[18] Born in Paris in 1887, he lost his father when he was two and was brought to this country in 1892, where he first lived in New York's Hell's Kitchen (around West Thirty-eighth Street). His talent for painting being discovered, he studied with Kenyon Cox and Robert Henri and then went to Paris, where he got to know the Steins and learned to appreciate Cézanne by borrowing one of his paintings from them and copying it several times over. In 1912 and 1913 he was a very promising figure in American art, and had three pictures and one sculpture in the Armory Show; his work was hung near Duchamp's *Nude Descending a Staircase*, which fascinated him, and as soon as Duchamp arrived in New York Dasburg sought him out.

Dasburg's *Homage to Mabel Dodge* pictures were painted around the time of the Show and after. Marsden Hartley, who introduced Dasburg to Mrs. Dodge, had a different relationship with her, because he was homosexual. But she was appreciative of his remarkable gifts as a painter and as an intellectual and arranged an exhibition of his work in her home town, Buffalo.

With Max Weber, her relations began with her purchase of his paintings. She had bought *Three Witches* in February 1912, before she left Florence, and a year later in New York she bought two more of his works. She and Hutchins Hapgood saw much of Weber that spring, when he wrote an essay in praise of Gertrude Stein and became very interested in the IWW and anarchism. In other words, he entered into the spirit of 1913. Dodge names him as one of those who liked to think aloud in her presence.[19]

Through Hutchins Hapgood, she also got to know the leaders of the IWW. Hapgood had been investigating social unrest for some years, describing the world of labor, of unions, and strikes. He published *The Spirit of Labor* in 1907, a study of the labor leader of the Midwest, Anton Johannson. Through him, the anarchists Emma Goldman and Alexander Berkman came to Mabel's Evenings; and so did Bill Haywood, the leader of the Paterson Strike. Several people considered the most interesting of all these occasions the confrontation between Haywood and the artists; Dasburg, Hartley, Marin, and Picabia were present, and Haywood challenged them to think of what function they would have in a truly proletarian democracy.

On another occasion the salon was apparently decorated with a red banner, and workers made their way there after a protest meeting. Frank Tanenbaum, who had been arrested for leading a column of homeless men into a church, was brought to the salon by Emma Goldman to meet Haywood. The editors of *The Masses* were invited there to exchange views with the editors of *The Metropolitan*—a radical magazine meets a fashionable glossy. And so on.

But Dodge's first meeting with Haywood was especially important to us, because it led directly to the Paterson Pageant. She had long wanted to meet him because of things Hapgood had written about him: that he was a strong, simple man with a unified personality. (Her own comments on Haywood imply that he did not meet *her* standards of strong simplicity: her standards were not favorable to political leaders.) At the time of their meeting he had just been released from a Paterson jail, and it was—by her own account, but confirmed by Hapgood—Mabel Dodge who suggested staging a pageant of the strike, to call all New York's attention to the workers' cause. And it was John Reed, also present, and just getting to know her, who took up the idea and brought it to fruition, with her help. He too had just got out of a Paterson jail, and had written about the experience for *The Masses*, under the title, "War in Paterson." (The various accounts of this meeting conflict, so it may be that it was before Reed went to Paterson.)

Mrs. Dodge was not always present when her salon met, but her presence or absence was always felt. On Andrew Dasburg's first visit, in December 1913, Hapgood and Steffens were the hosts, because she had followed John Reed, who had gone to Mexico to report the war there. Dasburg was so excited by the idea of her that he hung one of his abstract paintings on the wall to await her return, retitling it *The Absence of Mabel Dodge*.

The salon struck the imaginations of many people and has been reflected in many books written later, as well as in the gossip of the time, and in fiction as well as nonfiction. In Carl Van Vechten's novel of 1922, *Peter Whiffle*, Mrs. Dodge is called Edith Dale, who is not herself an artist or an intellectual, but who "spends her energy in living, in watching other people live, in watching them make their silly mistakes, in helping them make their silly mistakes. She is a dynamo."[20] He describes the effect Bill Haywood made at her salon: "The tremendous presence of the one-eyed giant filled the room . . . Debutantes kneeled on the floor beside him."[21] (We should not take the word *debutantes* too seriously: more likely they were Village women, perhaps schoolteachers, but the sexual magnetism Haywood had because of his background of violence is something Mabel and her friends insist on—it is of course, their kind of perception and expectation.)

Van Vechten's novel also refers to the Armory Show, which "has now become almost a legend, but it was the reality of that winter. It was the first, and possibly the last, exhibition of paintings held in New York which everybody attended . . ."[22] But the novel's major theme for 1913 is the threat of revolution, represented by Haywood and the IWW. "They all talk about the *Revolution*. It may come this winter. No, I don't mean the Russian Revolution . . . I mean the American *Revolution*. The second American *Revolution*, I supposed it will be called. Labor against Capital. The Workmen against the Leisure Class. The Proletariat against the Idler . . . There will be barricades on Fifth Avenue. Vanderbilt and Rockefeller will be besieged in their houses."[23]

Then Max Eastman's novel of 1927, *Venture*, was largely about the Paterson Strike. It presented Mrs. Dodge as Mary Kittredge, while the central character, Jo Hancock, was a blend of Eastman himself with John Reed. As he describes the salon, a supper table was spread at one end of the drawing room at midnight, which was one of the attractions for some of the poorer guests. Eastman does not deal with the Armory Show, but he does credit Mary Kittredge with a genuine passion for modern painting and genuine power to interpret it to others. His chapter 30 is about Haywood's visit to the salon and his debate with the artists. "He sits perfectly upright and perfectly motionless with his hands resting on his thighs. Bill's hands are very small, as the hands of a mountain would be, and they add to the massive appearance of his body."[24] He asks the aesthetes to imagine the life of a Pittsburgh steelworker: "Not only is art impossible to such a man, but life is impossible. He does not live. He just works . . . Since you have got life, and we have got nothing but work, we are going to take our share of life away from you, and put you to work."[25] Eastman depicts his hero as feeling himself to be "a small and unpleasantly complicated thing" in the presence of these ideas.[26]

Drift and Mastery, Walter Lippmann's 1914 book of political theory, does not depict the salon, of course, but it contains echoes of that milieu—in which many of its ideas were born. For instance, it evokes the atmosphere of 1913 by making reference to William Sulzer, to "the impeachment of a Tammany governor by a Tammany legislature."[27] Sulzer took office in January 1913, and was impeached and removed that October. This impeachment seems to have produced a moral effect like (though less than) that of Watergate half a century later, and Lippmann says, "The sanctity of property, the patriarchal family, hereditary caste, the dogma of sin, obedience to authority— the work of ages, in brief, has been blasted for us . . . We are not stifled by a classical tradition in art."[28] (He was no doubt thinking of the Armory Show's innovations when he spoke of art, but in music it was probably in 1913 that New York first heard instrumental improvising, and 1912 was the date of W. C. Handy's "Memphis Blues.") There were many innovations.

Lippmann himself was already moving toward conservatism. He wrote, "The battle for us, in short, does not lie against crusted prejudice, but against the chaos of a new freedom."[29] He was putting his faith into the scientific method and social science. In 1913, however, he was still one of Mabel Dodge's advisers and one of John Reed's friends. He brought A. A. Brill to the salon to expound Freud, and he helped Reed organize the Paterson Pageant.

It was not only Lippmann's political conservatism in the narrow sense which soon made him out of place in the salon. It was perhaps even more his need to formulate practical projects and commonsense criticisms—the prudent limitation of his sympathies with sheer experiment and sheer emotion. All limitations were suspect there. Even the crystallizing out of one's own ideas, though desired by the more political and theoretical, came to be distrusted by Mabel Dodge and her intimates. Alexander Berkman wrote in her copy of his *Prison Memoirs of an Anarchist* about his hope for "a more perfect crystallization of a definite goal." But Hapgood and Steffens and Mabel Dodge herself were hostile to all crystallization: after all, she believed in love, but not in marriage; in individuals, not in parties. This was an essential characteristic of the leaders of the salon and of the spirit of 1913.

As she herself said, *Song of the Open Road* was everyone's rallying cry. Even in Florence, she had had a Whitman slogan inscribed on her stationery in purple and silver: "If I contradict myself, well, then, I contradict myself."[30] In a poem of her own called "Magnetism," she wrote, "The supreme task of the soul is to encompass all experience."

The salon's interest in and enthusiasm for erotic values (which perfectly represented the eroticism of the Village as a whole) were also antipolitical in certain ways. It was, of course, a high-minded ideological eroticism: quite like that of the contemporary circle of D. H. Lawrence in England. (*Sons and Lovers* came out in 1913.) Margaret Sanger was, according to Mabel Dodge, "the first person I ever knew who was openly an ardent propagandist for the joys of the flesh."[31] And in magazines like *The Masses*, the drive toward erotic liberation was a political cause, as we have seen—one that somewhat jeopardized feminism. But the antipolitical side effects of the erotic and psychoanalytical concern become clear in Steffens's remark, "I remember thinking how absurd had been my muckraker's description of bad men or good men and the assumption that showing people facts and conditions would persuade them to alter them or their conduct."[32]

The salon cannot, of course, be taken as belonging to Greenwich Village. It belonged to Fifth Avenue quite as much, and was far too grand in style to suit most Villagers. Insofar as it was the work of a rich woman playing with radical ideas, it was indeed repugnant to them. From the point of view of the immigrants, however, or even the old inhabitants of the Ninth Ward, there was no great difference between the Villagers and Mabel Dodge. And even from the Villagers' own point of view, those of them that attended were able to make their best case for themselves and their ideas there, in a transcendent atmosphere of luxury.

Mabel Dodge, moreover, is not to be dismissed as easily as some people at the time, and most commentators since, have done. The intellectuals who really knew respected her. She was on the advisory board of *The Masses*, and was asked to edit an issue in 1914. Upton Sinclair asked her to attend meetings of the Socialist party; Joe O'-Brien asked her to set up a meeting of the IWW Defense Fund; John Collier asked her to head the executive committee for the Federal Commission on Industrial Relations (to decide its program and prepare the evidence it would review). In the world of the arts, her position and prestige were even clearer; she bought early Webers and Dasburgs; she gave Bobby Jones a room to work in; in July 1914, when Stieglitz devoted an issue of *Camera Work* to a retrospective of his gallery and journal, Mabel Dodge's tribute headed the series.

She was thus a worthy representative or heroine of the Village in even that heroic sense which is an abiding memory in American culture: in, for instance, Edmund Wilson's *I Thought of Daisy*, where the protagonist humbly remembers the leaders of 1913, "leaders of the true social idealism which cut under capitalist politics. To them the social revolution seemed as real as their love affairs; and I had often a guilty consciousness that it was not quite real enough to me . . . Her bad language and her great bare chest might represent the heroic braveries of some heart-breaking campaign—the devotion to some anarchist lover, deported or sent to prison; the shouldering of some burden of poverty; or perhaps some point-blank vindication of basic human rights in the teeth of the mounted police and the mob."[33] It is someone like (though not completely like) Gurley Flynn whom he has in mind.

Mabel Dodge, however, is not to be comprehended within these terms of a social faith and a joint enterprise. The ultimate source of the disapproval she has provoked from so many critics and historians is her treachery to all joint enterprises—her destructiveness—her irresponsible, arbitrary, and in some sense centrifugal, malice. Laying her soul open to every new idea, deferring to its spokesperson with total attention at first, she soon came to an end of him and it, while other people were just beginning to listen. Diagnosing his or her falsity, stupidity, vanity, she left him or her often paralyzed with the sense of having been found out.

But it is important to realize that this destructiveness was centripetal, too. The sharpest shafts of malice in her autobiography are aimed at herself. (She describes, for instance, her anxious maneuvers to prevent Edwin Dodge from seeing how short and dumpy she was.) This does not make her any the less destructive, but it makes her destructiveness moral and metaphysical—Dostoyevskian. She was an underground man or woman, and all the more impressive for her great generous power and wish to find the truth in art and the spirit—a power and wish exceeded only by her malice. (A famous example is her behavior with D. H. Lawrence, later.) She found it so easy, as everyone agrees, to pick up a new idea, even those parts of the idea that had not been fully expressed or worked out; and it was just this ease which made the world of ideas seem a fraud to her, when it stood on its dignity. She could not—to stay honest—take seriously an institution whose apprenticeship she had eluded so easily, whose tests and standards she had flouted with impunity. Thus her destructiveness is just what is most respectable about her, and the disapproval which high culture has visited upon her was a form of self-defense.

But because she held all the ideas of 1913 in solution—the bubbling solution of the spirit—and passed from modern art to radical politics with such quick bursts of insight, she is (in her admittedly disturbing way) the spirit of the age and the sardonic angel of this story. She was the spirit of her times, meaning both a manifestation of *Geist* and an irresistible solvent.

The Stein Salon

The Dodge salon, and Greenwich Village in general, marshaled the audience for our two events. The origin of these events, and their field of operation, was another matter, to which we shall now turn. In the case of the Armory Show we will take as that origin not the actual organizers, the Association of American Painters and Sculptors, but the circle of Leo and Gertrude Stein's friends in Paris, where the gospel of modern art was first preached as far as most Americans were concerned.

It was in 1903 that the two of them moved into 20 rue de Fleurus, and their brother Michael and his wife Sarah and their child Allan also moved to Paris. The rue de Fleurus connected the boulevard Raspail with the west side of the Luxembourg Gardens. This was Montparnasse, not yet famous as an artists' colony. The famous cafés of the future—the Rotonde, the Bal Nègre, and the Sélect—were not yet; and the Café du Dôme was not what it was to become.

Young American painters, however, already went to Paris, at least if they wanted to know what the new ideas and styles were. Alfred Maurer arrived there before 1900; Walt Kuhn in 1901; Edward Steichen in 1902; Patrick Henry Bruce in 1903; Walter Pach and Maurice Sterne in 1904; Max Weber and John Marin in 1905; Abraham Walkowitz and Morton Schamberg in 1906; Charles Demuth, Andrew Dasburg, and Stanton Macdonald Wright in 1907; Arthur Dove, Thomas Hart Benton, and William Zorach in 1908; Morgan Russell and Charles Sheeler in 1909; and Marsden Hartley in 1912.

By 1904 Leo Stein was in a position to instruct, for instance, Maurice Sterne, later to be Mabel Dodge's third husband. The latter came to Paris on a scholarship in that year, already a skilled draftsman but still devoted to Whistler and Puvis de Chavannes, and finding Cézanne and Renoir strange and repugnant. Then Leo "who was interested in my art education, introduced me to Vollard [the art dealer] who was very obliging and showed us half a dozen [Cézanne] canvases."[34] Two of these early works he quickly learned to appreciate, but the later, greater paintings were still a mystery to him. It took him time to realize that "To Cézanne, the appearance was not a point of arrival; it was a point of departure, a journey not away from the motif, likely to turn into a joy-ride by oneself (so freely indulged in at present) but a journey of exploration into the hidden secrets that reality may hold."[35]

What this alludes to is probably Cézanne's *primitivistic empiricism*, as Tashjian puts it; Cézanne "seemed to realize a pure sensation derived from nature . . . [He] was seen to have overcome the losses suffered by modern Western society."[36] We see this in his famous pictures of apples; getting rid of mythically and religiously and socially significant subjects, he offered his viewers the ontology or archetypal essence of, for instance, pieces of fruit. This was the aspect of his work most congenial to the life-values painters of New Mexico and aligned him for them with writers like D. H. Lawrence. Leo Stein approached Cézanne via Mantegna, we are told, and stressed much more the formal qualities of his composition.

Sterne says Leo Stein was the undisputed ruler of the Stein clan then, for Gertrude "had no taste or judgment in the visual arts."[37] This was a widely held view, and had perhaps some justice. (Mabel Dodge also says Gertrude did not take art seriously.)[38] Thanks to Leo, Sterne joined the saving remnant of those who appreciated modern art. There were, he says, only five among the American painters in Paris who did, and four of them were Russian Jews by birth—the fifth was Alfred Maurer. The other three Russian Jews were Samuel Halpert, Jacob Epstein, and Max Weber. The last, we shall see, discovered Cézanne at the Stein salon.[39] A little later, in 1910, Andrew Dasburg discovered Cézanne by borrowing one from the Steins and copying it over and over.[40] Katherine Dreier, who was then living in London, moving in the social circles of Sargent and Henry James, and influenced by Wilde and Fry, used to come to Paris to the Steins' salons, to meet the new ideas; the color schemes of the Fauves left her gasping. John Marin, on the other hand, shy and suspicious, never even met Leo and Gertrude Stein, the celebrity makers. "I was never one to push myself forward," he says.[41]

Gertrude and Leo had, thanks to Michael's prudent management of their finances, about one hundred fifty dollars a month to spend, and in 1905 they, or at least Leo, began to buy paintings—at first paintings by Fauves in general, and then, in 1906, Matisses in particular. In that year, Leo bought Matisse's *Femme au Chapeau* for five hundred francs and then made friends with the painter. Sarah Stein took painting lessons from him; she and Michael began to build a collection, too, almost exclusively of Matisses. Leo and Gertrude's collection included Cézanne, Renoir, and Picasso also. Picasso was to become a friend, especially of Gertrude, and painted a famous portrait of her, finished in 1906. Sarah Stein was like her sister-in-law in that both were exuberant personalities who frankly wished to shine—both aspired to be salon leaders. Sarah was first protector and then rival to Gertrude.

Both Stein households therefore held salons, which were frequented by most visitors to Paris who were interested in modern art. The four of them, it has been said, purchased and popularized one kind of art with such communal vigor that they were thought of as a unit.[42] Leo explained the pictures on the walls; more than that, he expounded a doctrine—he made propaganda for modernism in art. (*Propaganda* was his word.) It has been said that in the years before 1910, he was the most discriminating art connoisseur in the world.[43] Marsden Hartley compared the Stein salon with the famous Tuesdays held by the poet Mallarmé, which attracted the most brilliant minds in Paris: "That quiet yet always lively place in the rue de Fleurus is the only room I have ever been in where this spirit was organized to a similar degree."[44]

Mabel Dodge, a friend of the Steins in her Florence period and later, has left us vivid sketches of the two of them in their brown corduroy and leather sandals, walking energetically up and down the hills around Florence, Gertrude especially in a steam of perspiration. "Gertrude Stein was prodigious. Pounds and pounds and pounds piled up on her skeleton—not the billowing kind but massive, heavy fat. She wore some covering of corduroy or velvet and her crinkly hair was brushed back and twisted up high behind her jolly, intelligent face. She intellectualized her fat, and her body seemed to be the large machine that her large nature required to carry it."[45] She had a laugh "like a beefsteak."[46]

Leo, on the other hand, Dodge saw as having "the obstinate look of an old ram."[47] In his later self-analysis, he explained his assertiveness by saying, "I had to cling to myself or lose all assurance."[48] It seems clear that he was repressing strong feelings of masochism and self-hatred. He was out of touch with most other people, uncouthly polysyllabic in his speech, and demanding a special diet of fruit and nuts.[49] In 1913 he announced that he had taken to the simple life, walking everywhere and keeping out of towns.[50] He had become disillusioned with modern art and perhaps felt displaced in his relationship with Gertrude by her new friend, Alice B. Toklas. He had always experimented in cooking and diet and costume—he took from his fellow eccentric and Californian, Raymond Duncan, a preference for sandals, and his slang, his jokes, and his defiant judgmentalism were equivalent intellectual eccentricities.[51]

It is perhaps worth dwelling a moment on the Steins' sandals, because of the powerful social symbolism that footwear then carried. Sandals were associated with various figures in the simple life movement like Raymond Duncan and Edward Carpenter, both preachers of mystical socialism and erotic liberation. A 1901 book on Carpenter says that sandals free "the human foot from the stiff, impermeable leather boxes in which it is at present deformed and befouled. The boot is the symbol of the husks of which mankind must rid itself before it can attain to the human form divine, and blossom into the long-awaited unity . . . when at last man's feet are shod with the winged sandals of Hermes which free and do not confine them."[52] This language, though quite unlike the Steins' own, suggests the social geography in which they were to be found.

Mabel Dodge's sense of Leo Stein did not mean that she found him humorless—rather the opposite. He found *her* too serious. He told her that until he met her he had thought Hutchins Hapgood (an old friend, with whom he had made a round-the-world trip) the least frivolous person he ever met. The symptom of this seriousness of hers was her lack of appreciation for puns.[53] A lot of Leo's energy went into assertively frivolous activities like punning or parodying of Isadora Duncan's dancing; he hoped to achieve seriousness only within certain well-defined areas of thought and met other people in frivolity, while Mabel Dodge and Hutch were always seriously "questing," especially in their personal relationships. (Mabel scorned her second husband, Edwin Dodge, for his Bostonian humorousness, which seemed to her only to mask a spiritual cowardice.)

As a theorist about art, and a tastemaker, however, Leo had a great deal to teach his sister and Mabel Dodge. The latter tells us that he "always fulminated against any art expression that was merely the running of water downhill. Music for instance that sang itself, the clichés of melody whose bars followed one another in automatic fashion in one's mind after one heard the opening notes and phrases. Leo seemed to be an enemy of gravitation; he required more than just the natural laws when it was a question of art forms. The conventions of sound or painting were unutterably wearisome . . . 'Tension', he used to say, 'is the requisite for a living work of art.' "[54] This is no doubt one of the underlying presuppositions of modernism, and Mrs. Dodge cites Picasso as an example of the sort of painting that suited Leo's taste. She herself became a provocative propagandist for this iconoclastic modernism, even with traditional artists. While Jacques-Émile Blanche, an older man, was painting her portrait, she insisted to him that Picasso and Matisse were the painters of the day who were teaching the world to see again; and to the poet Edwin Arlington Robinson later she sang the praises of Gertrude Stein as an artist in language.

Modern art in the sense of formalism and abstraction was already well established in certain ways. Whistler had been painting pictures with titles like *Arrangement in Gray and Black* in the 1890s. But a battle was still to be waged on behalf of abstraction. That painting was after all better known as *Whistler's Mother*, and John Sloan, reacting against the suggestion that *he* should use Whistlerish titles, offered *Effect of Light on Stout Healthy Wench*—suggesting that such formalism was an affectation.[55] The big prices were still being paid for realism—at least for French academic realism. In 1900 Cornelius Vanderbilt came to Paris and bought a Bouguereau for one hundred thousand dollars and a Rosa Bonheur for sixty thousand dollars. There was still need for powerful propagandists on behalf of another, different idea of art.

Leo and Gertrude Stein were leaders among those propagandists. The cause of modernist art was congenial to them as an Apollonian mode of social rebellion. A notable feature of the Steins' psychological development was their rebellion against the patriarchal family. (This was one of the things they had in common with Mabel Dodge.) As the youngest two of a large family, they had banded together against both their older siblings and their parents. Gertrude says, "And so our life without a father began, a very pleasant one"; and she thought there was too much fathering in the world. "Mothers may not be cheering, but they are not as depressing as fathers." And their story is most striking in the success with which they freed themselves from the control of their elders.

Gertrude Stein, the youngest sibling, was born in America in 1874, but their parents moved back to Europe, to Vienna, the following year. Her father was a successful, if restive and reckless, businessman, and the Steins lived there in prosperous style, with a Czech tutor and a Hungarian governess for the children. In 1879 the family moved back to Baltimore, and then to Oakland, California, in 1880. It was there that Gertrude and Leo (two years older) had their childhood and adolescence. They were the youngest in a family planned to amount to five children; indeed, they would never have been conceived but for the deaths of two older siblings, and knowing this made them insecure as children, they claimed.

The family's changes of place and circumstance were due to their father's enterprising, restless, and domineering nature. Gertrude and Leo, precociously intelligent and self-aware, formed a pact while very young and rebelled silently against their father; indeed, they had little time for their mother, either, or for their older brother and sister, Simon and Bertha. (Later in life, Gertrude speculated about the ruthless way Jews cut themselves off from their families.) Instead they made an alliance with their oldest brother, Michael, though he was nine years older than Gertrude and no intellectual.

This rebellion made them natural citizens of Paris, for the artists' quarter there (like artists' quarters in other cities, but more so) was a refuge from patriarchy. One rather lurid example was the Steins' friend, Alfred Maurer, who lived in Paris, waiting for his father to die in New York. (When the old man finally did so, at the age of a hundred, the son killed himself.) They were *commedia dell'arte* communities. The rebellion against the academy in art was a rebellion against an alliance between art and the patriarchy. They, the new generation of artists, wanted to disentangle art from that alliance, to become purely rebellious.

The Steins grew up in California and then attended Harvard, where they found a revered teacher in William James. (Leo called James a colossal spirit and a brother soul to Lincoln.) Both he and Gertrude regarded themselves as in some sense universal geniuses, but up until about 1910 Leo was clearly the leader. They had studied philosophy and psychology at Harvard, but then Leo turned to art history, becoming friends with Bernard Berenson, and finally to modern painting. In 1900 he said there were no good books on art and would be none until he and Berenson wrote them. He was then primarily interested in old painters, but in 1904 Berenson told him about Cézanne. He had at that point never heard of van Gogh, Gauguin, or Seurat, but he soon mastered the whole field.

The idea of genius had a specific reference at this moment of American history and in the Harvard milieu. It bore on America's idea of herself and derived from the contrast between America, the land of liberty, and various European "tyrannies," but especially Russia, and especially the ghetto life it imposed on Jews. The idea seems to have focused on the image of a talented boy, born into those cramping confines, being transplanted to the free soil of America, where his gifts (his IQ) would so expand as to increase the range of human possibility. Two famous examples of this, both friends of William James, were Boris Sidis and Leo Wiener and their infant-prodigy sons, William James Sidis and Norbert Wiener. Men born into a privileged class like James seem at that moment to have been ready to hand over the torch of American learning to such young geniuses: no doubt the feeling was related to the privileged class's guilt and fear about the American ghettoes. Leo and Gertrude Stein fitted this pattern (not perfectly, but to some degree) and their claim to be geniuses surely owed something to it. At this time, daughters of privilege like Mabel Dodge and Virginia Woolf found gifted Jewish men like Maurice Sterne and Leonard Woolf especially interesting. And modernism in the arts, like psychoanalysis in the social sciences, was one of the fields they seemed to have a special competence to explain.

Leo was quoted in the catalog of the Armory Show, listened to with respect by Alfred Stieglitz, and wrote for the *New Republic* on modern art. He could explain why Cézanne was so important to the young painters, helping them to make a new system of indicating three-dimensional relationships. Though always an optical empiricist in some ways, Cézanne integrated the surface with the depths in his paintings, by means of *passages*, places where disconnected planes blended ambiguously.[56] From the 1880s on, he was organizing his subject according to separate acts of perception. Picasso went much further, of course, putting profiled noses on frontal faces as early as 1906.[57] In the *Demoiselles d'Avignon* (1907) the lower right figure had a mask-face, a back, and breasts all showing at the same time. Leo Stein felt, like any philistine, that this was "going too far," but he retained his enthusiasm for Cézanne and his interest in modern art as a whole.

Essentially Leo's doctrine was a variety of modern formalism. We can take some examples from Gertrude's *Lectures in America*, since there is no significant difference between the brother and sister in this matter. Both stressed the difference between a painting and its subject. Referring to her brother Michael's first response to Millet's *Man with a Hoe*, Gertrude said, "My brother said it was a hell of a hoe but what it was was an oil painting."[58] Thus Velázquez and Courbet "bothered" her, because their painting was too realistic. "One likes to be deceived, but not for too long."[59] The painters who excited her were modernist favorites: El Greco, not Velázquez, and Cézanne, not Courbet. They achieved a realism quite independent of the realism of appearances.

The paintings were arranged in several rows on the three walls of the pavilion on the rue de Fleurus, according to size. There were also portfolios of drawings, for instance by Picasso, for the visitors to turn over. People came on the recommendation of other people, and often it was a total stranger to the Steins who turned up at their door. Only the lower rows of pictures were visible by gaslight. On one wall, over a Henry Quatre buffet, was a row of Cézanne water-colors (of woods and mountains): above them, Matisses, Fauves, and Picasso's Spanish landscapes; the latter's nude youth leading a horse hung opposite Matisse's huge *Joie de Vivre*, (The latter is the supreme masterpiece of Fauvisme, according to some critics, to be compared with cubism's *Demoiselles d'Avignon*.) There were many nudes, in-cluding Cézanne's *Bather*, Picasso's nymphet with a basket of flowers, and Renoir's gamboling women. There were a long Renaissance table

69

and chairs, an iron stove, and some bronze Buddhas, plus Matisse's sculpture, *The Slave*. Overflows were put in Leo's study ("le salon des refuses") or the bedrooms—Gertrude slept beneath Picasso's *Hommage à Gertrude*.

Leo lectured his visitors, apparently taking the other person literally by the buttonhole. Gertrude, in the years she lived with him, seems to have mostly listened and to have been remarkable for her silences. This did not mean that she was an ineffective presence: her hearty laugh was commented on, and she in fact constituted more of a social center than he, though she did not hold forth in the same way until after he was gone.

However, Leo disliked *Demoiselles d'Avignon*, and the whole cubist movement that followed from that. He began to turn his attention away from art, toward psychoanalysis. There was a connection with his earlier interests; Lois Rudnick says he studied his psyche as if it were an aesthetic object, and thus objectified his problems. She suggests that both Gertrude and Mabel learned from him how to recreate the self, in freedom—as a version of the "imperial self"—by the means of language.[60] Thus he continued to be a powerful influence on them, though less directly than before, and not in this matter of modern art.

In 1913 he and Gertrude, who had been inseparable so long, parted company. She stayed in the rue de Fleurus house, with her friend, Alice B. Toklas, and continued his work of propaganda for modernism, while he moved around the world and took up various interests without finding a lifework again.

Gertrude Stein's ideas were to become commonplace in the discourse of modernism, but they were radical then. She made, for instance, a distinction between art and official art so absolute it amounted to an opposition or antithesis between them.[61] And she declared that emotion must not be the cause of a painting.[62] From these two principles most of the laws of twentieth-century taste can be deduced, or at least the ways it differed from nineteenth-century taste.

Her idea of modernism was exemplified above all in cubism and Picasso, and she based much of her claim for her own work on the similarity she saw between the two of them. She developed this

70

similarity idea in various ways—by describing both Spain and America as countries of abstraction,[63] and by saying that painting had been French until the end of the nineteenth century, when it became Spanish.[64] We remember that American writing (also abstracted from its social context) was due to supersede English literature in the twentieth century.

According to her interpretation, cubists presented objects without either emotion or allegory;[65] and it was because Matisse failed to do that that she turned away from him to Picasso. Indeed, it was generally said that the cubists, especially Picasso and Braque, were highly intellectual painters, engaged in "research"; this idea was blended with a sense of how difficult it was to understand their pictures. It is clear that Duchamp, for instance, was attracted to cubism because of this aspect—though he immediately became anxious to cast off the shackles and to burst out of the straitjacket of being a mere follower. Cubism was freedom for Picasso and Braque, but conformity for everyone else, and at the big cubist exhibition of 1911 they, the great cubists, did not exhibit. This was another aspect of modern art, the constant competition in authenticity and originality, in prestige conflicts and power plays, an aspect with which Gertrude Stein was well equipped to deal.

Cubism, according to John Golding, was the threshold over which many painters, not all to be called cubists, stepped into total abstraction: it was the pivotal movement of the period 1900 to 1950, just because it set going the seesaw between abstraction and representation.[66] And if this is true primarily of analytic cubism, the later, synthetic kind has its own importance, because it paved the way for surrealism.

Mark Roskill, on the other hand, reminds us of the conservative and negative or contracted aspects of cubism. By 1909, Picasso and Braque were painting half- or three-quarter-length figures, or tabletop still lifes;[67] and by 1912 "a shallow space in which lighter or darker forms and planes are sandwiched in between plates of glass, with an extreme complexity of transitions and inter-relationships." During analytical cubism, they suppressed colors, flattened objects, and bled them out, detached floating planes and emphasized discontinuities and ellipses.[68] All this opposed the love of speed (seen in the futurists' work) and of dance (seen in Matisse's work).[69] The cubists were also markedly unerotic, and compared with contemporary movements, unresponsive to social and political stimuli.[70] During and after the war, they stressed order, harmony, tradition.

Edward Fry also points out that while Fauvism had been obviously influenced by African and oceanic art, cubism turned back to the landscape of Paris studios: Picasso's portrait of *Ambrose Vollard* of 1910 took its own formal language as its subject. But Fry does not see this as a turning back. He says that the decade ending in 1914 was "as will one day be recognized, one of the golden ages of Western civilization,"[71] obviously referring primarily to art, and that cubism first posed the fundamental questions that were to preoccupy artists for the first half of the century. It also set a pattern by the speed of its evolutions: time-units of months or weeks replaced the years and decades by which earlier developments of a style were measured.[72] It tried to make the plastic image reveal the essence and permanence of beings, as Jacques Rivière points out, and so dismissed perspective and lighting.[73]

In *Picasso*, Gertrude Stein says, "I was alone at this time in understanding him [Picasso], perhaps because I was expressing the same thing in literature."[74] Both of them were seeking "to express things not as one knows them but as they are when one sees them without remembering having looked them." And asked about the meaning of her *Portrait of Mabel Dodge at the Villa Curonia*, she said, "Well, Pablo is doing abstract portraits in painting. I am trying to do abstract portraits in *my* medium, words." (By stressing the idea of medium, and insisting that one person could have only one, she made it more plausible to claim to be his twin in literature.) Other people took up this idea; in 1914, George Soule spoke of Gertrude Stein's "cubist literature" in the first issue of the *Little Review*,[75] and in the same year Max Weber published his *Cubist Poems*.

Thus, the Stein salon was, among other things, a kind of echo chamber in which certain enthusiasms and art theories and reputations were enhanced, intertwined, and further mystified at the expense of the intellectually insecure. It was also an anteroom where would-be disciples waited in hope of meeting the painters themselves, in hope of entering their world. The painters were the source of all truth and the focus of all glamour. Thus as important as the official *ideas* of cubism was the *taste* of Picasso and his friends ("la bande à Picasso"), a taste for all sorts of fantasies, tricks, and practical jokes. André Salmon said, "We invented an artificial world with countless jokes, rites, and expressions that were quite unintelligible to others."[76]

The central idea was to defy traditional values and in some sense values as such. Salmon himself mocked Leonardo da Vinci as "the eternal thief of energies" and complained that the Gioconda's smile had been the sun of art, the source of all light and heat. Now it was time to abolish the old gods and the old suns.

These friends, like Salmon, Jacob, and Apollinaire, and Picasso himself, cited Baudelaire, Rimbaud, and Mallarmé among writers, but also Fantômas and Buffalo Bill—strictly popular culture. Perhaps their most important hero was Alfred Jarry, whose *Ubu Roi* of 1896 celebrated the god of the grotesque, lewd, and licentious. This taste, as much as their actual painting techniques, distinguished Picasso's intelligence from the more refined and moderate cubism associated with Albert Gleizes and Jean Metzinger. (Their book, *Du Cubisme*, came out in 1912 and was immediately widely translated.) Duchamp's older brothers practiced their other cubism, and he did some work in that style, but in spirit he had more in common with the anarchic humor of "la bande à Picasso."

So had Gertrude Stein, and thanks to the force of her personality and the enigma of her work, she was associated with the Armory Show from the first, and at every level of commentary in America. The explosion of publicity surrounding the Show coincided with that moment in her career when she was emerging from under Leo's wing. She had always been frankly avid for *la gloire*. It was one of the things that linked her to Picasso and distinguished her from Leo. (He was probably less avid, and certainly less frank.)

But it was not just she, but the Stein salon, or indeed both Stein salons, which were an important resource for the organizers of the Show—who came to Paris to consult them. Of the many precursors, the most important was perhaps Walter Pach. He brought Walt Kuhn, and later Arthur B. Davies, to both the Stein houses when the two men were in Paris seeking paintings for the Show. (After leaving

Michael and Sarah's house on the rue Madame, Davies bowed toward the door, as toward a temple of Matisse's art.) Both pairs of Steins loaned paintings to the Show (Matisses and a Picasso and a Duchamp-Villon), and they were invaluable in sending the two men to the right dealers and private collections.

The Wobbly Hall

In the case of the Paterson Strike, the origins of the radical event cannot be found in any salon like Mabel Dodge's or Gertrude Stein's. The nearest equivalent one could name is the IWW leadership, of Bill Haywood, Gurley Flynn, Carlo Tresca, Joseph Ettor, and so on. But to concentrate on the leadership at the expense of the membership, or even to concentrate on the IWW at the expense of the strikers, would probably be a mistake. So at least argues the Strike's most recent historian, Steve Golin. So it seems best to follow a different method in this case, and to describe group actions and general ideas rather than individuals.

(We could of course, look at the Pageant in isolation from the Strike, and study the committee which John Reed formed to devise it. But that would eliminate most of what was interesting in the Pageant. Even the theater reviewers on the day said that the few individual performers and speakers on stage were less impressive than the over a thousand strikers, who did not act but presented their experience to the audience. If we ignore that experience to concentrate on their art, we shall diminish the event; it could then be judged by aesthetic criteria appropriate to the Armory Show, but the idea of this comparison is to bring into play and then reconcile different sets of criteria.)

The comparable breeding ground for Wobbly ideas was perhaps the Wobbly Hall, a phenomenon to be found in most western cities with a sizable number of migrant workers (sailors, harvesters, loggers, etc.). These were of course cheap structures, designed to give shelter and minimal comfort and a meeting place for men out of work and drifting; they usually provided a stove on which the men could cook the mulligan stew that was the staple food of hobo life (many Wobblies were hobos, though in some sense the aristocrats of the hobo life) and a collection of songbooks, pamphlets, and even books. Apparently authors like Marx and Darwin were often to be found there, and Voltaire, Spencer, and Paine. There was not so much fiction, except for Jack London, and in particular his *Iron Heel*. Another favorite set of books included Frederick Jackson Turner's histories of the West and the frontier; these were in some sense incongruously matched with Marx and Paine, but as we know, a love of the West was as dominant a passion in the IWW as a hatred of capitalism.

This was a very different setting from the two salons we have looked at, and other American institutions of their ilk, but the difference is not to be located in a lack of ideas in the Wobbly halls, or in an absence of the imaginative arts. There was, for instance, a great deal of singing there—verses by Joe Hill and Ralph Chaplin set to well-known tunes from the Salvation Army or from Tin Pan Alley, from the hymn book or the commercial songbook. It is even said that there was some "epic" composing of poetic narratives, or prolonging and continuing of narratives already begun. It seems likely that such poetry, like the music, was predominantly satiric, and so parasitic on earlier poetry; but it may nevertheless be proper to call it epic because of the circumstances of its composition. Certainly this non-literary setting was more likely to produce epic poetry than a salon was.[77]

The Wobbly ideas that were in some sense the equivalent of the cubist ideas (of course in substance they are quite different, and similar only in function) included the inevitability of war between the working class and the owning class; the need for direct industrial action, as opposed to the indirect action of working through the established political party system; a unionism based on the principle of one union for all the workers in one industry—as opposed to the AFL principle of one union for all the workers with one skill—so that all railwaymen, whatever their craft, would be united in a railwaymen's union, which could move en bloc against the owners. By extension, there was the idea of one big union that would represent all the working class of a country, and of the general strike that would shut that country down and install the working class in power; and finally the idea—but this was a different sense of the word idea—of violence.

These people, like the artists, saw the bourgeois class and state as the enemy. They did not avenge themselves upon the bourgeois's sense of sight, but on his sense of security, his sense of property, his sense of law. Above all, they wanted to change political and economic facts, to seize power over the state and expropriate the expropriators. But their period of intense revolt began at the same point of history as that of the artists in nineteenth-century France and Germany. Marx and Bakunin were their great precursors. In late nineteenth-century and turn-of-the-twentieth-century America, there were various groups working to redeem the working classes: socialists, communists, anarchists; and the IWW seemed for a time the best American hope. The men of the West saw the middle class encroaching on that last zone of freedom (perhaps more mythical than real), the frontier. They saw the opportunities of the new continent and the new start in life for the immigrant millions snatched from them to swell the endowment of the exploiting class, literally in the form of individual wealth or imaginatively in the idea of adventure, as dude ranches, safari holidays, or artistic or entertainment materials.

Last among the Wobbly ideas was violence. Violence was never explicitly advocated by the leadership, and often explicitly renounced, but a sense that the IWW was ready for violence was part of the excitement the organization had, for its members and for others, and for those who feared violence as well as those who welcomed it.

Of course this violence disguised itself as something like adventure or romance to those who responded to it. Ralph Chaplin, explaining his attraction to radical labor movements, wrote, "To me, the WFM [the Western Federation of Miners, the progenitor of the IWW] was full of glamorous courage and adventure. I considered men like Bill Haywood and Vincent St. John as the knights-in-armor of the labor movement."[78] But though he invokes a romantic chivalric past, it was in fact the American West with which he associated the IWW. The stories his father told as a boy, which inflamed his imagination, were of wild horses, Indian raids, and notorious frontier characters in Kansas, he says.[79] His father always dreamed of moving west himself.

He explains this by saying, "Youth has a logic all its own, and the IWW was an organization of young men."[80] Gurley Flynn also said, "The Western half of the IWW were young men who had followed Horace Greeley's advice to grow up with the country . . ."[81] Their attitude to, for instance, white-collar workers, was scornful. "You had to wear overalls, be muscular, you had to work. If you were a pen-pusher, you were not a worker, according to the IWW."[82]

In the talk of 1962 from which this is quoted, Flynn is expressing disapproval of the IWW for its incomplete socialism, its divisiveness about the working class. But as a young woman, she had fallen in love, literally, with just that macho flamboyance. Her husband, Jack Jones, was a miner, and as Vincent St. John said, an embodiment for her of all western miners. Thus the IWW's striking success in the New England and New Jersey strikes expressed a mastery of the eastern imagination by that of the West. Flynn had been brought up a socialist and found that dull, while the IWW was exciting.

The Wobblies saw themselves in these terms at the time. In their newspaper, *Solidarity*, for November 21, 1914, we read, "The nomadic worker of the West embodies the very spirit of the IWW. His cheerful cynicism, his frank and outspoken contempt for most of the conventions of bourgeois society, including the more stringent conventions which masquerade under the name of morality, make him an admirable exemplar of the iconoclastic doctrine of revolutionary unionism . . . His anomalous position, half industrial slave, half vagrant adventurer, leaves him infinitely less servile than his fellow worker in the East . . . Nowhere else can a section of the working class be found so admirably fitted to serve as the scouts and advance guards of the labor army. Rather they may become the guerrillas of the revolution—the francs tireurs of the class struggle."[83] Such language links the IWW with both the idea of violence and the adventure novels of Scott, Dumas, Kipling, and Cooper.

This idea of the West was a part of standard American culture, as Flynn's mention of Greeley reminds us. Mark Twain, for instance, has a striking passage on the young men of California, in *Roughing It*:

It was a driving, vigorous, restless population in those days. It was a *curious* population. It was the *only* population of the kind that the world has ever seen gathered together, and it is not likely that the world will ever see its like again. For, observe, it was an assemblage of two hundred thousand *young* men—not simpering, dainty, kid-gloved weaklings, but stalwart, muscular, dauntless young braves, brimful of push and energy, and royally endowed with every attribute that goes to make up a peerless and magnificent manhood—the very pick and choice of the world's glorious ones. No women, no children, no gray and stooping veterans—none but erect, bright-eyed, quick-moving, strong-handed young giants—the strangest population, the finest population, the most gallant host that ever trooped down the startled solitudes of an unpeopled land.[84]

Such ideas fitted into the orthodox culture of even eastern cities and their bourgeoisie. An extremely popular book of 1911, for instance, was Ernest Thompson Seton's *Two Little Savages*, about two white boys who put all their passion into imitating American Indians in everything—from living in tepees to painting their faces and walking with their toes turned in. It is made clear that this is just a phase in their development, to be replaced in due time by a return to middle-class standards, but that it is an irreplaceably valuable phase—a period of training and a rite of passage. Although this is a book for children, the nature religion of the Indians is explicitly contrasted to its advantage with the Bible religion of one of the boys' mothers. (It is worth noting that this book, an important document in the history of the American Scout movement, is still in print today, and in five editions simultaneously.) Thus the myth of the West, in one or other of its myriad forms, was to be found nearly everywhere in American society.

The English Wobbly, Charles Ashleigh, contrasted the eastern states, where industry was permanent, with the West, where capitalism was still in a preparatory stage:

In the steel industry, in the textile industry, and others of like magnitude, it is nothing out of the ordinary for several generations of workers to have lived always in the same spot and to have worked always at the same process . . . Also women and children—whole families employed together . . . the nerve-and-body-racking monotonous nature of the work, the close and unhealthy atmosphere, and, sometimes, chemical poisoning or other vocational diseases, and the speeding up system, all make for loss of nervous tone and physical vitality and the creation of bodily weaklings.[85]

Whereas

The striking feature of the Pacific country is that it is a man's country. Conditions render it impossible for the worker to marry . . . [and] the arduous physical toil in the open air does not have the same deteriorating effect as does the mechanical, confined work of the eastern slave . . . the wandering proletariat of the West. In health and in physical courage he is undoubtedly the superior of his Eastern brother . . . A mighty wave of fertility sweeps up through the various states into British Columbia, drawing in its wake the legions of harvest workers.[86]

Richard Brazier says that the wanderings of the IWW members were governed to some degree by their sense of the beauty of certain landscapes.[87] It does seem as if imagination played a larger part in directing their lives than it does in most workers' lives.

In areas like Coeur d'Alene and Cripple Creek, where the WFM and the IWW were active, modernization occurred almost overnight; but the miners were, unlike the immigrant workers of the eastern states, not uprooted or isolated. There were no ghettoes in their towns, and their leaders appealed to American precedent, not European ideology. Haywood, for instance, harked back to the model of 1776, and the redcoats then were what the militia were in 1890 and 1900.

These ideas the IWW brought from the West to the industrial towns of the East, like Paterson, where they met and blended with somewhat similar syndicalist—and socialist—ideas from Europe. This meeting can be exemplified in the coming together of the leaders mentioned: Bill Haywood, from Utah and the Western Federation of Miners; Gurley Flynn, from Brooklyn and the socialist clubs of New York City; and Carlo Tresca and Joseph Ettor from Italy. They all met in Lawrence, Massachusetts, where the IWW under their leadership led a very successful strike in 1912, immediately before the Paterson Strike. And to complete our sketch of the genesis of the latter, we must complement the general picture so far presented by detailing some particular conditions and tactics followed in those two events.

In Paterson in 1913, out of a population of 125,000, 50,000 people worked in the town's sixty silk mills, which together made 60 percent of the country's silk. These had originally been cotton mills, but were converted to make silk in the nineteenth century. However, the mills of Pennsylvania were doing better in the making of cheap silk because they were making each worker supervise several looms at the same time. Between 1907 and 1913 those Pennsylvania mills increased production by 97 percent, while the mills of Paterson increased their output by only 22 percent.

The strike was a protest against the mill owners' introduction of the multiple loom system into Paterson, too. The first walkout occurred in the Doherty Mills on January 27, when the bosses fired four workers who were members of a league demanding an eight-hour working day. A thousand operatives stopped work to protest the firing. And on February 25, IWW leaders arrived to advise and help organize the strikers. Gurley Flynn called a mass meeting the day they arrived, and twenty-five thousand workers left their tasks to attend.

At that moment the IWW was at the peak of its career. It had just led a strike to a successful conclusion, in Lawrence. There sixty thousand out of a population of eighty-six thousand depended on textile mill work. There was little unionization before the strike began, on January 12, 1912, but the IWW sent Joseph Ettor from New York, and he organized a successful range of committees, one for each ethnic group among the workers, and with an elaborate system of replacements for committee members sent to jail. The workers picketed the mills—at that time an innovative tactic—and Mayor Scanlon called out the police, and the state and local militias. The local membership of the IWW grew from three hundred to ten thousand by the time the strike ended on March 12.

Lincoln Steffens wrote, "This is an IWW strike. It's a western strike in the East; a strike conducted in New England by western miners, who have brought here the methods and the spirit employed by them in Colorado, Idaho, and Nevada . . ."[88] What this "method and spirit" meant was, in part, a semireligious exaltation. Ray Stannard Baker wrote in *American Magazine* in May that year, "It is not [far] short of amazing, the power of a great idea to weld men together

. . . There was in it a peculiar, intense, vital spirit, a religious spirit if you will, that I have never felt before in any strike."[89] But it was also, in another part, the spirit of violence. At 12:30 that January 12 in Lawrence, "From room to room the Italian workers ran, stopping the motors, cutting the belts, tearing the cloth, breaking the electric lights, and dragging the other operatives from the looms; knives were brandished before workers who refused to walk out, and bobbins, shuttles, and anything else that came to hand, were thrown at other employees who hesitated. Within 30 minutes, work at the mills came to a standstill."[90]

The engineer at the wood mill was threatened with death if he did not turn off the power. Motors were smashed, looms disabled, and all five thousand workers rushed out of the building. They went from there to the Ayer Mill, where they broke through the iron gates, broke down the doors, shut off the power, and crashed bolts of cloth to the floor. All two thousand employees joined the crowd, which went from there to another mill, where this time the police were strong enough to stop them.[91]

In Lawrence (and again in Paterson) one of their most striking maneuvers was to dramatize the plight of the workers' children (a tactic proposed by New York Italians and derived from strikes in Europe). First, Flynn and Haywood brought the children into the strike by holding meetings for them specifically, in which they explained the strike and told the children how heroic their parents were being. Haywood was a big hit because he brought with him a touch of the wild West, with his Stetson hat and his western drawl and his tall tales. Speaking with his hands in his pockets, he would call himself a two-gun man, and snatch his hands out, one holding his IWW card, the other his SPA card.

Then it was announced that the children were suffering from lack of food and proper clothing, and they were to be sent out of town, to be cared for by well-wishers in New York and Philadelphia. On February 10, 1912, a hundred and twenty of them, representing a large number of nationalities, marched to the railway station carrying banners and black-draped flags. There they were given a medical examination by Margaret Sanger, a trained nurse (who reported that only four of them had underwear), who escorted them via Boston to New York City, where a crowd of five thousand awaited them at Grand Central Station. When the children wrote letters home from their foster parents, these too aroused sympathy. And when another such crusade of 150 children was forbidden and interrupted with some brutality by the police and two companies of militia, a great scandal was aroused, which redounded to the strikers' advantage.

These were days of triumph, Debs polled a million votes in the presidential campaign of 1912. Internationally, the Lawrence strike coincided with labor unrest in Canada and England—on Clydeside, in South Wales, in Dublin. When Hapgood came to Lawrence, to replace Ettor, he was met at the railway station by fifteen thousand people and addressed twenty-five thousand on Lawrence Common. They sang him the "Internationale" in all their native languages.

Paterson, just fifteen miles from New York, had seen a lot more labor organizing than Lawrence, and the IWW had led a small strike there in 1907.[92] Flynn tells us that it was known as Red City and that the first strike there, of women and children, occurred in 1828, with another in 1830.[93] In the late nineteenth and early twentieth centuries, the town was popularly associated with Italian anarchists and revolutionaries like Malatesta. In fact, in November 1912, the socialist candidate for mayor got five thousand votes, only two thousand fewer than the man who won, while in the neighboring town of Haledon, Gene Debs won a plurality of votes as presidential candidate, and a socialist mayor was returned to office; and in North Haledon some socialist city council members were returned to office. (This fact was to be very useful to the strikers and their leaders— when forbidden to meet in Paterson, they simply marched to Haledon and held their meetings there.) Thus, hopes for the Paterson strike, after the success in Lawrence, ran high.

Paterson was a city with a quite special importance in the history of American industry. It had been a key place in Alexander Hamilton's scheme to make the new United States into an industrial state, instead of—as Thomas Jefferson wished—an agrarian republic. In 1791 Governor Paterson of New Jersey signed a charter of incorporation for such an industrial city, and the following year two of Hamilton's agents reported that of several sites, the Great Falls of the Passaic was the best, in terms of power and in other ways, for his Society for Establishing Useful Manufactures. Seven hundred acres were to be developed and given the governor's name. The planner of Washington D.C., Benjamin L'Enfant, was assigned to be its architect. And though the grand scheme collapsed as early as 1797, Paterson did in fact become one of the first industrial cities in the country.

Bill Haywood described the town thus: "Paterson, the silk city of New Jersey, is built near the mosquito-infested swamp lands of New Jersey. It is a miserable place of factories, dye-houses, silk-mills, which are operated by from 20,000 to 25,000 workers. There is not a park in the workers' quarter for the children to play in, no gardens or boulevards where mothers can give their babes a breath of fresh air. Into this town there had thundered weekly a silk train from the West, bringing the raw material from Seattle, where it had been shipped from Japan. The mammoth Doherty mill, owned chiefly by Japanese capitalists, and the other mills, the dye-houses and the factories were all closed down by the great strike of 1913." The work he describes as follows: "After the cocoons were unwound and the silk was whipped into skeins, it was dyed with the glorious colors seen in this costly fabric. All of it went through a process called 'dynamiting,' where it was loaded with metals of different kinds— lead, tin, and zinc. From a quarter to a third of the weight of the silk was of these adulterants, which shortened the life and durability of the finished goods. The owners of silk garments could not understand how a folded or hanging gown would rust and break in the creases until this exposé was made by the strikers."[94]

It had in fact been a cotton-mill town, originally; that is, from its founding by Alexander Hamilton in the last decade of the eighteenth century. In the mid-nineteenth century its mills were adapted to silk weaving, and English operatives from the silk mills around Macclesfield came to work there. Paterson had two great advantages as a silk mill center: its proximity to New York City, with its garment industries and its soft water, which facilitated dyeing.[95]

Steve Golin, a modern historian of the strike, thinks that the strikers there organized themselves and that the work of the IWW was less important than labor historians have said.[96] In fact, he suggests that it was only ancillary. Bill Haywood said as much at the time, but it is of course flattering to labor ideology to propose that "the people" were acting autonomously.

But however suspicious we may be of that proposition, Golin's account of the structure of the Paterson work force and its various traditions of protest and strike action deserves our attention. He divides them into three groups: the ribbon weavers, the dyers' helpers, and the broadsilk weavers. Of these the first—mostly English—were the most skilled, and had the proudest sense of their rights. Originally, they had owned their own looms, and still in 1913 some of them owned their tools. They had a tradition of striking, and were seen by the owners in the 1880s as "communistic."[97] A strike of theirs in 1894 was so successful that the owners began to invest in mills outside Paterson in the rival new mill centers in Pennsylvania, a tactic which helped them during the 1913 strike, because they were able to maintain production in those other mills. From 1901 on, these workers were organized by the United Textile Workers Union, which belonged to the AFL.

The dyers' helpers earned a weekly wage comparable with that of the ribbon weavers (twelve dollars as opposed to fourteen dollars), but in fact they were usually out of work six months of the year. They were largely Italians, with a tradition of anarchism. "During the 1890s, Paterson became the international center of Italian anarchism."[98] In 1900 the king of Italy was assassinated by an anarchist from Paterson, and the anniversary of his deed was honored there. In 1902 they engaged in the bloodiest strike in Paterson history: nine people were killed in a single clash with the police. They were organized by the IWW, but by 1913 they had strong feelings against violence.

The broadsilk weavers were mixed in their national origins, but they included many Jewish immigrants from Poland and Germany, some of whom tried to maintain German or Yiddish cultural and socialist traditions—in music, writing, and social work. They are described by Golin as "seasoned veterans of labor," and they initiated the 1913 strike.[99] They were organized primarily by the Workers'

International Industrial Union, also known as the Detroit IWW, whose leading theoretician was Daniel de Leon. They had struck in 1912 under that union's leadership, and some people referred to that as the Jewish strike, and to the strike of 1913 as Italian. [100]

The city of Paterson had had a policy of strict neutrality in labor disputes, which had made possible labor victories like that of 1894. But the violence of 1902 had aroused public alarm and enabled the owners to make some changes: the police force was increased by 50 percent, some Italian detectives were hired, and above all a new police chief was appointed, John Bimson, who was effectively on the owners' side. He acted decisively in 1913, arresting Haywood, Flynn, and Tresca as soon as they arrived in Paterson, but this provoked the ribbon workers to enter the strike. (For this reason, Golin entitles his article, "Bimson's Mistake.") But if the police move backfired in that case, the owners' close organization and militancy, and above all their disposition of their property outside the town as well as inside, enabled them to break the strike in the end.

Anne Huber Tripp thinks that the IWW should either have brought out strikers in the Pennsylvania mills or else have accepted shop-by-shop settlements in Paterson. In fact they had set their faces against any such settlements—partly because the bread-and-butter issues varied from trade to trade—and had concentrated on making this a general strike, and a battle in the class war. They were playing for high stakes, she thinks. Their demands, if granted, would have constituted "a success of enormous proportions. Following the victories in Lawrence and Little Falls, the IWW would then have to be recognized as a potent force in the country . . ."[101]

Thus Haywood, at the first mass rally he addressed, at Haledon, avoided the concrete issues in favor of the symbolism of the flag. "We will have a new flag, an international flag. We will take the flag of every nation, dip them in a common dye pot, an international flag—the red flag, the color of the working man's blood, and under that we will march."[102] And to a significant degree the owners used the same imagery: they declared March 17, 1913, a flag day and had the Stars and Stripes flying from every mill in town, though it does not seem that this persuaded the strikers to return to work. Instead, they responded with a parade, at the head of which they carried a banner saying, "We weave the flag, We live under the flag, We die under the flag, But damned if we'll starve under the flag."[103]

The strike leaders, however, made a significant error with their flag imagery when the Englishman, Frederick Sumner Boyd, sneered at the national flag in an English accent, on March 31 and April 1. He said the stars were police badges and the stripes were prison bars, and this turned public opinion against the strikers and many of the strikers against the IWW. Later, indeed, some of the leaders thought Boyd had been an agent provocateur. But the point for the moment is just the prevalence of the flag imagery, with its high ideological content.

There was also again a stress on the participation of the strikers' children. Haywood explained the strike to them, and suggested that they, like their parents, should form strike committees; and in fact the children picketed the schools when the teachers made remarks unfriendly to the strike. But he also explained life to them. "I told the children that the world is young, and ever-changing, explaining to them the elemental forces continuously at work, the glaciers ever moving, the effects of earthquakes, volcanoes, and cloud-bursts, the erosion of the earth's surface and the reaction of heat and frost. . . ."[104] Haywood's considerable eloquence always referred to the geological history of the earth, and then he turned to metaphor. "The hardest thing to change is the minds of old people . . . It is they who fasten on the people besotted governments, bigoted religions, and frightful diseases."[105] Children, he said, everywhere wanted cities as close as possible to nature. Thus the youth-and-growth, nature-and-innocence rhetoric of Greenwich Village found a counterpart in the rhetoric of the IWW.

T H E

Leaders

4

Why should I have been interested in the stupid education of our time? We take young, soaring imaginations, consumed with curiosity about the life they see all around, and feed them with dead technique: the flawless purity of Washington, Lincoln's humdrum chivalry . . .
— JOHN REED in Granville Hicks, *John Reed*

I force myself to contradict myself so as to avoid conforming to my own taste.
— MARCEL DUCHAMP in Michel Sanouillet,
Salt Seller

I have lived like an artist, and I shall die like an artist.
— JOE HILL, from his last message to
the people of Utah

Dynamite! Of all the good stuff, that is the stuff! Stuff several pounds of this sublime stuff into an inch pipe (gas or water pipe), plug up both ends, insert a cap with a fuse attached, place this in the immediate vicinity of a lot of rich loafers who live by the sweat of other people's brows, and light the fuse. A most cheering and gratifying result will follow.
— ALBERT PARSONS, *Alarm*, February 21, 1885

*I*n chapter 4 the three themes of chapter 3 will be developed further, but biographically, and principally by focusing on a man and a woman in each case: on Mabel Dodge and John Reed for the Greenwich Village audience; on Gertrude Stein and Marcel Duchamp for the Armory Show; and on Big Bill Haywood and Elizabeth Gurley Flynn for the Paterson Pageant. By examining the origins and the relationships of these men and women, we shall be able to understand what they were aiming at in their work and what those events meant to them, and therefore to others. The relationships were of different kinds: Mabel Dodge and John Reed were lovers; Bill Haywood and Gurley Flynn were comrades; Gertrude Stein and Marcel Duchamp were twin stars of modern art. But, however different the three cases, the gender identities play important parts in all of them. And finally, as we trace the individual places of origin and lines of development, we shall see a convergence of many strains and drives in American life (and indeed from outside America) upon the two events of New York, 1913.

Mabel Dodge and John Reed

John Reed (1887–1920) was born well-to-do in Portland, Oregon, a city which in 1887 still observed some New England proprieties, we are told, but also included "leathery cowboys just off the range, grizzled miners hoping for a stake, lumberjacks with a fistful of change, prostitutes, card-sharps, and con-men."[1] Reed was born on the genteel side of the line dividing Portland, but was aware of the other side—the docks, bars, and opium dens. Such things were part of the vitality of the West, and only officially deplored, so there was no firm barrier between the two. (This ambivalence is not to be associated with men exclusively. Reed's grandmother is supposed to have said about her two grandsons, "Harry is a lamb but Jack is a lion. I prefer lions."[2] Harvard, on the other hand, preferred Harry, and called Jack a grandstand player.)

In other words, Reed was born close to, but separate from, the postfrontier America which Bill Haywood and the IWW claimed to represent. (To Reed, however, for the first twenty-five years of his short life, it seemed to be represented by Theodore Roosevelt.) Reed's grandfather, Henry D. Green, had built a mansion called Cedar Hill on a five-acre estate at the top of B Street when Portland was less than thirty years old, a little town carved out of the Oregon forests, with streets deep in mud and the wilderness coming down close around it. These are Reed's phrases, and he also describes his grandfather as "coming round the Horn on a sailing ship."[3] "Through this my grandfather drove his blooded horses to his smart carriages, imported from the East—and from Europe—with liveried coachmen and footmen on the box."[4] Reed's sense of himself was thus closely involved with his frontier-adventure sense of his country.

Mabel Dodge, born in Buffalo eight years earlier, did not have the same sense of the frontier and its closeness to her. Buffalo was older and more established than Portland. In the 1890s there were sixty millionaires living in Buffalo, and new money was looked down on by old money. But it is worth noting that her first husband, Karl Evans, had lived with an Indian tribe for months at a time; its members had given him beadwork, saddleclothes, etc., and a chief's dress made of buckskin which he loved to wear. He was a fantasy Indian. And so was her other principal beau, Seward Cary. Thus she, like Reed, shared the upper-class myth of America as a frontier nation. Karl Evans in his buckskins looked, she says, like a young buck, with his brown skin and flashing white teeth. When they exchanged wedding gifts, he gave her a silver-mounted rifle, and she gave him a pair of hunting dogs; and their honeymoon was two weeks of deer hunting.[5]

But her key experiences, described in her autobiography, were rejections of patriarchal America—because her values at the time of writing were antipatriarchal. Thus her first mechanical toy, given her by her mother one Christmas, was an iron policeman which came walking toward her, swinging its club, and terrified her. "My first mechanical toy! I have always hated machinery. I wonder if it has anything to do with that Christmas morning. And how I have always loathed policemen!"[6]

Then, when her grandfather Cook gave her a silver dollar, he made a solemn moment of the presentation. The child was impressed, "and yet at the same time a feeling of revulsion and disdain and inward ridicule and irony that has rejected so many other symbols for me all through this life, the sense of clarity and irony that tears away veils . . . 'Oh nonsense! What do I care for your old dollars!' "[7]

Her stress in describing Buffalo falls on the sexual inhibitions and prohibitions and the private unhappiness of the rich people she knew. Her book's values are erotic, and by them her parents and most people she knew failed. The book's heroine might be said to be Isadora Duncan, who danced at the Cooks' summer home at Lennox, and danced out-of-doors, turning all nature into a theater, a theater of life. (This has a cultural and even political significance. A recent study of American radicalism says that Isadora Duncan was a cultural goddess to all the radicals of *The Masses*.)[8] "Isadora, the embodiment of undisciplined rich upswelling life and the wonder of life. The vestal who has served Dionysos . . ."[9] At least in her autobiography, Mabel Dodge was herself a sister vestal, of a slightly different kind.

Reed grew up determined to make himself answer to a current idea of America as young, big, natural, brawny, brawling. Many descriptions of him sound like Robert Hallowell's of 1920: "He was big and brisk and breezy, with the body and mind of a man who could fight, and the temperament of a knight of romance."[10] Art Young says Reed "entered a room hitching up his pants, rough and ready, with he-man shoulders which he would shrug with an amusing coyness."[11] Max Eastman describes him in terms of the same teenage gestures —hitching up his pants and scratching under his arms and giving a gentle, shamefaced smile.[12] Reed had no regard for regularity, in food or in work, and enjoyed outwitting anyone in authority.[13] One of his precursors, as a writer, was Richard Harding Davis; another, more strikingly similar, was Jack London.

Anna Strunsky Walling wrote some "Memoirs of Jack London" for *The Masses*, July 1917, which suggest the way both London and Reed fitted into the range of left-wing enthusiasms of their time. (She and her husband, William English Walling, were leading socialists.) She wrote, "For who shall say when that of wonder and beauty which was Jack London will pass from the earth? . . . He was youth, adventure, romance . . ."[14] an indescribably virile and beautiful boy . . ."[15] He is the outgrowth of the struggle and the suffering of the Old Order, and he is the strength and the virtue of all its terrible and criminal vices."[16] He was a great boxer, fencer, swimmer, sailor: he wanted everything, and he wrote about himself just the way she wrote about him. At twenty-three, in 1899, he wrote her calling himself "a bird of passage, splashing with salt-rimed wings through a brief moment of your life . . . a rude and blundering bird, used to large air and great spaces, unaccustomed to the amenities of confined existence."[17] Reed and Eugene O'Neill were direct heirs of London's sense of self and gesture.

This personal and erotic glamour was inseparably linked to his political radicalism. At twenty-five, London began to sign his letters, "Yours for the Revolution," and thousands copied him. Like Reed, he loved the IWW and Mexican revolutionaries. Walling regrets that he died too soon to see the Russian Revolution. Reed of course saw it for the rest of the world, and in many senses took London's place.

While Reed was still alive he became legendary, and so in some sense unreal. His friend Walter Lippmann wrote about him, "He is one of those people who treat as serious possibilities such stock fantasies as shipping before the mast, rescuing women, hunting lions, or trying to fly around the world in an aeroplane."[18] To Reed and his friends, of course, it was a fatal mistake on Lippmann's part to dismiss these possibilities as "stock fantasies." They were part of his heritage, the heritage of his class. Reed's uncle Ray claimed that he had been made king of Guam (there is a Richard Harding Davis story with that plot) and to have led a successful revolution in Guatemala, after which he gave an official ball and declared war on Germany—tales again close to actual Davis stories. (Reed says, reporting these boasts, "How true his tales were hardly mattered." Meaning that, even if untrue, they announced a crucial courage of the imagination.)[19]

He loved romantic tales about knights as a boy, and at his prep school (in Morristown, New Jersey) saw himself as Sir Galahad. At Harvard he was unpopular for his bumptiousness, but won fame as a leader of the singing and cheering at football matches. Lippmann tells us he would curse the crowd, bully it, sneer at it, but he always captured it.[20] His work on the Paterson Pageant was a continuation of that Harvard role, both literally and metaphorically. He was national cheerleader for the IWW and then for the Russian Revolution, just as Mabel Dodge was their national hostess and social arranger. He and she managed the audience, between them.

After graduating, Reed traveled around Europe "having adventures." A typical example of his exploits was that he bathed, uninvited, in the Duke of Marlborough's pool at Woodstock and did the same in a Michelangelo fountain in Rome. Thus his audience was invited to imagine him leaping into sacred waters, defying the law in the name of his own virile body. A whole series of young men of letters, from Byron to Richard Halliburton, have flaunted their bodies thus, to the admiration of their readers.

He arrived back in New York in 1911 and got a half-time job on *The American*, thanks to his father's friend, Lincoln Steffens. *The American* was a muckraking magazine, taken over in 1905 by Ray Stannard Baker, Ida Tarbell, and other investigative journalists— the muckrakers. For it Reed wrote stories about immigrants, big business, and similar subjects. He met the painters who organized the independent exhibitions of 1908 and 1910 and the Armory Show: John Sloan and Robert Henri and others, a group who often dined at Petitpas' on Twenty-ninth Street. (A central figure in the group was Jack Yeats, father of W. B. Yeats, the poet.) Reed also met Theodore Roosevelt, then to him an impressive embodiment of vitality and virility. They both wrote for the *Metropolitan*.

At this point in his career, Reed was described by the Village poet Harry Kemp, thus: "The huge, genial, broad-faced youth presented the hulking appearance of a full-grown bear, yet still somehow, in spite of its growth, a powerful cub that life had not yet licked into shape."[21] His biographer says, "For Reed, being a man had something to do with drinking, swearing, fighting, enduring hardship, and making the kind of principled stand that might lead to destruction."[22] Hence his need to apprentice himself to a series of exemplars of manliness: Roosevelt and Haywood, and then Villa and Lenin.

Describing the New York he knew, he wrote, "Within a block of my house was all the adventure of the world; within a mile was every foreign country. In New York I first loved, and I first wrote of the things I saw, with a fierce joy of creation—and knew at last that I could write . . . through the swarming East Side—alien towns within towns—where the smoky flare of miles of clangorous push carts made a splendor of shabby streets; coming upon sudden shrill markets, dripping blood and fish scales in the light of torches . . ."[23] This is adventure prose. Reed—like his precursor, Jack London—had learned to write from Kipling and Roosevelt.

In *Historical Essays*, Roosevelt wrote, "The Bowery is one of the great highways of humanity, a highway of seething life, of varied interest, of fun, of work, of sordid and terrible tragedy; and it is haunted by demons as evil as any that stalk through the pages of the Inferno."[24] This could be Kipling on Lahore; but in this essay, "Dante in the Bowery," it is Roosevelt reproving American painters for failing to exploit New York. Reed followed Roosevelt's recommendation.

Soon he moved to Greenwich Village, to 42 Washington Square, with old Harvard friends such as Robert Edmond Jones, and Steffens moved into the same building. Reed made the house famous in his farcical poem, "A Day in Bohemia." And a natural complement of this Bohemianism was politically radical opinions. He visited Lawrence just after the strike there and wrote to a friend, "I have become an IWW, and am now in favor of dynamiting."[25] (The language of dynamite is both a feature of 1913 in general and a mark of our subjects in particular, because of its promise of explosion.)

In summer 1912, *The Masses* reorganized itself under the leadership of Max Eastman, with the managerial help of Dolly Sloan, the painter's wife. Reed joined the magazine and wrote its manifesto. "The broad purpose of *The Masses* is a social one; to everlastingly attack old systems, old morals, old prejudices—the whole weight of outworn thought that dead men have settled upon us . . . We intend to be arrogant, impertinent, in bad taste . . ."[26] The magazine's contributors included people who figured in both our two events—John Sloan, Arthur Davies, George Bellows, Mabel Dodge—as well as other famous names, like William Carlos Williams, Carl Sandburg, Upton Sinclair, and so on. Like most of them, Reed took a libertarian, antireformist view of sex, attacking for instance the Committee on Amusement and Vacation Resources for Working Girls: "What business it is of anyone," he protested, "to quarrel with the working girl's sense of beauty?"[27]

Reed went to see the Armory Show more than once, and Lippmann says that he compared the cubists with the IWW, as two kinds of radical. But his taste in art ran more to the impressionists and the ashcan realists. And—leaving aside his love of adventure—his aesthetic sensibility was subordinate to his political passions. In this he was unlike Mabel Dodge, and in some anecdotes (for instance, those of Muriel Draper) he seems to feel at a disadvantage among her friends.

Mabel Dodge used the language of dynamiting about the Armory Show. (She saw herself blowing up New York as she bustled about in the Show's cause.) She wrote Gertrude Stein, on January 24, 1913, about the Show, that it would be the "most important event that has ever come off since the signing of the Declaration of Independence, and it is of the same nature . . ."[28] Among her concerns the visual arts and the idea of art as a spiritual project, subversive of civilization, were much more powerful than they were among his.

Mabel Evans was married and widowed young in Buffalo. She was left with a baby boy. (She said her period of pregnancy was the only time she felt fulfilled and at peace.)[29] In 1902 she sailed to France, and on the boat met Edwin Dodge, an architect and son of a wealthy Boston family. Her feelings seem to have been less strongly sexual for him than for the two French women she was on her way to meet in Paris (her early sexual orientation seems to have been lesbian), but she married him, and they went to live in Florence. There they bought and rebuilt the Villa Curonia, and moved among English and American expatriates and Italian nobility, all (as she presents them) aesthetes or decadents.

The *gran' salone* was ninety feet long at the Villa Curonia, the dining room was decorated and furnished in Renaissance style, the kitchen in New England colonial, the Yellow Salon in eighteenth-century French, and so on. She had great success as a hostess, and soon felt very superior to her husband. In her own, self-satirizing account, "Sweep the long terrace, making a long line from shoulder to earth. Head back and eyebrows so disdainful! (Weltschmerz) . . . I so deep, so fatal, and so glamorous—and he [Edwin] so ordinary and matter of fact."[30]

The work of redecorating and entertaining was absorbing for a time, and there were outside projects such as the one she and Gordon Craig discussed, for a cinquecento pageant in Florence. They planned to take over the whole town for three days, and exclude all manifestations of modern life, in order to reestablish, briefly, the Renaissance, in dress, food, work, and so on. They would "turn all Florence back to the cinquecento . . . where there would be no audience but only actors . . . revive the old costumes, and the old customs . . . bring people in from all over the world, so that it might be a revival of Art and Beauty . . ." and make everyone ashamed of the ugliness of modern industrial civilization.[31] But by 1912 she found Florence "aesthetically and emotionally bankrupt."[32]

She first met Reed, it appears, the evening they both went to meet Haywood, who was just out of jail in Paterson and was staying in the Village apartment of his mistress of the moment. He complained that there was a news blackout on the strike, and two days later Reed went to Paterson with his friend Eddy Hunt to report it for *The Masses*.[33] He found his way to the picket line, and stood with other people to watch what would happen. A policeman told him to move on and arrested him when he refused. He was sentenced to twenty days in the Passaic County jail, and was locked up with the IWW leader, Carlo Tresca. The latter was suspicious of Reed at first, until the next day Haywood, himself again jailed, could give Reed his endorsement. Released four days later, Reed wrote "War in Paterson," saying that law and order in Paterson were being endangered not by the IWW, but by the authorities. (Hapgood says, "Reed, escaping from the jail at Paterson, was put in jail by Mabel—a far more difficult prison to escape from."[34] But in fact she was the more resolute in breaking off the relationship finally.)

This jail sentence made him a hero of the strikers, who asked him to speak at at least one of their Haledon rallies. He also led them in singing the "Marseillaise," the "Internationale," and various Harvard football songs with new lyrics. This was a rehearsal for one of the episodes in the Pageant. When a committee was set up to organize a Strike Pageant, he was the leader and the most committed member.

But commitment was still an expression of Reed's enthusiasm, rather than vice versa. As Walter Lippmann wrote in 1914, "Revolution, literature, poetry, they are only things which hold him at times, incidents merely of his living. Now and then he finds adventure by imagining it, oftener he transforms his own experience."[35] This refers to his artistic side, but it holds true for his politics, too. He wrote to his mother on June 18, 1913, "Don't believe the papers that say I am tying up with the IWW, or any other limited, little bunch. I am not a Socialist any more than I am an Epicurean. I know now that my business is to interpret and live life, wherever it may be found—whether in the labor movement or out of it."[36] He belonged to the audience, not to the action, till the Russian Revolution changed him.

This was the philosophy he had been taught by his mentors in the Village. Steffens wrote about him after his death, "I tried to steer him away from convictions, that he might play; that he might play with life; and see it all, live it all . . ."[37] That was Mabel Dodge's doctrine, and the Village's. In *Movers and Shakers* she wrote, "That was my only philosophy in those days. Let It happen, let It decide . . . Have faith in life and do not hamper it or try to shape it."[38] She quotes both Hapgood and Steffens as being against "crystallization" and for "fluidity."

In her struggle with Reed, this was in some ways the crucial issue; they both claimed to be for fluidity, but they had different ideas of what fluidity should mean. For her it meant the supremacy of love —of personal relations, in all their changingness. For him it meant a movement to and fro between personal relations and achievements in the world of men.

There were of course comradeships between Reed and men in the Village which did not threaten Mabel's relationship to him. He walked with Bobby Jones from the Villa Curonia to Berlin in 1913; he took

Andrew Dasburg to the front with him in 1914; he was friends with
Marsden Hartley and George Cram Cook. But none of them belonged
to the world of men, as Haywood did; and so Reed's feeling for
Haywood and the IWW, his readiness to apprentice himself to Haywood as a master of manliness, threatened her.

Thus in Venice in 1913, she tells us, "I was jealous of the way
he said, 'Men!' I jumped into the automobile and returned to Florence,
leaving him there to it." What he had said to her was " 'The things
Men have done! But I wish that I could have been here at the *doing*
of them, or that they were doing it *now*.' " Mabel Dodge says she
"hated to see him interested in Things. I wasn't, and didn't like to
have him even *look* at churches and leave me out of his attention."[39]
She wrote him that nothing could compare with the odor of the jasmine
at the window or the warmth of the sunlight, with Nature, which she
felt to be in alliance with love and with woman.

This battle for Reed's allegiance she in effect lost, though not to
Haywood, who did pass out of Reed's life after 1913. She may have
won that battle. It seems to have been his experience in Mexico in
1914 and 1915 as a war correspondent that was decisive. In Pancho
Villa he found a hero who represented the world of men still more
powerfully, and who made him present at what men do. He met Villa
on December 26, 1913, and found him, "the most natural human
being I ever saw"; but he was using *natural* in a sense quite different
from Mabel's—"most natural" in the sense, as he says, of nearest to
a wild animal. "Hands, arms, trunk, moved with the swiftness and
sureness of a coyote." His dark eyes were absolutely hot and
steely—the eyes of a man who could kill. Pancho Villa was a living
legend, the subject of many poems and ballads, and his government,
Reed said, was what the rule of the IWW might be if it came to
power. Villa was (like Haywood) a passionate gambler, a big laugher,
and sexually rapacious.[40] And whereas Mabel Dodge had in some
sense neutralized the charge Haywood had for Reed, she was unable
to make contact with Villa. (And later, of course, he found an even
more impressive man in Lenin.)

However, their relationship was also a love affair, and can be
understood also in the conventional terms: attraction, desire, rapture,

jealousy, boredom, entrapment, mutual exasperation. In Florence, Reed wrote about her thus:

> *Through the halls of the Medici, queenlier far than they,*
> *Walks she I love, half peasant, half courtesan—*
> *In her right hand a man's death, in her left the life of a*
> *man—*
> *Beware which you choose, for she changes them day by day;*
> *Sea and wind in the room of her soul, and all the beasts that*
> *prey.*[41]

Gertrude Stein and Marcel Duchamp

Gertrude Stein and Marcel Duchamp were, I have suggested, two stars of the Armory Show. They were names in lights outside the theater; inside, their performances had little to do with each other, except that both exemplified modern art. They were both part of the action and not the audience, in the sense here given to those terms, for they did not see themselves as central, average, or normative.

The Steins marked themselves out as deliberate eccentrics early, defying all social norms. Their mother died when they were young, and their father in 1891. Their brother Michael thereupon became vice president of the Market Street Railway Company in San Francisco, and from then on Leo and Gertrude, who lived simply, never had to bother about money. They relied on Michael for financial matters, and he relied on them for ideas, taste, amusement. In 1893 he married a woman, Sarah Samuels, who though not as brilliantly clever as they, was also interested in art and ideas; Leo and Gertrude opened up to Michael and Sarah a life which the latter found exhilarating.

This escape from patriarchal power, both metaphorical and literal, and their replacement of it with a mild, admiring protector, is an important clue to Gertrude's philosophy and attitudes. When she wrote, "Fathers are depressing, mothers may not be cheering, but they are not as depressing as fathers," obviously she was referring to something larger than their own domestic situation. In the 1930s, with her eye on the political climate of Europe, she wrote, "There is too much fathering going on." And the world of artists in Paris, to which she (and Duchamp) came, was a congregation of refugees from patriarchy.

In Oakland they were neighbors to the Duncan family, of whom Isadora and Raymond were to be briefly friends to Leo and Gertrude in Paris, and permanently an instructive contrast. The Duncans were considerably poorer than the Steins, and it is said that Raymond was one of the boys who robbed the Steins' apple orchard. What California primarily meant to both sets of siblings was the Bohemian atmosphere of life-experiment, which we can associate with the artists' colony at Carmel; but it is worth noting that when Leo and Gertrude wandered far on foot, he would carry a gun, even as a boy. In other words, Oakland was still close to its frontier past. And Gertrude's idea of America (which was, like John Reed's, closely tied to her idea of herself) was a matter of breadth and freedom, movement and experiment.

She described herself, in *The Autobiography of Alice B. Toklas*, as "completely and entirely American."[42] Perhaps one aspect of this was her simple and frank appetite for success—for what she called *la gloire*. Her early friend, Mabel Weeks, says that she talked freely of this as early as 1900. And "Hurrah for gloire!" was her reply when Mabel Dodge sent her the Armory Show essay. ("Do send me half a dozen copies of it. I want to show it to everybody.")[43] Leo's primary characteristic, on the other hand, was a fear of responsibility, and therefore of life itself, according to Weeks again. This marks the largest difference between them, a difference in the balance between self-doubt and self-confidence, which in him inclined to the former, in her to the latter. A later biographer, John Malcolm Brinnin, described her as being "as self-satisfied and as full of contented whimsies as a cat on a hob . . . she tended to see everything as concentric to herself."[44]

She read enormously, from early on, and apparently identified herself with Maggie Tulliver, the heroine of *The Mill on the Floss*, another intellectual girl with a dominant older brother. This is an identification incongruous with the personality of the later Gertrude Stein, so jolly and hearty and sure of herself. But her self-consciousness during adolescence was apparently painful and murky (no doubt in part because of her nascent lesbianism).

She saw herself as an anxious type.[45] Such people, she said, always have fear in them; they need to keep feeling their hands, to know if they are still alive, and they demand admiring praise from their friends. She also saw in herself, and in Leo, their father's short-lived enthusiasms and failure to push things through to a successful conclusion. Clearly, her public persona disguised such feelings.

She and Leo, at least while growing up, both seem to have been moralistic, and to have feared the moral and psychological consequences of losing self-control, so that later she in some sense repudiated her youth. She henceforth associated adolescence with unwelcome emotions and melodramas and with music—apparently making Wagner rather than Mozart represent music. She claimed that some lucky people managed to completely avoid that time of trouble.[46] "Fifteen is really medieval and pioneer and nothing is clear and nothing is sure, and nothing is safe and nothing is come and nothing is gone. But it all might be." William Vaughn Moody noted the emotional intensity of her writing while she was a student at Harvard, and she spoke herself of her explosive laughter and belligerent attitudes there.[47] Where she felt at home was in the Enlightenment; or with contemporary heroes of Enlightenment values, like William James. John Malcolm Brinnin speaks of her as a last daughter of the Enlightenment.

Because she had, apparently, a happy childhood, as the baby of a large family, she kept in touch with her babyhood even as she repudiated her adolescence. Even as an adult, everyone looked after her—especially Alice B. Toklas—and friends called her Darling Baby and Baby Woojums. Leo and she both used baby language and slang, in letters as well as in talk; discussing a painting, "It's a bully picture all right."[48] But of course this aspect of her was complemented by, for instance, her formidable cleverness, and by a simple directness and naturalness which made it easy for her to talk to people quite remote from her, socially and intellectually. And her friend, Etta Cone, said of her, "Gertrude is great fun." Indeed, enemies—like Wyndham Lewis—also remarked on the baby aspect; he described her as "a huge, lowering, dogmatic Child."[49]

Having been something of a favorite pupil of James's at the Harvard
Annex, she entered Johns Hopkins Medical School in 1897, but lost
interest and joined Leo in Paris in 1901. There she took a natural
place in that congeries of artistic rebels against bourgeois life. Su-
perficially, her style was eccentric in that setting: in an early work,
Q.E.D., she claims to be the apostle of middle-class values—honesty, respectability, content, affection. And her life-style in some
sense confirms her claim. But her *ideas* were modernist, and, she
says (and claims that Picasso agrees with her) "when you are way
ahead with your head, you are naturally old-fashioned in your
daily life."

Her work seemed modernist in many ways. It was compared in
1911 by Hutchins Hapgood with the "fragmented and excited talk"
of Anton Johannson, a labor leader whom Hapgood admired. "A
temperament that can express with vitality the turbulent reaching out
and reaching up for a new life of submerged masses of men has
something esthetically and emotionally similar to an artist who is
strenuously seeking to express feelings and words hitherto unex-
pressed in art forms, and to express which means the breaking of the
academical habits."

We can get one clue to her inspiration in her language experiments
from a remark of her great teacher, William James. "If we look at a
printed word, and repeat it long enough, it ends by assuming an
entirely unnatural aspect. . . . It is reduced by this new way of
attending to it to its sensational nudity."[50] This suggests the psychological experiments in which she and her friends engaged under his
direction at Harvard.

Having escaped the authority of her father—and later that even
of Leo—she refused all other familial relationships. More than that,
she refused all those intellectual forms in which the principle of
patriarchy and hierarchy lurked. She refused history (i.e., the sense
of necessity and strict causation), preferring geography (i.e., the broad
open sense of possibility).[51] In art, she refused paintings with obvious
centers (subjects and anecdotes), preferring composition (where every
square inch of the canvas was as important as every other); she liked
Cézanne because his paintings were decentered.[52] She refused human
nature (the claim to know what people will do and feel and think),

preferring the human mind (the limitless possibilities of thought and action). Human nature, she said, might as well stop, if it could do no better than it had done. This was modernism in art and thought, as Stein represented it.

Marcel Duchamp was born in 1887 in "that part of Normandy where the Bovarys have not displaced the Grandets."[53] He was born, like Gertrude Stein, into a prosperous family with five children, among whom he was the youngest boy. His father seems to have been rather remote, while of his mother he remembered a determined placidity and indifference to himself, which hurt him, until he made those same qualities his own to defend himself against the outside world.[54] When his older brothers left home, Pierre Cabanne says, Marcel felt very lonely, because his mother openly preferred the younger children, who were girls. So he assumed a haughty detachment in self-protection.[55] Thus there is a developmental likeness between Duchamp and Stein, in that both apparently found adolescence a time of pain or disappointment, and both found themselves in young manhood or womanhood—and after crossing the Atlantic to another continent.

Also, according to some observers, Duchamp cherished a grudge against his brothers (one which found expression only after their death) because they brought him the message of the rejection of his *Nude Descending a Staircase* from the Section d'Or exhibition of 1912. He told Lebel that from then on, his always antipictorial painting became also antisocial and antifamilial.[56] And Cabanne agrees that this was a shock which strongly affected his life and work.[57]

He began to paint as a boy, thanks to his brothers' example, and was influenced first (among contemporary schools) by the impressionists, Cézanne, and the Fauves. He attended the Académie Julian, like so many American artists, but by his own account spent his days playing billiards rather than studying. His brother Gaston (who painted under the name Jacques Villon) earned his living by drawing illustrations for Paris newspapers. Marcel did some illustrating himself, but recoiled from the prospect of a lifetime of such work, which was not what being an artist should mean.[58] Typically, however, he concealed his aesthetic idealism beneath cynicism. "We paint because we want to be free. We couldn't go to the office every morning."[59]

Villon, he said, "Aimed at fame. I *had* no aim. I just wanted to be left alone to do what I liked." And no doubt his temperament *was* profoundly quietist and anarchistic. "I consider working for a living slightly imbecilic from an economic point of view."[60] He avoided both marriage and military service, treating both love and war with disdain. And these are attitudes which his disciples are likely to develop. We find them echoed in, for instance, the autobiography of Man Ray. "I wondered: perhaps love had come to me too easily, as it had to Duchamp . . . [and Duchamp's work] while not as world-shaking as war, certainly has outlived the latter. The survival of inanimate objects, of works of art through great upheavals is one of my consolations. My justification, if need be."[61]

When it came time for his military service, he took advantage of the partial exemption offered skilled workmen, by training to be a printer. There was nothing military or civic or patriotic about Duchamp's temperament, or his interests: during both World Wars, he absented himself from France. Gertrude Stein, on the other hand, was interested in the history of the Civil War; and was, at the end of her life, highly patriotic. But perhaps these aspects of her behavior should be called whimsical (in relation to her modernist ideas, which occupied the serious part of her mind), a self-indulgence which Duchamp did not permit himself.

Having endured military service, he joined his brothers in Paris, and lived *la vie d'artiste*, though making strong inner protests against its clichés: the painter in beret and smock, as he says, with his soul full of beauty and aesthetic theories on his lips, and all the quarrels over precedence and the resentments of bruised egos. He compared life in France to a basketful of lobsters clawing each other.[62] Yet he also said, "In my time we artists were pariahs, we knew it and enjoyed it. But today [in the USA] the artist is integrated," a state of affairs he deplored.[63]

He was strongly attracted to the Pierrot poet, Jules Laforgue, especially to the latter's *Moralités légendaires*, such as his ironic revision of *Hamlet*. Duchamp's painting, *Portrait d'un jeune homme triste dans un train* was inspired by a Laforgue poem, "Encore à cet astre," and that painting clearly led him on to the *Nude Descending a Staircase*. For Duchamp, titles were very important; Laforgue's were very evocative, and his own were each as much an element of the picture it belonged to as its color or its drawing. *Célibataire* is a key concept and image for both painter and poet; though both married, each painted or wrote out of a self that could not be subsumed in marriage or citizenship. And Duchamp shared Laforgue's nostalgia for popular culture and for fairgrounds; both *La marieé mise à nue par ses célibataires, même*, and his last large work, *Étant donnés*, have fairground associations. This resemblance is an important index to Duchamp's kind of refined aestheticism, the kind which asserts or defends itself by the means of vulgarity, like Laforgue's (and that of the early T. S. Eliot, another Laforguian).

His brothers belonged to a different part of the Paris art world from Picasso, and practiced a different sort of cubism, the less rigorous sort associated primarily with Gleizes and Metzinger. But Duchamp shared many interests with Picasso and his gang. He in fact got to know Apollinaire in 1911, attended the performance of Raymond Roussel's *Impressions d'Afrique*, admired Jarry and other princes of eccentricity, like J. P. Brisset, the Douanier Rousseau of philology, and Maurice Princet, an amateur enthusiast for non-Euclidean geometry. These pundits, sometimes unwittingly, turned the structures of seriousness on their heads—subverted whole sciences—which is what Duchamp, like Picasso, was looking for.

Duchamp's cubism was more like Cézanne's version than Picasso's.[64] His *Portrait of the Artist's Father* displayed filial piety to both its subject and Cézanne, he said. Via Villon he adopted from Cézanne a tenderly colored, transparent surface, an aquarelle-like overlapping of translucent facets: these facets are in themselves flat, but the picture as a whole is not, as it would be in a true cubism. Duchamp left remnants of perspective—holes punched in the canvas, as one critic puts it, and chiaroscuro modeling.[65]

He discovered the Fauves in 1910, after his enthusiasm for Cézanne, he says. Matisse, Van Dongen, Braque, and Derain were then "the wild men in the zoo of painting," in his words. Then came the pictures he painted in Munich in 1912; typically *The Passage from the Virgin to the Bride*. "The small canvas is an intricate web of dissected flaps, tubes, filaments, and modules which blossom across a fluid field of glowing color in a rococo network of sensitively spaced waves and distensions."[66] In this work he produced a velvety smoothness by hand-kneading his pigments; but in all his subsequent career he seems to have felt disgusted by the smell and touch of oil paint.

Finally he met and fell under the influence of Francis Picabia, who always contradicted, Duchamp says.[67] He showed Duchamp a world other than that of his brothers, or of all the professional painters. Picabia, Duchamp tells us, smoked opium every night—that was just one of his contradictions. Looking back, Duchamp said Picabia revealed to him a new idea of—of the artist? his interviewer suggested. "No, of man," Duchamp said.

Some of his favorite reading was the periodical almanacs, for instance the *Vermot* (founded in the 1880s, and still printed): this was/ is a collection of proverbs, vulgarities, puns, spoonerisms, riddles, obscene jokes, recipes, horoscopes. He loved schoolboy verbal games of distorting words and phrases. (This corresponds to Gertrude Stein's baby talk and Leo Stein's puns.) Even late in life, Duchamp liked looking through old catalogs of, for instance, the gun and cycle factories. But this was combined with a taste for Mallarmé (because he is so simple) and for other modernists of literature, like Huysmans, Lautréamont, Rimbaud.

He often talked about his love-hate of science, which has induced some scholars to credit him with more command of such subjects than is likely. Looking back, he himself insisted that he never understood non-Euclidean geometry or the fourth dimension. They simply suggested to him games he might play. Irony was the breath he breathed. He found even Picasso's friends too fulsome and self-important. He described to Cabanne a lunch he and Picabia shared with Apollinaire and Jacob; it was unbelievable, he said; the latter two were still talking like the symbolists of 1880; he was torn between anguish and insane laughter. (The symbolists represent the grandiose pretentiousness of the generation against which Duchamp's generation reacted.)[68]

In 1905 or 1906 Gertrude and Leo Stein were introduced to Picasso by Henri-Pierre Roché, later a close friend of Duchamp. Roché was also the intermediary through whom the Steins met other people—

notably Alfred Jarry, the precursor of dada. (Duchamp's mock science, in the Notes to *The Large Glass*, owes something to Jarry's pseudoscience, Pataphysics.)

Gertrude constructed an elaborate system of psychological types, and the one to which she assigned herself and Picasso she called the Bazarovs—people not capable of experiencing the full reality of other people. (The word comes from Turgenev's novel, *Fathers and Sons*. Bazarov is a son in rebellion against all fathers.) The danger that hangs over the Bazarovs is of fanaticism, and of a "dirty" sexuality. Picasso (and presumably she too) was saved from this threat by the intensity of his aesthetic experience; for instinctive creativity and consciousness to the point of genius have to do with relating to the world more than to oneself.[69] She saw Picasso as like herself: greedy, childish, laughing, a bit rough. She also described him walking with his friends as having "the isolation and movement of the head of a bullfighter at the head of their procession."[70] Clearly, he stimulated her imagination, and in ways which evidently seemed to him appropriate, so that her claim to be his twin is in some ways justified.

Matisse, on the other hand, she thought of as blind, and she seems to have associated him with the image of her father. His blindness made him stick to his experience and be "slow," while Picasso was "quick in gesture."[71] She hates his "brutal egotism." She saw more life in Madame Matisse than in him, no doubt because of his bourgeois traits. He told an American journalist, "Oh do tell the American people that I am a normal man; that I am a devoted husband and father, that I have three fine children, that I go to the theatre, ride horseback, have a comfortable house, a fine garden, that I love flowers . . . just like any man."[72] This was very unlike Picasso.

At the time she met Picasso she was translating Flaubert, whose story "Un Coeur Simple" inspired her "Good Anna." In the spring of 1906 she finished that story and *Three Lives*, of which it is a part; she was there experimenting with something like a stream of consciousness—an idiosyncratic monologue in which a psychological type and certain moral problems reflected themselves. She also sat for her portrait for Picasso. (*Three Lives* was published by a vanity press, and appeared with blurbs by Hutchins Hapgood and his wife, Neith Boyce.) Having trouble with the face, he solved the problem by substituting a mask derived from Iberian sculture; and in so doing set himself on the path to the *Demoiselles d'Avignon*, and so on to cubism.

The years 1906 to 1911 are sometimes called the heroic period of analytical cubism.[73] This was the time when Gertrude Stein worked on her long "novel," *The Making of Americans*, which also sacrificed many of the colors and forms of conventional fiction, reducing plot and scene and dialogue to a monotonous continuity. She studied Cézanne's *Portrait de Madame Cézanne* which Leo had bought, and no doubt saw it in the terms he had suggested: that is, seeing Cézanne as a painter like Mantegna (in his *Crucifixion*) and focusing on his use of color, his simplified forms, and his subordination of the illustrative to the compositional interest. She spoke of Cézanne's revolutionary sense of composition and his realism which superseded that of the objects depicted, and she thought writers had to practice composition in that way. She was also ready to say that she was the first writer to get that idea. Works of art were henceforth to have no center, no ideational structuring.[74] Everything was to be offered with equal emphasis. The essential struggle of the twentieth century, she thought, was to be to "flatten" experience—to remove the films of philosophical tradition which clouded the observer's vision.

"I was there to kill what was not dead, the 19th century which was so sure of evolution and prayers, and esperanto and their ideas."[75] To kill the nineteenth century, art must decentralize composition and present objects in a form that itself becomes an entity, as the cubists did.[76] She rebelled against "that socially elevated tone, the orotund authorial voice, the elegant drawing-room diction" of nineteenth-century fiction—the details, the descriptions, the plots, the psychological analysis, of for instance Henry James. She pointed out that Proust and Joyce, and she, had no plots.

Mabel Dodge invited her to the Villa Curonia and enthusiastically described her work habits and what she produced to her friends: how Stein wrote at night, banishing all preconceived images, and waiting for words to rise up from her subconscious.[77] Dodge also saw the whole proceeding in more skeptical and satiric terms, like a baby's fascination with its own excreta—with Toklas as the mother who admired whatever baby had produced. But Stein calmly told the world that she was "the only one in English literature in her time."[78]

All this self-confidence had its effect, and found receptive hearers. She was taken to be a cubist writer, and the American connoisseur of modern painting. In 1912 Alfred Stieglitz wrote her, saying he would like to publish in *Camera Work* some photographs of work by Matisse and Picasso, together with her "portraits" of both. Her claim to be doing in prose what they did in paint was something Mabel Dodge was ready to repeat (she called herself "your faithful and uncomprehending Boswell") in the essay introducing the Armory Show.[79]

In February 1913 Leo Stein sold his Picassos and left Paris for Settignano with sixteen Renoirs and two Cézannes. "The general situation here is loathsome with its cubico-futuristic tommy-rotting . . ." he wrote a friend on April 2, 1914—"nothing better than an exploitation of ingenuity."[80] This left Gertrude and her friend Alice in possession both of 20 rue de Fleurus and of the role of interpreter of modern art. (Her collection finally included thirty-eight Picassos and nine paintings by Gris.)

Gertrude Stein's passion for *la gloire* was perhaps part of her modernism. Her old friend, Raymond Duncan, was another artist of notoriety. And Maurice Sterne attributes the same passion to Mabel Dodge and to the archetypal artistic modernist, Picasso: "For *la gloire* he became a monotheist, who believed in no other God but himself."[81] It is worth noting that Picasso once defined genius as "personality, with a pennyworth of talent," which—since he and Gertrude were both bent on *being* geniuses—is surely a congruous insight. Duchamp had a more complex and conflicted attitude to fame, perhaps suggested by his appearance. Cabanne describes him as looking like a sly cleric—a comparison also applied to Laforgue and Laforgue's disciple, T. S. Eliot: lean-faced, thin-lipped . . . a penetrating gaze but a soft voice . . . a rather disconcerting serenity.[82]

In some ways, Duchamp reminds us of the great literary dandy, Nabokov (and in other ways of the philosophic dandy, Derrida). To a friend whose wife had died, Duchamp wrote, "We all play a miserable game, and generalities and generalizations are the inventions of amateur magicians," which could have been written by Nabokov.[83]

Another of Duchamp's epigrams, "I object to responsibility," is worthy of Humbert Humbert, or any other of Nabokov's heroes. The passion for chess they shared is another clue. A game of chess is a drawing, Duchamp said, a mechanical reality.[84] It creates very beautiful things, but in the domain of movement, not of pigment. Moreover, it has no social purpose, which is very important. Duchamp found the milieu of chess players more sympathetic than that of painters. The former are "madmen of a certain quality," the way artists are supposed to be.

This could remind us of several Nabokov heroes, and Duchamp's one encounter with or vision of Raymond Roussel was as a chess player; Roussel looked very strait-laced and high-collared, all in black, very "avenue de Bois," another "clergyman," in the French sense. All this, we realize, is exactly to Duchamp's taste. And when Duchamp reminds us that Roussel killed himself, we think of another dandy writer, Beckett, and his novel *Murphy*, in which the autobiographical hero finds happiness at last in playing chess with a suicidal madman called Mr. Enders.

As for Derrida, Duchamp told Cabanne that he believed in nothing: "The word belief is another error . . . I don't believe in the word 'being'. The idea of being is a human invention."[85] This is very close to Derrida's philosophy of deconstruction, as is Duchamp's philosophy of art. "I shy away from the word 'creative' . . . fundamentally, I don't believe in the creative function of the artist." He preferred the word *craftsman*.[86] Nor did he believe that art had any significant function of veracity, of truth.

Gertrude Stein was by no means so ready to debunk art; and her attaching herself so decisively to Picasso, and not to Duchamp, signals a big difference between them. However, there are connections, especially if you compare them as phenomena of reputation, of public image. Duchamp, looking back over his career, said, "I've been a little like Gertrude Stein. To a certain group, she was considered an interesting writer, with very original things . . ."[87] (One such group —probably the one he was thinking of—was the Arensberg circle in New York, which constituted itself Duchamp's milieu and claque when he first arrived in this country.) And one book on Duchamp begins by quoting Stein: "It is awfully hard to go on painting . . . Having done anything you naturally want to do it again and if you do it again you know you are doing it again and it is not interesting."[88] And both of course were admired for the gay insolence with which they defied and perhaps defrauded their publics.

Both broke away from their families early and avoided marriage and children themselves. They maintained a personal style independent of generation—self-born out of their own heads—with a hidden bitterness against the father in Stein's case, and the mother in Duchamp's. The early allies against the parents in both cases were elder brothers, but that alliance was soon broken, and the mentor quietly but ruthlessly rejected. What they aimed at, and achieved, in personal style was a serene cheerfulness and a dazzling wit that would attract others, to build a life of friendships and admirations. And these personal traits are reflected, indirectly but powerfully, in their work and in the character of modernism as they have shaped it.

Haywood and Flynn

The modern artists and the Wobblies were both rebels and therefore conscious of being minorities. But the former renounced the pursuit of social power, as the latter did not. This means that the former were culturally or spiritually rebellious, while the latter were politically so. Judged by some criteria, the first rebellion is more profound—by other criteria it is a form of compromise.

Bill Haywood and Gurley Flynn jointly represented the working class of America; and, unlike our other two couples, they represented their constituency organizationally. But they represented significantly different ideas of that class, a western and masculinist idea versus an eastern and feminist idea. Their interrelationship was also different from those we have been discussing. They were comrades; unlike Stein and Duchamp, they worked together, shared ideas, supported each other, spoke on the same platforms. But unlike Dodge and Reed they were not attracted to each other. Indeed, though they were mutually appreciative and for a long time loyal, one guesses at a positive lack of personal warmth between them—each was less close to the other than to other people in their movement. They had

111

their quarrels: one was over the Paterson Pageant; another, more serious one, occurred in 1915 when Haywood reproved Flynn, and she in effect ceased to work for the IWW.

But for most of the great decade of IWW history, 1905–1915, they worked together efficiently as members of a collective leadership. They embodied different kinds of labor radicalism, as we know, but they were mutually complementary; in them man and woman came together, young and middle-aged, the western United States and the eastern, the frontier and the city, the pioneer and the socialist, tall-tale humor and socialist club rhetoric. Coming together, their different styles formed the IWW charisma and promised a new life to the American labor movement, especially benefitting the unskilled and the immigrants.

Bill Haywood was born in Salt Lake City in 1869. That city was then only twenty-two years old, and was unusual among western cities in that it had been settled by families rather than by men alone; more than half its population was female; there were colleges and debating clubs, and permanent public buildings with some style. But the Haywoods were neither Mormons nor substantial citizens. Bill's father was a Pony Express rider from Ohio, whose forebears had been soldiers of fortune. (Another Wobbly hero, Vincent St. John, was the son of a Pony Express rider.) He died at about twenty-five, leaving a nineteen-year-old widow and one son. Mrs. Haywood had belonged to a family of immigrants from South Africa.

When she remarried, she and Bill went to live in Ophir, Utah, a mining camp seven thousand feet above sea level, with copper and gold, lead and zinc mines. Founded in 1870, the little town had died by 1880, its 2,500 ore locations having shrunk to 150. Its history seems to have been typical of such towns, and its imprint can be found on Haywood's mind much later. His imagination was geological; he saw society shifting and growing, sometimes in huge slow movements, like the earth, sometimes in avalanches; and he judged people by frontiersman standards. The two or three streets of Ophir stood in a canyon, and mountain lions prowled around the town at night.

As a boy, he saw a shootout in which Slippery Dick left Marny Mills dead on the street; and like Mark Twain in Hannibal, he met violence and physical cruelty as a recurrent part of social life. He lost the sight of one eye early, which gave a sinister aspect to one profile. He took his first job at the age of nine, going down the Ophir mines. And later, back in Salt Lake City, he was a boy of all work for a farmer for six months.

At fifteen he took a job in the Humboldt County mine in Nevada and remained there three years, staying on as a guard when the mining operation closed down. He liked to fight and gamble, and told Western stories about his experiences. These stories, and even quite literally the places where they are set, are familiar to readers of Mark Twain, especially of *Roughing It*; but it is worth noting certain differences. Haywood gives books a greater role in that culture; his stepfather introduced him to Voltaire, Byron, Burns, Milton; and there were related activities, like playing chess and reciting Shakespeare. (In jail in Idaho in 1906, Haywood spent time committing Kipling poems to memory, and he wrote poetry himself.)

He also expresses, in his writings, a much less racist frontier mind than Twain does. His accounts of Indians, Negroes, and Chinese cooks are prejudice-free. He gives two accounts of a massacre of Indians—the event as described by a white participant, and as described by an Indian victim. "Old Sackett's tale seemed to pull a lot of the fringe off the buckskin clothes of the alluring Indian fighters I had read about in dime novels. There was nothing I had ever read about, with heart palpitating, of killing women and little children while they were asleep."[89] The sequence of such stories, he tells us, "began when the earliest settlers stole Manhattan Island. It continued across the continent. The ruling class with glass beads, bad whisky, Bibles and rifles continued the massacre from Astor Place to Astoria."[90]

On the other hand, Haywood is recognizably of that roughly masculinist pioneer culture and uses that language against his political rivals, like Samuel Gompers of the AFL. "It was amusing to see the big broad-shouldered men of the West taking the measure of this undersized individual that called itself the leader of labor. This squat specimen of humanity certainly did not personify the membership of the AFL. Sam was very short and chunky with a big head that was bald in patches, resembling a child suffering with ringworm. He had small snapping eyes, a hard cruel mouth, wide with thin drooping lips, heavy jaws and jowls. A personality vain, conceited, petulant and vindictive."[91]

In the mid 1880s there was a technical and social revolution in mining, which had its roots earlier. The year of Haywood's birth was the year the railway lines from the East Coast met those from the West, in Utah. The linking up made it possible to bring in mining machinery, and thus made it profitable to mine in many new locations. This attracted capital from far away. For instance, British investors financed twenty enterprises in Utah between 1871 and 1873, with fifteen million dollars of initial capitalization. (Haywood's stepfather worked in a British-owned mine.)

Up to this time, prospectors had been placer-miners, who sifted pure metals from the sand and gravels of creeks; such work cost no money, for such men built their own rockers, and moved on when the claim was exhausted.[92] And if they did not need capital from outside, they did need cooperation from other men in the same work: they helped each other build rockers and sluices; typically a site was developed by a group. In the camps, theft was allegedly unknown, and men went into other cabins in the owner's absence, to make themselves a meal. This was the past (legendary or not) which inspired the new unionism to rebel against the new work conditions in mining. Haywood reported being outraged when someone did rob his cabin in 1895.

Under the new conditions, the majority of prospectors became wage earners, but they kept up traditions of independence—for instance, sneaking nuggets home at night, concealed in their clothing, which officially belonged to the owners. The unions that sprang up at this time were, therefore, a natural expression of that independence and cooperation. "The socialism of the Western Federation of Miners was rooted in the traditions of the prospector, not in the tomes of Marx and Engels."[93]

The conditions of work changed radically, with the new ownership. Thus the Ohio mine at which Haywood worked in Nevada was only half-heartedly exploited, because it was sixty miles from the railway. But the Brooklyn mine to which he went in 1887 was absentee-owned, mechanized, and run strictly for profit. The miners worked in lung-choking, eye-smarting powder gas, and suffered from lead poisoning, as well as rheumatism and tuberculosis. If a man worked ten years in the hard-rock mines, as Bill Haywood did, he had one chance in three of suffering serious injury, and one in eight of being killed.[94]

In 1889 Haywood married Nevada Jane Minor, who soon began to suffer from arthritis, which crippled and finally killed her. He prospected, worked as a cowboy, and then tried working a homestead. He delivered his own child, and had to do a lot of nursing of his wife. But relations between them went sour early, partly because she turned to faith healing and Christian Science. Haywood was hostile to all piety and every religion, except for his passionate faith in labor politics.

In 1894 he left his family and went to Silver City, Idaho; he hoped to find a skilled mining job there, but had to shovel ore, as a car man. In 1896 his hand was mangled in machinery, and would have been amputated had he not protested. In that same year the Western Federation of Miners held two organizing meetings in Silver City, and Haywood joined. He got elected to the finance committee and later became treasurer. In 1898 he was sent as a delegate to a convention in Salt Lake City and got elected to the executive board. In 1900, at a meeting in Denver, he became secretary-treasurer of the federation, a full-time job, and so left the work of mining, and moved to Denver to live. His career as a labor leader had begun.

He was already a picturesque figure who compelled people's imaginations. A few years later, *McClure's Magazine* described him thus: "A powerfully built man, built with the physical strength of an ox. He has a big head and a square jaw. A leader here is judged by the very force of his impact. Risen from the mines himself, 'from the bowels of the earth', as he describes it, this man has become a sort of religious zealot, and Socialism is his religion. He is a type of the man not unfamiliar now in America . . . [Mary Heaton Vorse also spoke of Haywood's type as familiar and representative in America then, which testifies to his authority.] . . . Take a character like this, hard, tough, warped, immensely resistant, and give him a final touch of idealism, a Jesuitic zeal that carries the man beyond himself, and you have a leader who, like Haywood, will bend his people to his own beliefs."[95] He was a gambler, a womanizer, and a heavy drinker—though it has been suggested that diabetes may have been the cause of his addiction to drink.

Elizabeth Gurley Flynn was born in the Bronx in 1890 to Irish socialist parents. The whole family attended the Harlem Socialist Club every Sunday. Mr. Flynn, an often unemployed civil engineer, checked his daughters' school essays for their political content. There were three daughters, of whom Elizabeth was the oldest, and a quiet and retiring brother. The center of the family was the mother, who thought, we are told, that her husband used Marxism as an excuse for his laziness in looking for work. She was something of a feminist—going to hear Susan B. Anthony speak, and consulting women doctors—as was Elizabeth.

At the age of fifteen, in January 1906, Elizabeth addressed the Socialist Club on "What Socialism Can Do for Women," and attacked marriage, quoting from Paine and Gorky, from Marat and Mirabeau. She had already won prizes for public speaking and for her school essays—one from *The New York Times*. Now she began to go with her father to street meetings, and to address crowds, where she soon won a hearing, because of her youth and sex, but also because of her powerful voice and force of conviction. She always wore a red scarf, to announce her sympathies. One newspaper reported her remarks under the heading, "Mere Child Talks Bitterly of Life," and David Belasco offered her a career on the stage; but Theodore Dreiser, then the editor of *Broadway Magazine*, called her the East Side Joan of Arc.[96] This was, as we know, a time when journalists were very alert to stories of labor and the East Side. She said later that she had felt that socialism was just around the corner, and that she must hurry if she was to take part.[97]

At just this time, after his acquittal in Idaho, Haywood was offered a career by lecture agents, and he too refused. This was a moment when both might have been seduced, or suborned, or deflected from their chosen path of political protest, by spokesmen for entertainment. They belonged to the world of action; they meant to act upon the labor movement, and the rest of society would be their audience. Flynn told Belasco that she intended to speak her own piece: no one was going to write her lines for her, and her lines were of course to be burning brands.

In her autobiography she says that her father dragged the children to too many meetings, and read aloud to them, and dictated the essays they they should hand in at school—which they secretly rewrote to please themselves. But this revolt was not against his socialism but against his masculinism. "It developed a dislike of my father and his methods and also a distaste for meetings . . . none of us to this day reads aloud or can bear to listen."[98] The *us* means her sisters and herself: her father, her brother, and later her husband and her son seem to have played second fiddle to the women. She read Wollstonecraft and Bebel on women, and her mother hated household drudgery and belonged to a Bellamy Club. Her father thought the Socialist Club should have asked him to speak on women; he was, she tells us, what would now be called a male supremacist.[99]

In 1906 she spoke in New York and Schenectady on behalf of Haywood, when he was accused of murder. She had joined the IWW Local 179, which included other intellectuals. In 1907 she worked on a strike in Bridgewater, Connecticut, speaking and collecting money, and the same year she was her local's delegate to the IWW Conference in Chicago. She also spent seven days in Paterson, speaking in the Wobbly hall there. In Chicago she met the leader, Vincent St. John, and Jack Jones, a miner from Minnesota, who persuaded her to go on a speaking tour of the West, and whom she was soon to marry.

The West and the IWW were glamorous to her, and in specifically youthful and masculine ways. In her "Memories of the IWW" she says that just *because* her parents were socialists, "we of the younger generation" were impatient with the Socialist party, and felt it to be stodgy. Its leaders were professional men, and often professors. The IWW were young men, who had gone west to grow up with the country.[100] The union had also some striking women, like Mother Jones, who led an army of strikers into New York in 1903. In Chicago, where Gurley Flynn at eighteen got to know Jones, she feared her sharp tongue, and once fainted at her lurid pictures of bloodshed, but clearly she was not dull.[101] Flynn had heard about anarchism in high school—enough to alarm her parents, who gave her Marxist pamphlets to counteract the influence. By temperament she was far from anarchist, indeed morally conservative, but for this moment in her development, she responded to the West's call of adventure.

St. John said that she had fallen in love with the West and its miners and had married Jones because he was the first one she actually met. In her autobiography she acknowledges the truth of this.[102] She also says, "It was in a spirit of high adventure that I set out in the summer of 1909, to see my country and to meet its people."[103] "Her country" was primarily the West, seen with radical but not very political eyes. She describes it in romantic language—Pittsburgh, for instance: "the great flaring mills on both sides of the Ohio River, the roar and crash of the blast furnaces, the skies lit up for miles at night, the smoke, gas-laden air, the grime and soot that penetrated every corner. Industries fascinate me and wherever possible I visited them . . ."[104] As for the miners, "To me [they] were, and have remained, the unsung heroes of labor, who daily take their lives into their hands that we may have light, heat and power."[105]

She admired St. John very much, and as a westerner. He was "a fabulous figure who came out of the class-struggle of the West."[106] But the stress in her account of him falls on the West rather than on the class struggle. "His father before him had been an adventurous figure who rode the Wells Fargo pony express [as did Bill Haywood's father] carrying the U.S. mails through the South West, and lost his arm, shooting it out with Indians during a hold up." St. John himself had been tricked into lending his gun to someone else, in Goldfield, and then was shot in both hands by a stool pigeon. She explains that "To bear arms is the constitutional right of every American," and that this is, and even more was, especially true in the western states. "Dance halls, gambling houses and saloons crowded the main streets and men carried arms as a characteristic part of their dress."[107] It seems clear that she felt the glamour of the West the way most Americans did—as something partly outside the range of her socialist categories.

Bill Haywood, as secretary-treasurer of the WFM, helped direct a series of strikes in Colorado, which began in 1901 and became a full-scale labor war in 1903. He negotiated with owners, wrangled with judges, joined in fights with his fists and his gun, and was often arrested. By 1905 he was nationally known among those concerned with labor issues. And he was coming to a larger, national vision: himself. He saw that something was wrong with American society and that direct industrial action (as distinct from ordinary political action) was the way to put it right. Of course he meant direct action by unions, organized according to industry, and including unskilled as well as skilled labor.

There was violence on both sides in these conflicts—certainly floggings and reputedly murder—and the miners often employed dynamite. This was true of the strike at the Bunker Hill smelting mill in Idaho in 1899, which the miners blew up with three thousand pounds of dynamite. Governor Frank Steunenberg (elected as a Populist, but having become a Democrat) declared a state of martial law, and brought in federal troops. As a consequence fifteen hundred miners were locked up in jail for a year. Local governments were often sympathetic to the miners, but state governments supported the owners throughout the mining West, except in Colorado. Educated by these experiences, Haywood and the president of the WFM, Ed Boyce, joined the Socialist party in 1901.

As secretary-treasurer, Haywood organized smelters and mill workers around Denver to demand an eight-hour working day, by direct action. Here he displayed for the first time his striking talent for propaganda, by drawing a Stars and Stripes flag, with an accusation of the Colorado government on each stripe (for instance, "Habeas Corpus Suspended in Colorado") and the legend, "Is Colorado in America?"

On Election Day, 1903, he was attacked by deputy sheriffs. They had knocked out his colleague, Charles Moyer. "One of them struck me on the head with a gun. I dropped on my knees off the curb of the sidewalk, and drew my revolver. The captain's nephew was rushing up to give me another blow; I shot him three times in quick succession. He staggered back and started to run. I got to my feet and the other deputies ran away pell mell."[108] He was booked at the station, where the police surgeon stitched up his head. Later he describes how he hit Captain Wells in the face, and soldiers came to Wells's help; "and with the butts of their guns they struck me over the head and knocked me back between two cars. One pulled his gun down on me. I could see the hole in the barrel. I said, 'Pull it, you son of a bitch, pull it,' "[109] and so on. Telling these stories made it clear that Haywood had participated in the adventure of the West (which was so much a matter of violence) and carried that authority with him.

But he was also expanding his political horizons, both in theoretical matters and matters of practical politics. In 1904 he wrote pamphlets in support of Debs for president which urged collective ownership of national resources. In 1906 he himself got sixteen thousand votes for governor of Colorado, even though he was at that time in jail in Idaho, as we shall see.

On December 30, 1905, ex-Governor Steunenberg was killed by dynamite at his home in Caldwell, Idaho; and on February 17, 1906, Haywood and Moyer and another WFM member were secretly arrested and charged with the crime in Colorado and then (illegally) transported over state lines into Idaho. The trial did not begin until May 7, 1907, almost eighteen months after the crime. (In jail, Haywood studied Buckle, Voltaire, Carlyle, and Marx and learned Kipling poems by heart.) It was by then a very famous case, especially in labor circles; in Boston, fifty thousand people marched in sympathy with the accused; in New York, twenty thousand. The leading lawyers were famous men; for the prosecution, William Borah, for the defense, Clarence Darrow. Theodore Roosevelt declared Haywood and Moyer (and also the millionaire, Harriman) "undesirable citizens," which became a famous phrase.

Louis Adamic says, "Everybody believed him [Haywood] guilty of complicity in Orchard's deeds: he never really denied anything definitely or emphatically. He believed in violence, openly advocated it and practiced it. . . . Some of those who publicly denounced him secretly admired him."[110] Other historians sum things up differently; there is no consensus as to Haywood's guilt or innocence, as there is no consensus about Joe Hill's trial for murder, eight years later; the split between radicals and conservatives goes too deep to allow any objective consensus as to what happened.

Labor feeling was very strong at the time. Frank Heslewood armed several hundred men to march on Boise to free Haywood; and Gene Debs was all for the scheme, but other IWW leaders dissuaded them.

The accused were acquitted, which occasioned great rejoicing, especially in the West and among the miners. Haywood says perhaps tons of dynamite were exploded in the mining camp celebrations, and the men danced in hobnailed boots on their mahogany bars, drinking whisky in triumph.[111] Haywood was offered large sums to lecture on his experiences. The Tuileries Gardens in Denver offered him seven thousand dollars for a week, and a California agent offered fifteen thousand dollars for forty lectures. He actually spoke to crowds of fifty thousand and sixty thousand in Chicago. Thus it was a very famous man with a lurid reputation who attended Mabel Dodge's salon in 1913.

Elizabeth Gurley Flynn married Jack Jones from Minnesota in January 1908, before she was eighteen. She describes him as being in his thirties, youthful and vigorous, with deep blue eyes and a friendly smile; according to her obituary in *The New York Times*, he had been sent to jail for ten years for arson. They went together to the IWW meeting in Chicago that year, and stayed on afterward. She spoke in alliance with the "overalls brigade" from the West against Daniel de Leon and his Socialist Labor party. She got to know people with whom she would be working for the next few years, like Vincent St. John and Joseph Ettor, the Italian immigrant who would lead the early stages of the Lawrence strike, and Ben Williams, the editor of *Solidarity*. She lived in a Wobbly rooming house near the Radical Bookstore and bore a child prematurely.

In the spring of 1909 St. John, then the secretary-treasurer of the IWW, sent her west on a speaking tour, to Minneapolis, Montana, Seattle, and British Columbia, the strongholds of the union. She was valued primarily as a speaker (her youth and sex adding piquancy to her professionalism) but she was also a capable organizer and strategist, as which she earned twenty dollars a week. She settled for a time in Spokane as writer for *The Industrial Worker*. She also went to Missoula, Montana, where Jones had been working as a miner, and they spoke against the employment agencies which exploited the migrant workers. When they were forbidden to speak, they organized one of the IWW "free speech" campaigns, bringing Wobblies in from far and wide to stand up in public and speak about anything, just to defy the ordinance and to crowd the city's jail. Flynn defied the authorities to arrest her, finally spent some time in jail, and caused a scandal about the conditions of prison life.

After another period in Spokane, alone, she returned to New York to bear her only child, a boy called Fred, or Buster, who was to be in effect brought up by her sister, Kathie. Her marriage was not a success. Her mother resented Jones, feeling that he should not have married Elizabeth so young. Mrs. Flynn apparently saw a likeness between Jones and her own husband, as sources of poverty and large families. "It was bad enough to have one man around the house out of work," said Flynn, "spouting ideas and reading books, while she toiled to keep our small crowded quarters clean and make ends meet—but to have two of them was just too much."[112] Flynn sums up, "It was an unhappy time for all of us."

Jones went back to Chicago alone. In all the months of their marriage they had not spent many weeks together. She had soon felt that "I could make more of a contribution to the labor movement than he could."[113] Apparently he tried to devise a plan of industrial organization that would be an improvement on Father Hagerty's, drawing bright-colored diagrams on oil cloth. "His hobby was 'system.' He nearly drove me crazy in Chicago with his wheels and charts."[114] When her father asked her what she meant to do about her marriage, she said he bored her.

In later life Jones became locally famous because of the Dill Pickle Club he founded in Chicago. This was a radicals' night club that was one of the centers of Bohemian life in the city. He was still a radical, but soured on the labor movement. People like Haywood and Flynn scorned what he stood for, as a squandering of radical potential. (One story about him was that he invested his time in inventing a mechanical duck—at just about the time that Disney popularized Donald Duck.)

On December 20, 1910, Haywood's and Flynn's lives came together, when she presided over a huge IWW meeting in New York to welcome Haywood home. He had been attending a Second International meeting in Copenhagen (which Lenin also attended). Elizabeth's thirteen-year-old sister, Bina, recited a poem entitled "Revolution." Her other sister, Kathie, was then secretary of IWW Local 179. All the Flynn sisters were now involved in the movement.

Haywood was now a workers' hero, but he was still involved in bitter clashes between, on the one hand the IWW and the socialists, on the other, the IWW and the anarchists. The socialist congressman, Victor Berger, said the IWW was anarchist, and he himself didn't believe in murder as propaganda, or in theft as expropriation, or in replacing the "Marseillaise" with "Hallelujah, I'm a Bum." The IWW was irresponsible and unrespectable, by socialist standards.

But Haywood was evolving, forging new alliances, and leaving behind old ones. He did not attend either his wife's funeral, or that of one of his codefendants at Boise. One change was that as he became a national figure, he became more cautious about being seen to endorse violence. Conlin says that he avoided doing so after 1907.[115] Instead he declared that if the workers just laid down their tools, or kept their hands in their pockets, they would win. He refused to join Emma Goldman and Alexander Berkman when they wanted to arrange a mass funeral for three anarchists who killed themselves preparing to assassinate John D. Rockefeller. He paid a price for this prudence; Berkman said Haywood "showed the white feather," and some of the strikers at Paterson were alienated by his persistent pacifism.

His tactics were certainly unlike what they had been earlier in the West; he was trying now to follow the tactics that had been so successful in Lawrence, where the indignation aroused by police brutality turned into a strong force of public opinion for the strikers. Haywood was trying to conciliate a part of middle-class opinion which was becoming fascinated by the union story (there were comparisons drawn between the persecution of the IWW and the persecution of early Christians) while still preserving the union's old reputation for reckless young manliness.

He was not changing his principles, but he was changing his audience. He was speaking to the Greenwich Village audience, who were ambivalent about violence, but who wanted him to stay a figure of force and action. That audience was strongly attracted to Haywood. *The Independent* for January 9, 1913, remarked scornfully on his attraction for "artistic people"; "They follow Haywood much as a bunch of giggling girls go wild over the physical prowess of a quarterback."[116] But we should not assume that only insignificant people felt that fascination; one who did was Frederick Sumner Boyd, the

English radical leader, and later the close friend of John Reed; another was John Reed himself. Young men of force and brains found in Haywood the model of manhood they needed.

In 1912, Haywood and Flynn worked side-by-side for the first time and devised a new IWW modus operandi. Not only did two streams of labor radicalism converge, but both were in a context new to them. A textile town in New England, where the workers were largely immigrant and the worker leadership was Italian was something new to Haywood, and not really familiar to Flynn. Moreover, the workers were both men and women, and the presence of the latter seems to have been felt more than it ever had been in the West: "Bread and Roses," for instance, is a song sung by the women of Lawrence. Women from outside rallied to the cause, moreover. Margaret Sanger played a prominent part in the strike, and Vida Scudder, a professor at Wellesley, risked her job by going to Lawrence to declare her sympathies. Flynn, who continued her work of feminism, had appealed for women socialists to come and see the strike for themselves. Mary Heaton Vorse, the journalist, was one who accepted that invitation, and the two women formed a long-lasting friendship there.

Mobilizing the Lawrence workers, disciplining them into a political force, leading them to victory, Haywood and Flynn persuaded the world that American workers constituted a national entity, and labor radicalism was a new force with unlimited potential. It was America's version of the international labor movement. There were some 9,000 English-born workers in the Lawrence mills, 12,000 French Canadians, 2,000 Poles, 2,500 Jews, 2,700 Syrians, 6,500 Greeks, 8,000 Italians, and so on.[117] A march of 10,000 in the first week of the strike had the "Marseillaise" being sung in all fifty of the languages which, it is said, were spoken within the square mile of which the mills were the center.

This was made dramatic by the conservatives' hostility to the immigrants. *Harper's Weekly* said that only 8,000 of the workers were of "full American stock". The immigrants had of course been inhibited by their status as immigrants, citizens on trial. They had been lured to America by the promise of easy money; they had the shipping company posters still on the walls of their rooms. When they arrived they found themselves a class with no rights, at the mercy of their employers. To take control of their destinies, in the strike, was an Americanizing experience. It was also, to Haywood's consciousness, an experience like the general strike the IWW dreamed of, when whole cities would be taken over by their working classes.

The IWW was invited into Lawrence only after the plants closed, when Local 20 wired the headquarters in New York, which sent Joseph Ettor, only twenty-five years old, chosen because he could speak several languages, notably Italian. He created ethnic group committees and imposed discipline and thus ended sporadic violence; but he also assembled such large and enthusiastic audiences that the mayor panicked and called out 250 local militiamen to patrol the mill district. The owners first planted dynamite on Ettor, and then when that plot failed, got him and other leaders indicted for murder when a woman was shot in a street action. Ettor (and Arturo Giovannitti) were put in jail, and kept there for a year. To replace him, Haywood and Flynn came, together with Carlo Tresca, who was to become Flynn's lover.

Tresca was fifteen years older than she, and of a well-to-do family in Sulmona, Italy, where the peasants knew him as Don Carlo. At twenty-two he was secretary of the Italian Railroad Workers' Union. He was arrested in 1904, and though defended by famous lawyers, condemned, so he left the country for America (having a quarrel with Mussolini on the way—Mussolini being then a rival socialist). In the United States he edited an anarchist paper called *L'Avvenire*, and is described by Eastman as "the most pugnaciously hell-raising male rebel I could find in the United States." (Eastman names Tresca as one of the Heroes I Have Known.) He was arrested thirty-seven times for blasphemy, sedition, criminal obscenity, conspiracy, and murder; and was shot at, bombed, and kidnapped by fascists, and had his throat cut. At Paterson alone he was arrested seven times, tried three times, and held on thirty thousand dollars bail.[118]

He became a legendary figure in New York, still known as Don Carlo, wearing a floor-length cape and a slouch hat, and a beard to cover the scars. He was fiercely anticlerical and antibourgeois; he felt "a natural satisfaction of my ego in being feared by the upper classes."[119] Since he openly recommended violence ("an eye for an eye and blood for blood") the police came to question him after every explosion that seemed to be related to radical politics, and he drank wine with them as they talked.[120] In Lawrence he organized mass marches and meetings; at one meeting thirteen thousand people listened to Flynn in English and then eight other speakers in eight languages, on eight platforms, all flying the red flag. His own rhetoric was flowery and fiery.

The liaison between him and Flynn was open in Greenwich Village, and notorious in New York, but concealed in Paterson. It lasted from 1912 to 1925, but was always stormy, because of his unfaithfulness. Like Jones, he seems to have resented her political activities—in which she was more prominent than he. His inability to master English limited his political effectiveness: Eastman calls him an amateur and says, "Fighting for the rights of labor is with him an art, and not a profession."[121] But also the Italian socialists, and even anarchists, did not welcome public action by their women. When the couple finally broke up it was because he had a child by her younger sister, Bina. But she mourned his death in 1943, when he was murdered mysteriously, perhaps by emissaries of Mussolini.

Despite this personal link, it was not perhaps Tresca so much as Haywood from whom Flynn learned most at Lawrence. She had been trained in an old-fashioned style of oratory: she clenched her fists while speaking and made semaphoric pothooks, dots, and dashes, and so on, according to a newspaper description.[122] She herself spoke of the fervid oratory in which she was trained: "We gesticulated, we paced the platform, we appealed to the emotions . . . We spoke loudly, passionately, swiftly. We used invective and vituperation . . ."[123] Haywood's voice was, at least by contrast, quiet and his manner, simple.

Mary Heaton Vorse says, "When he talked about the children shucking oysters or peeling shrimps he made you see actual children, hands wrinkled with water and painful with salt-water sores."[124] Flynn says he taught her and others to talk to the immigrant workers in the English their children brought home from primary school, which avoided both long words and slang.[125] This was obviously a more modern rhetoric and could be compared with the reform which Gertrude Stein and Hemingway were soon to introduce into the fictional prose of the twentieth century. She says Haywood's speech was "like a sledge-hammer blow, direct and simple . . ."[126] He used only a few very simple gestures, like spreading out the fingers of one hand to show the feebleness of a number of separate unions, and then clenching his fist to show the power of One Big Union, and he himself was "the living symbol of that unity [and that power]. When he walked through the streets of New York, he towered over other men. Workers would turn to look at him and say, 'Why, that's Bill Haywood.' "[127]

Hapgood tells us that Haywood changed during his stay in Greenwich Village. He visited Robert Henri's studio. "What did he find at Henri's? Did he find a new view of life, a way in which he could refresh himself by another kind of reality, the reality of art?"[128] Though this is a rhetorical question, Hapgood answers that Haywood was not allowed to find that new view, because even in the studio people insisted on talking to him about the strike. They treated him as a curiosity, which left him, according to Hapgood, depressed and lonely, "because he cannot cultivate the broad human relationships and enjoyments springing from art, books, human society. . . . Bill Haywood was essentially a poet, and he even tried his hand at writing verse; for after meeting writers and artists among the groups who sometimes went to Mabel's salon, sometimes going to a painter's studio or talking with an expressive woman, Bill would sit in Washington Square and write poetry." But "this becoming known among his followers caused some of the labor people to say that Bill was weakening and being corrupted by contact with the bourgeoisie."[129]

Flynn did not respond to Greenwich Village with such readiness for radical change, and the Village was not half so interested in her. She came from a world they knew, or thought they knew. This split was to work to the IWW's disadvantage over the next few years. But in 1912 Haywood and Flynn were still loyal comrades, and were leading a movement of almost limitless promise. Mabel Dodge and John Reed were ready to devote their formidable gifts to calling the world's attention to the IWW, as well as to the challenges of modern art.

T H E

Organizations

5

A history of the IWW needs "the poetic under-standing which should invest any history of a militant church. From 1905 to the 1920s, the IWW was just that—a church which enlisted all the enthusiasm, idealism, rebelliousness, devo-tion, and selfless zeal of thousands of mainly young, mainly migrant workers."
> —WALLACE STEGNER,
> *The Preacher and the Slave*

Art is produced by a succession of individuals expressing themselves; it is not a question of Progress. Progress is merely an enormous pre-tention on our part. . . .
> —MARCEL DUCHAMP in Michel Sanouillet,
> *Salt Seller*

In 1912 Bill Haywood said, "No Socialist can be a law-abiding citizen. . . . I again want to justify direct action and sabotage." The latter was the artistic credo of the Greenwich Village bohemians in political terms.
> —DANIEL AARON, *Writers on the Left*

In America we have a certain view of art history that comes down to us from the Armory Show.
> —ROBERT SMITHSON in Joseph Mashek, *Marcel Duchamp in Perspective*

■

I n this chapter I will focus on the organizations, individuals, and ideas that stood behind and produced our two events, rather than on those which in retrospect stand out as dominant or most brilliant. And because both events were shaped by more than a single organization, I will add to the discussion of the AAPS something about Alfred Stieglitz's influence, which can be seen in the Armory Show, and to the discussion of the IWW something about the contemporary enthusiasm for pageantry, which can be seen in the Paterson Pageant.

The AAPS

The group that organized the Armory Show was the Association of American Painters and Sculptors, consisting by the time the Show was put on, of twenty-five members. The AAPS was founded on January 12, 1912, by some New York artists who proposed to follow the example of those independent artists who had held a free exhibition (one in which anybody could show whatever works he or she chose) in April 1910, at 29 West Thirty-fifth Street. Many members of the AAPS had been independents, and both groups wanted to promote new kinds of art and a new organization of artists—*new* meaning more modern and more free than the National Academy of Design allowed art to be. The independents' show had run four weeks, but had not been a success financially.

The new organization was rather heterogeneous. Those members who had most of a group identity and something of a theoretical core had exhibited together in 1908, and were known as the Eight. (Only seven pictures were sold at that two-week exhibition, but seven thousand people attended, and it was counted a success, which will help us measure the much greater success of the Armory Show.) They consisted of Robert Henri and four of his disciples, labeled the New York realists, plus an impressionist, Ernest Lawson, Maurice Prendergast, sometimes called a postimpressionist, and Arthur B. Davies, who belonged in the fantasy tradition of Odilon Redon, Marées, Hodler, and Puvis de Chavannes.[1] The man elected first president of the AAPS was another impressionist, J. Alden Weir, but he resigned as soon as he discovered how aggressively hostile to the National Academy the new organization meant to be. He was succeeded by Davies, who was ready for a big new enterprise, and for burning the bridge which connected them all to the Academy.

To understand that predecessor and the tradition against which they were rebelling, we must step back a little in time. The New York Academy of Design had a long tradition (it had been founded in 1825) and gave an annual exhibition and operated a school. (Maurice Sterne studied there from about 1900 to 1904.) Some of its members split away in 1877 and called themselves the Society of American Artists, holding an exhibition of their own in 1878. But the power of the old institution was too great. The rebels found the path of independence nonviable, and in 1906 remerged with the parent institution, to become the National Academy of Design.[2]

The title of Associate of the National Academy carried a lot of prestige, and membership was self-perpetuating; in the annual exhibition the jury that decided which works should be hung carried white cards that exempted their own works from judgment. Their aesthetic creed has been summed up as a belief in composition, the study of the human figure, the primacy of drawing over color, and the models of the past.[3] If we interpret these slogans by reference to the paintings of the great Renaissance tradition, we shall see well enough how far they were from what we call modern art.

The genres included portraits, landscapes, interiors, battlefields, historical scenes, and legendary and literary scenes, but they could all be seen as celebrating the culture's achievements or as recruiting spiritual energies in some traditional way. The new art treated quite different topics, and with quite different conventions. Moreover, the painterly effects of traditional art ranged from Raphael's geometrical balance to Caravaggio's lurid colors and shadows, from Dutch realism to French impressionism, but were limited to one or another version of realism. This again was something that modern art was to attack, in the name of new possibilities. Both Katherine Dreier and Georgia O'Keeffe say that, as students, their teachers made them feel there was nothing left to paint—that every subject worth doing had been painted. Only modernism saved them.

The National Academy was essentially a traditional institution. It was also an establishment and elitist institution, and its demands for publicly funded larger quarters, on the grounds that only then could American art be adequately presented in great exhibitions, won the rival AAPS (privately funded) some approval and backing from journalists.

At that time, American art lived in bondage to the Renaissance tradition and to Europe. The greatest contemporary names—Whistler, Sargent, Cassatt—lived abroad. The greatest prices were paid for French paintings, and for old-fashioned painters like Bouguereau and Bonheur. These reputations were dead in Paris by 1910, and the Armory Show was to obliterate them in America, but Bouguereau, for instance, had been a prominent figure at the Académie Julian, where many American artists trained in Paris. Art Young, in his autobiography, explained Bouguereau to the next generation as someone "possessed with the desire to paint the skin of the human body, to which he gave a kind of transparent loveliness" and as able to make "hands and feet look more beautiful than any hands and feet that ever were."[4] This will suggest the flattering idealization of fashionable people against which the New York realists, and all the schools of modern art, reacted.

They were even more scornful about the American expatriates; John Sloan said Whistler turned etchings into boutonnières;[5] while Sloan's friend, Van Wyck Brooks, called Whistler a cut flower.[6] Sloan said Sargent turned everything he painted into satin,[7] while Brooks called him "the apotheosis of an ostrich plume."[8]

133

The American painters of that time who were admired later were then ignored as peripheral—Thomas Eakins, Albert Pinkham Ryder, and Winslow Homer. Of these three, the last lived in Maine in seclusion, and the other two painted largely for themselves: Eakins had some effect on other painters in Philadelphia, via his disciple, Thomas Anshutz, but Ryder was almost entirely unappreciated. Better known were Boston genre painters like Edmund G. Tarbell and Frank W. Benson; those in the Munich tradition, like William Merritt Chase; and the impressionists, like Lawson, Weir, and Childe Hassam. There had been an exhibition of French impressionists in the mid-1880s, organized by Paul Durand-Ruel, and as late as 1913 most Americans thought impressionism was the latest thing. Walter Pach says that in that year perhaps fewer than a hundred Americans knew anything of postimpressionist French painting. But quite a lot of people knew that there was such a thing, and that it was scandalous.

We should also remember a difference in art matters between France and the United States, or rather between Paris and New York: a difference of sheer numbers. According to Pach, there were about forty thousand artists living in Paris in the decade before 1913, plus another thirty-five thousand working in the art trades—numbers with which New York could not compete.[9] Such statistics alone made Paris the art capital of the world, in terms of production and appreciation and the artist's life. It was the place everyone interested in art felt some compulsion to visit.

Some American artists, however, felt a strong need to escape this compulsion by inventing kinds of art that would be specifically American or specifically modern. One such group, central to our story, was the New York, or ashcan, realists. (*Ashcan* was a label applied to them some years later.) They in some sense stayed at home in America, and in its cities, to fight both native philistinism and expatriate sophistication.[10] Their names were John Sloan, Robert Henri, Albert Glackens, George Luks, Everett Shinn.

These men, like the painters of Paris, wanted to break the grip of bourgeois taste (representing bourgeois interests) on the ideas of beauty and art. But they did so primarily by asserting a vulgarity of topic and a vigor of manner—by introducing new subject matter, which offended against propriety. They continued to aim at visual realism, unlike the modernists of Paris, and so they failed to profit by the excitement of the latter's project of changing the very idea of art and dominating the public's sense of sight.

Robert Henri had returned from a trip to Europe in 1891 and gathered around him in Philadelphia a group of young men interested in art. They, the men just named, all drew for newspapers and magazines and so depicted events in ways that satisfied "the average man." Luks worked for the *Bulletin*, Glackens for the *Record*, Sloan for the *Press*, and Shinn for five papers. (Stuart Davis's father, Edward Davis, was art director of the *Press*, and so Davis began by painting in the style of the Eight, though he became a modernist after the Armory Show.) Henri stimulated their ambition to become serious painters; they had learned from the *Punch* artists, Keene and Leech, before falling under Henri's influence. He introduced them to more ambitious French and Spanish models—Daumier, Gavarni, Guys, and Goya. He also gave them a creed of life values, which blended into an enthusiasm for the American scene around them.

This was all part of the revival of American art and ideas which climaxed in our two events of 1913 and which differed in character from city to city. In Philadelphia it was strong primarily in the visual arts; in Chicago it was primarily literary—the names are Dreiser, Sandburg, Anderson, Veblen. In New York, where it developed a little later, it was more intellectual and reformist, with less of populist optimism.

The realists owed something to Anshutz, and via him to Eakins; but the dominant artist on the Philadelphia scene, judged by any ordinary criteria, was William Merritt Chase, to whom they owed nothing. Chase followed the Munich school; he admired Frans Hals among the painters of the past, and Whistler and Sargent among contemporaries.[11] He had invented a grand-gentleman style of clothes and manner for himself. All of this the realists were to reverse. But the only alternative to this theatricalism, when they began, was what Pach calls the "confident positivism" of Winslow Homer; what Hartley calls Homer's "flinty and unyielding . . . mania, almost, for actualities . . . not an atom of legend."[12] Hartley says this was Yankeeism

turned to creditable artistic account, but it was no more attractive to
the realists than Chase—no doubt because of the association of these
actualities with traditional heroic adventure on the sea, the confident
and conservative positivism of the Anglo-Saxon tradition. The realists
wanted to paint the people of the city, many of them immigrants, in
their unheroic actuality.

Luks, Glackens, Sloan, and Shinn moved to New York City around
1895, and at the same time began to take their art seriously. Glackens
and Shinn were the worldlings among them who painted the people
of fashion and the theater. In 1904 George Bellows came from Ohio
to study with Henri at the New School of Art, and he joined the
group. He saw the artist as a superman and was compared with Jack
London, Kipling, and Walt Whitman. They were all interested in city
scenes, and in the *truth* of them—i.e., their uglier, more ignoble or
embarrassing aspects. One of Sloan's pictures is of an old woman
finding a pair of corsets in an ashcan. Luks painted *Hester Street* in
1905, and Bellows, *Cliff Dwellers* in 1917. Jerome Myers, who had
arrived in New York in 1877, had already begun to paint the Lower
East Side. In 1900 he sold two of his paintings to the Macbeth
Galleries, which gave him a show in 1904. But he made the poor
picturesque, while the realists tried to avoid that; Brown says that
Luks made them vital and flamboyant, while Sloan saw them with
pity and tenderness.[13]

Myers was one of those first involved in organizing the AAPS and
the Armory Show, though he was also one of the most bitter, after
the event, at the Show's betrayal of American art and artists—the
ascendancy it reestablished for France—the rebinding of American
art's bondage. The attempt at social realism was in fact what modernism was to displace, quite as much as the old academic styles of
the National Academy. And this seemed a betrayal not only from a
patriotic point of view, but from that of social and political responsibility. The new formalist art showed, as Brown says, "With only
minor exceptions, no evidence of war, post-war depression, prosperity, industrial expansion or impending catastrophe."[14]

Why was New York realism so easily defeated? Brown says, "The
cultures which produced Matisse and Picasso, Proust and Joyce, were
far different from that which produced Dreiser and Sloan."[15] He is

pointing to a narrowness and drabness in the American cultural tradition which separates it from the European, and explains the defeat of such realists by modern art in 1913. But there are many strands to a culture, many kinds of imagination. America was poor in some kinds, privileged in others—notably as the site of adventure, a form of imaginative life which historians of culture often ignore. In that kind of imagination, there was no such gap of inferiority between, say, Twain and Kipling; it was the Englishman who learned from the American, because the frontier tradition of the West was a powerful stimulus, and one which Americans found it easy to appropriate. (Indeed, the opposite activity, of denying the frontier tradition, was taught to English writers by Henry James and T. S. Eliot—Americans.)

That frontier tradition could be felt in, for instance, Henri—it was part of his personal vitality, and so part of his life values. Pach says the dead ideas about art had to be blasted out and that "Henri had the dynamite for the job. Tall, broad-shouldered, a bit rough in his ways, he could make convincing allusions to the men with revolvers he had known in the far West of his youth. Jesse James was pretty near a hero to him. Something of the fascination, of the sense of danger and adventure of the old West hung about his talk and flashed from under his dark brows . . ."[16] Similar things were said of George Bellows, as we shall see, and of Walt Kuhn, in his ten-gallon hat. (Henry McBride said Kuhn was the most masculine painter since Bellows.) The group called themselves Henri's stock company, because they met so often; they valued their masculine camaraderie.

This was part of the gospel of "life" which influenced so many of Henri's pupils. That his painting was, according to Milton Brown, inferior to Sargent's and even to Chase's—the brushwork slick and the vitality all in the surface—did not diminish the authority of his personality.[17] It is natural that it was his studio which Bill Haywood visited during his Village period. Hutchins Hapgood describes the visit, and Haywood's being pestered by admirers there.[18] Henri's values, and even his paintings, could seem congenial to the Wobbly mind. Haywood's visit to Stieglitz and his gallery, called 291, Haywood's encounter with modern art, was more combative.

We can see this affinity of values again in the comments of Guy

Pène du Bois, an associate of the New York realists, on Henri and his friends. "They were natural men, liking life enough to want to tear off the veil thrown so modestly or priggishly over it by the prevailing good taste."[19] Henri had learned to see men as men, and taught his friends to side with Dreiser in the matter of fiction and to grin at historical novelists—Howard Pyle was one of their bêtes noires.[20] "An artist must be a man first. He must stand on his own feet, see with his own eyes, the brave eyes of bold manhood, and report his findings in the straightforward unfinicky manner of the male."[21] Du Bois too uses western language; he describes Henri's class as "rough-riding," and delights in anecdotes of Roosevelt and his artist friend, "Sheriff" Chanler. (Luks and Glackens went on the Cuban campaign of 1898, like Remington and Russell. We cannot imagine Duchamp or Picasso in that setting.)

It was not preordained that these values would lose out even among men of culture to the opposite values embodied in the formalist art of Paris. Most artists, indeed most men, still wanted to see themselves as adventurers. Roosevelt aside, this masculinism was very congenial to Haywood and the IWW, for instance. And there are cases of men initiated into the styles of Paris art, who turned back to the myth of the West; one we have mentioned was Stanton Macdonald Wright, the founder of synchronism, but later the friend of Thomas Hart Benton. That these masculine life values *did* lose out was an event, a decisive event, whose causes and effects deserve study.

Sloan, though a less flamboyant figure than Henri (the latter once said Sloan was the past tense of *slow*) took a similar line. He drew for magazines like *The Masses* and Giovannitti's anarchist *Il Proletario* and illustrated the writings of muckrakers like Ernest Poole. From our point of view, he is the central painter in the realist movement. His paintings exemplify their common doctrines much better than Henri's.

Sloan worked on the Armory Show Hanging Committee, and had two pictures and five etchings on display. (Pach says he did the lion's share of the work for the independents' exhibition, also.) Floyd Dell called him "a very vigorous and combative personality, who was himself hotly propagandist."[22] The heat expressed his faith in nature, in naivete, in youth.

In 1958, in *The Critic*, Adelaide Garvin said that Sloan was always the angriest of angry young men; the object of his anger she was referring to was abstract art, while Dell was referring to Sloan's refusal to follow *The Masses'* ideological line in 1916. Different though the two cases are, one might say that both times Sloan was protesting in the name of humanism. This sort of humanism is what is expressed in this typical quotation from his journal: "The streets seem pulsing with human life and warm blood and a feeling of animal love, honest animal affection."[23] Sloan loved the Lower East Side, and *human* was one of his favorite words. In *Gist of Art* he said, "Drawing is a human language, a way of communicating between human beings . . . Don't be afraid to be human. Draw with human kindness, with appreciation for the marvel of existence."[24]

Clearly Sloan, like Hapgood and other exemplars of the spirit of 1913, set a high value on human warmth. He was suspicious of all ideas that seemed to foster detachment or unfeeling scrutiny, which included all ideas and certain artistic postures. He did not like to be compared, for instance, with Stephen Crane or Theodore Dreiser, despite their prestige with the left wing because "I never liked their idea about the artist needing to have experiences in order to understand or to gather subject-matter from life."[25] When Haywood made a sarcastic attack on socialism, Sloan interrupted angrily.[26] His art judgments were primarily moral, and he was once called an unbearded Tolstoy.[27]

He and Henri were good friends, though so unlike. Sloan was the provincial pragmatist, the figure of virtue, and Henri the worldling and posturer. In 1902 Sloan refused the other man's offer to finance a trip to Europe for him. He said he was not interested in the life of art students in Paris, and he didn't want to lose his independence by getting into debt. But it was clearly intellectual and artistic independence he cared about as much as the financial kind. "I found the courage to stay in this country, to put down roots . . . It was a time when many artists had become expatriates—imitating the Europeans and often tempted to paint sentimental or picturesque subjects."[28] Though this now seems a shrewd as well as brave decision, it was not then a quick road to success. Sloan got his first picture exhibited (at the Carnegie Institute) in 1900, but he did not sell a picture until 1913 (to his former classmate, the collector Albert Barnes). By 1921, when he was fifty, he had sold only eight, but he was part of an exciting current of ideas.

Henri was above all an inspiring teacher. He told his students in 1892 that he wanted them to express their ideas: "What do you get out of nature? Why do you paint this subject?" This interested him more than their skills or technique. "Be willing to paint a picture that does not look like a picture."[29] He himself painted children, gypsies, dancers, laborers—other races and other classes. They should suspect slick brushwork and foggy aestheticism.[30] "Never think of beauty or use small brushes."[31]

Henri, like Bellows, inclined toward anarchism, and both taught at the anarchist Ferrer School; *anarchism* was another word of the day, like *radicalism*, much feared by the establishment, quite popular among artists. Hapgood, in *The Spirit of Labor* in 1907 had called anarchism the fine art of the proletariat.[32] Margaret Anderson was to say, in her *Little Review* in March 1916, "Anarchism and art are in the world for exactly the same kind of reason."[33] Emma Goldman taught modern drama at the Ferrer, and Steffens and Clarence Darrow were also on the staff.

Sloan, on the other hand, belonged to the Socialist party. His wife, Dolly, was organizer of Branch 1 of that party in New York. In February 1912, she helped arrange the reception of the children sent from Lawrence during the strike; she led them from the railway station they arrived at to the Third Avenue El and the Labor Temple, and again in March she had great baskets of sandwiches and oranges and a hundred quarts of milk waiting for another such group when they arrived. She was secretary-manager of *The Masses* in the first months of Eastman's editorship—until May 1913, when the magazine moved to 91 Greenwich Avenue. Eastman described her as "a tiny, vital, scrappy, devoted, emotional, secretary of socialist locals, organizer of socialist picnics, collector of funds for strikers."[34]

At the Ferrer School, one of Henri's pupils was Man Ray, one of the next generation of painters most influenced by the Armory Show. We can feel the gulf between the generations when we are told by Henri's admirers that, "Perhaps the one quality that dominates his work is vitality, a vigor that is both intellectual and physical."[35] He felt that technique was often overemphasized and was himself "always white-hot with conviction."[36] It is a long way from this heat to the coolness of Ray and his friend Duchamp.

Brown suggests the historical importance of these New York realists by pointing out that Frank Norris and Theodore Dreiser depict contrasting representatives of art in their novels, who differ in personal traits as well as in schools of art. Sheldon Corthell, in Norris's *The Pit*, 1903, is an academic painter, cultured and cosmopolitan, a figure of refinement and not of force; but Eugene Witla, in Dreiser's *The Genius*, 1915, is full of American vitality. Witla is a realist; it is usually said that Shinn was the model from whom Dreiser drew him. "The living counterparts of Eugene Witla," says Brown, "are to be found in that group of realists which began its activities in Philadelphia in the early 90s."[37]

Henri recommended Zola and Flaubert to his followers, but also Walt Whitman, and the realists in general believed in a mystical and erotic democracy. One sign of this was their enthusiasm for Isadora Duncan, whom they often connected with Whitman in their minds. Henri said that when he saw Isadora dance he heard the great voice of Whitman and saw a new age of full natural expression for all people.[38]

This was an enthusiasm felt by the other realists and by the editors of *The Masses*. Isadora is one of the heroes Max Eastman describes in his collection, *Heroes I Have Known*, and he says she was much greater than comparable theater stars like Duse or Bernhardt because she was a creative and moral force.[39] (Like Gurley Flynn, she spoke her own piece.) Her dancing was a "divine revelation" to him.[40] That is why we see this connection of Isadora with Whitman, and then the substitution of her for him; this transformation of the idea of life, its transfusion with the feeling for free womanhood. Previously *life* had been associated with men as much if not more than with women, and with cities as much as with nature. Now that was changing.

In either manifestation, life was the cult of these painters and not of the cubists or most of the other Paris schools. We can refer again to Marsden Hartley's interesting essay on "the two great primitives and pioneers"—the models for his generation—Whitman and Cézanne. Clearly the realists were influenced by Whitman, the French painters by Cézanne.

Cézanne had been accepted in Paris only recently, after his commemorative exhibition of 1907. Van Gogh had been accepted only after 1901 and Gauguin after 1903, in both cases after retrospective exhibitions. But by 1913 their reputations stood high, even with buyers. Cézanne's *Femme au Chapelet* arrived at the Armory Show with a price tag of $48,600, and a Gauguin came priced at $40,500. Thus Americans knew that there was a powerful new force emanating from Paris, a maelstrom of value changes, but what was happening was as hard to understand as the literal Stock Exchange would be to a stranger. Most Americans who considered themselves connoisseurs found themselves on the fringe of a crowd, where only the innermost circle could understand what everyone else was trying to catch a glimpse of. They were largely puzzled and offended by many of these new pictures, even those by these giants of the recent past, while the contemporaries, like Picasso, were little more than names. The Show was thus an expected and rehearsed revelation, though its effects were not those its organizers had calculated.

Other figures who stood as godfathers to the Show included Walter Pach, Alfred Stieglitz, and Arthur B. Davies. Pach, born in 1883, had been overwhelmed by the Cézannes at the 1907 exhibition and forthwith turned away from the taste and the idea of art he had learned from his teacher, William Merritt Chase. That same year he met Matisse at the Steins' villa in Fiesole and took painting lessons from him; he arranged that painter's first one-man show in New York in 1915. He also acted as American impresario to Marcel Duchamp and his brother Raymond Duchamp-Villon, from 1913 on.

Pach, according to Sandra S. Phillips, understood the import and importance of modern French art better than any other American in the years before 1913. He acted as ambassador between French and American painters, for instance, showing Winslow Homer's work to Matisse, and Albert Pinkham Ryder's to Odilon Redon. He conducted the organizers of the Show, Kuhn and Davies, to the Steins and to other collectors and galleries in Paris. He was a friend of both Steins:

Gertrude wrote a portrait of him, but when the brother and sister split up, he gave his loyalty to Leo.

He is sometimes said to have been responsible for the broadly historical and educational aspect of the Show, as an explanation and justification of modern art. Probably he deserves credit for that no more than Davies does, but then the two men were collaborators and friends in the years between 1909 and 1914, and no doubt ideas passed to and fro between them. Pach certainly translated Elie Fauré's essay on Cézanne, and wrote essays on Redon and Duchamp-Villon, all of which were published by and for the Show.

He is generally acknowledged to have made an important contribution to the shift in American taste away from impressionism and symbolism toward cubism and formalism in general. At the same time, he was soon outdistanced by the movement in taste which he had initiated. His book of 1928, *Ananias*, attacking false artists, aroused such unfavorable comment that he left the country; and in a story by Francis Steegmuller, Pach and his wife are depicted selling off their collection in their declining years for miserable prices.

Arthur B. Davies suffered a similar fate. Already in 1913 Dasburg, and later Rosenberg, found his work effeminate. When he died in 1930, his reputation was falling sharply, because his paintings failed to satisfy the modernist taste he had so successfully propagated. He had, for instance, been adviser to Lillie P. Bliss in the collection she built, but when that collection went to the Museum of Modern Art in 1931, to form the core of that museum, none of the Davies paintings were hung in main galleries; and the Tate Gallery in London refused the two Davies pictures bequeathed it by Miss Bliss.

Davies's *Sleep* of 1905 (the figures were added in 1908) is like Hodler's *Night* of 1890 and Puvis's *Sommeil*. These are in some loose sense symbolist paintings. In England and France, Burne-Jones and Redon did similar work. But Davies was very responsive to fashion. From 1910 on he introduced a lot of movement into his subjects; as in *Crescendo*, which might remind one of Isadora Duncan. *The Dancers* (1914 to 1917) might be called cubist, but it is more like Delaunay than Picasso or Braque: Davies was not so concerned with mass and space, but more with design and lateral movement.

Davies was personally an enigmatic figure. Brown describes his work on the Show thus: "This man of fastidiously aristocratic bearing, a painter of poetic sensibility bordering on the ephemeral, this shy, reticent, and coolly formal person . . . [had turned out to be] a hand of steel in a suede glove."[41] He was so shy he would leave any public space, like a gallery, if more than two or three people joined him there, and at meetings he was usually the most silent and reserved member. But as Marsden Hartley described him, he was a "propagandist for and admirer of the ultra-modern movement."[42] And Brown says that he proved himself, as an organizer, energetic and ruthless—dictatorial. He delegated authority with political skill, and drew meticulous sketches of each room in the Armory, showing the place each picture was to occupy on the wall. There was a parallel paradox in his private life: this very proper man was discovered, when he died, to have been living a double life, with an unofficial wife and child, with whom he lived half his days under an assumed name. And finally there was the contradiction between his own pictures of dreamy landscapes and the modernists he loved, who included Duchamp, Brancusi, and Matisse.

Royal Cortissoz, one of the main enemies of modernism, praised Davies for his sense of beauty. That word, as a slogan, was one of the points at issue between schools of painting then; it will be remembered that Henri exhorted his pupils never to think of beauty; but it was a key word for Davies as a painter. Ellen Berezin says he was "consistently a painter of beauty. To him, painting did not need to depict objective reality."[43] In turning away from realism, Davies was of course in step with the modernists, but his devotion to beauty was as repugnant to them as to their predecessors. He stepped back from realism, while they stepped forward.

Unlike the other two, Alfred Stieglitz deserves to be discussed not just as an individual, but as the leader of that movement often labeled 291, after the address of his gallery on Fifth Avenue. Though he behaved as the rival of the Armory Show, as much as he behaved as its promoter, he had in fact prepared its way and quite properly profited by its success much more than its actual organizers, the Eight. (He had consciously separated himself and his followers from the Eight: none of the Stieglitz group showed in the 1910 exhibition, and they were underrepresented at the Armory.) The Show in fact confirmed Stieglitz's authority as the prophet of modern art, and it was *his* painters who in the next two decades moved to the center of avant-garde taste. Famous names like John Marin and Georgia O'-Keeffe were strongly identified with Stieglitz in the art world.

Mabel Dodge paid her first visit to 291 (where she met Francis Picabia and his wife) between January 24 and February 13, 1913. The exhibition room was only twelve feet by fifteen feet, with the walls covered with light gray burlap. In the month before the Armory Show, Stieglitz showed twenty-eight watercolors by Marin, of both the Berkshires and Lower Manhattan. During that February he showed his own photographs, as a "synchronous contrast to the Show," to bring out the opposition between the character of painting and that of photography. There were sixteen photographs, mostly of Manhattan.[44]

Stieglitz had led his followers out of the New York Camera Club in 1902, in order to save their work from drowning in the flood of mediocrity, and founded the Little Galleries of the Photo-Secession. (*Secession* was a word in vogue then—a signal of modernism just beginning.) His early photography was congenial with the paintings of the realists; for instance, a study of industrial city landscape like *The Hand of Man*. But as Homer says, "His tastes in painting followed quite another track at this time. It is as though he had two sets of standards of what was 'artistic'."[45] But those two sets of standards overlapped in time only partly. Partly the one followed after the other: Stieglitz can be seen to change the stress of his interests from photography to painting a few years before the Show, and the subject of his own photography changes from *The Hand of Man* to his hundreds of studies of Georgia O'Keeffe's body after the Show. (Again we see life values coming to be embodied in a woman's body.)

Stieglitz was a formalist, believing in a direct equivalence between certain shapes and certain emotions. In this his ideas were not unlike those of the Bloomsbury group in England; for instance, Clive Bell's idea of *significant form*. He joined to this, as did Bloomsbury, a somewhat Platonic idealism. To Stieglitz, art was creativity: it was an end, not a means, and an all-justifying end.[46] And creativity was linked to two other concepts—spirituality and life. In 1913 the thirty-ninth issue of *Camera Work* included a two-page black-edged spread entitled "In Memoriam," written by Hapgood and reprinted from his newspaper, the *Globe*. It contrasted the deadliness, the death-in-life, of Kenyon Cox criticizing the Armory Show, with the life of Virginia Myers dancing—she was the six-year-old daughter of Jerome Myers. That is a good example of *Camera Work*'s life values; other examples, also to be found in the journal, were a poem by eight-year-old Mary Steichen and a letter from the sculptor, anarchist, and political prisoner, Adolf Wolff.

Thus he showed Rodin and Matisse drawings at what were then called his Photo-Secession Galleries as early as 1908, and later Marin, Toulouse-Lautrec, Rousseau, Weber, Cézanne, and Picasso. In 1909 his friend Edward Steichen took him to see both Stein collections in Paris. Leo lectured them on the inferiority of Whistler to Picasso, and Stieglitz, impressed, offered to publish anything Leo might write about art.[47] Later he solicited Gertrude's "portraits" of Picasso and Matisse.

This magazine, as misleadingly named as the gallery, since it was so largely concerned with modern painting, ran for fifty issues, from January 1903 to 1917. By then it had only thirty-seven subscribers left, due in part to the disruptive effects of military patriotism on the art world.[48] The issue of the war produced quarrels, for instance, between Steichen and Stieglitz, because the former wanted the magazine to commit its support to the Allies, or at least declare its opposition to Germany. But during those fourteen years, *Camera Work* was a very important promoter of modernism in art.

Perhaps the best proof of that is the hostility Stieglitz provoked among the antimodernists. In 1935, Thomas Craven, the spokesman for the American Scene painters like Thomas Hart Benton, wrote in *Common Sense* that "No place in the world ever produced more idiotic gabble than 291."[49] He called Stieglitz a "Hoboken Jew without knowledge of, or interest in, the historical American background."[50] Craven and Benton had turned against cosmopolitan modernism, and blamed Stieglitz for its fashionableness.

Important as he was, however, Stieglitz was primarily a propagandist and impresario, not a thinker. His ideas were commonplace for the times and amounted to a stress on spiritual values and life values, which tended to blur into each other. He picked up forms of modern taste from, for instance, Steichen and later Weber in Paris, and later still from Marius de Zayas and Picabia. These lines of taste were all modern, but in other ways they ran in different directions. Picabia and de Zayas promoted in effect a kind of dada, while Marin and O'Keeffe thought in life values terms.

Thus de Zayas wrote an article called "The Sun Has Set" in *Camera Work* in 1912, saying that art was dead because a religious worldview had been replaced by a positivism. Art had succumbed to industry, and the modern artist was all consciousness and premeditation, while the primitive artist was unconscious. A life values artist (like Marin or D. H. Lawrence) could assent to that in general and in theory, but in particular and in practice, he believed *he* could still create living art.

It was Stieglitz's friends, like Steichen, de Zayas, and Weber, who seem to have had the more interesting ideas. Weber wrote a lost article about Gertrude Stein in 1913, and he was one of the few who made a certain sense out of the vague idea of a fourth dimension. He thought experimentally. In a catalog introduction of 1913 he wrote, "Surely there will be new numbers, new weights, new colors, new forms, new odors, new sounds, new echoes, new rhythms of energy."[51] All these ideas interested Marcel Duchamp also, though Duchamp put them to ironic and playful uses uncongenial to Weber. The latter came of orthodox Jewish parents, hard-working and frugal. "I never knew the joys of young life. Wildness was not for me. There were no escapades. I suppose that whenever I was tempted to do something of that sort, I felt a sense of shame, thinking as I did of my parents." His studio was, he said, his synagogue.[52] It may be this old-fashioned temperament—so unlike Duchamp's—which prevented Weber's being one of the great modernists, despite a quite remarkable intellectual equipment. The *ideas* all attracted him, even the wildest; Stieglitz says that, under Mabel Dodge's influence, Weber even became an anarchist in 1913; and he was in some ways the most thoroughgoing American cubist. But, unlike Duchamp, he needed to make sense of life—as did most of Stieglitz's painters.

During the Paterson Strike, Bill Haywood lived in Greenwich Village and visited its institutions, among which was of course 291. Stieglitz records that Haywood asked him what a big man like him was doing in a dinky little place like the gallery and told him that "the workers don't believe that art will ever win their fight," to which Stieglitz made a wordy reply: when what Haywood asserted and did proved to be true, he would find Stieglitz fighting at his side, but not till then, for Stieglitz could not hate.[53] Both men assumed that the other was on the same side, but neither could recognize the other's mode of action, nor win his recognition for his own.

The IWW

The political radicals had to ask themselves how to bring the socialist adventure to a successful conclusion. They saw a rising curve to history, punctuated by the great dates of revolution, primarily in France (1789, 1848, 1871) and then in Russia (1905), now to be transferred to America; and in Germany there were the great works of theory, above all Marx and Engels.

The IWW stood behind the Paterson Pageant in a way different, obviously, from the way the AAPS stood behind the Armory Show. From the Wobbly point of view, it was the Paterson Strike that was important; the Pageant was designed by a small group of enthusiasts who were not even members of the union. But the Pageant turned out to have an important effect on the Strike—and therefore on the IWW.

To begin at the beginning, it was in Chicago on June 27, 1905, that about two hundred delegates from thirty-four labor organizations formed the Industrial Workers of the World. Eugene Debs, Mother Jones, Daniel de Leon, Bill Haywood, and his friends from the Western Federation of Miners were there to form a new union of unions. Haywood, as chairman, denounced the American Federation of Labor for conservative leadership, craft unionism, a non-class-conscious politics, and for refusing to admit immigrants and blacks to its unions. The WFM, which had joined the AFL in 1896, had withdrawn the following year, because the larger organization was too conservative and offered too little support. The 1905 meeting called itself the Continental Congress of the Working Class, thus aligning itself with the history of the United States, and Haywood opened the proceedings by saying that they were there to confederate the workers of the country into a working-class movement.

On the preceding January 2, some thirty leaders had met to draft an Independent Union Manifesto, which had been sent all around the country, to arouse interest in this meeting. The secretary to the Constitution Committee was Father Thomas J. Hagerty from New Mexico, a convert to Marxism from before his ordination in 1892, and suspended from his priestly functions by his archbishop in 1903. He helped frame the manifesto, wrote the preamble, and drew the chart of industrial organization, with its eight departments (what Samuel Gompers of the AFL was to call the Wobbly wheel of fortune). But the intriguing presence of this Marxist priest was very temporary; he soon disappeared from Wobbly history, and the union was dominated by western workers, miners, or migrants.

The preamble to the constitution said, "The working class and the employing class have nothing in common. There can be no peace so long as hunger and want are found among millions of working people, and the few who make up the employing class, have all the good things of life." And two sentences added in 1908 ran, "It is the historic mission of the working class to do away with capitalism. The army of production must be organized."

The new organization thus had a revolutionary aim, and a syndicalist philosophy. It wanted One Big Union, nationally and even internationally, with individual unions organized according to industries and on a national scale, just the way the employers were at that time, notoriously, getting organized into trusts. (Eugene Debs had been advocating industrial unions ever since 1893, when he organized the American Railwaymen's Union.)

The departments of industrial organization of the One Big Union would be a shadow and reversed version of American capitalism, organized on the same scale and prepared to step in and take over after a workers' revolution. Then an injury to any individual worker would be felt as an injury to all; the wage system would be abolished; the working class would rule the country, and eventually the world.

This would come about by the means of direct industrial action, by strikes, not through the country's conventional political system, with its parties and elections and House of Representatives and Senate. Daniel de Leon, who as a socialist disagreed with this, had a clause about political action inserted into the preamble, but the western delegates (Haywood's WFM was the largest single group there) were scornful of what they called the capitalist ballot-box. Many of their constituency, being migrant workers, had never voted, and they feared that their new organization would be taken over by Daniel de Leon's Socialist Labor party or by Victor Berger and Morris Hillquit's Socialist Party of America, both of which had their primary affiliations with the eastern half of the country and with intellectuals, often belonging to the professional classes.

However, the largest single difference of politics lined Haywood up together with de Leon and Debs, as all in the loosest sense socialist, against the anarcho-syndicalists, who included Father Hagerty, Mother Jones, and Lucy Parsons, widow of one of the Haymarket martyrs. The power went to the first group, but some of the ideas of the second group stayed with the IWW throughout its history; for instance, the abolition of the state, the practice of sabotage, and the cult of violence reminiscent of Bakunin.[54] And the example of French syndicalism inspired them. Trade union activity, suppressed in France after the Commune of 1871, began again in 1884, inspired this time by Proudhon and Sorel. (Indeed, their sense of world history was French; its main events were the Revolution and the Commune; their main hymn was the "Marseillaise," a main symbol the Bastille; but this of course was socialist as much as syndicalist.) The backbone of the French labor movement, the Confédération générale du travail, had been formed in 1895 by uniting two federations. The doctrine that there would always be a militant minority to arouse and lead the majority was also a syndicalist idea; and though it was not too popular with the IWW as a whole, it was held in practice by Haywood and most of the other leaders.[55] The IWW's big difference from its French model was that it set itself up as a rival to the established AFL, whereas the French recommended boring from within and taking over existing union structures.

In 1908 the political action clause was expunged from the second paragraph of the preamble, and de Leon was expelled from the IWW by Haywood with the help of twenty of the "overalls brigade"—

western delegates who stole rides on trains across country to get to the Chicago meeting and swing the vote. Both those who won and those who lost shared the feeling that the bums were taking over the union. Vincent St. John, a westerner and only thirty-four years old, became secretary-treasurer, the most important officer.

As early as 1906 the IWW had gotten rid of its presidency, and declared itself a party in which everyone, or no one, was the leader. (In Paterson, in 1913, Haywood said this to Rabbi Mannheimer, a liberal sympathizer who wanted to talk to the strikers' leaders; it is difficult to measure the empirical truth of the claim, for it seems clear that its prime function was rhetorical and doctrinal.) But up to 1909 the radical groups within the union fought each other, one faction seeing it as a strictly economic organization, another as attached to the SPA. In 1909 it was recalled to effective action by the success of the Free Speech movement in the West, and by the strike at McKee's Rocks, in Pennsylvania, which the IWW organized and won after fifty-seven days.

Charles Ashleigh's autobiographical novel, *Rambling Kid*, describes the attraction the IWW exerted, its call to radical commitment. The story begins in London and ends with the hero on a boat to Moscow in 1917, but the action is all about the American Wobbly identity. "They fascinated Joe . . ."[56] There was an atmosphere of recklessness and daring about these fellows, who strolled along the streets in their blue overalls, or khaki trousers, with gray or blue shirts, open at the throats, and their black slouch hats. They knew the western states from British Columbia to the Mexican border, from Chicago to Portland, Oregon. In all the vast territory where great railroads are still being built . . . giant reservoirs . . . forests . . . [they] travel illegally, hiding upon freight or passenger trains."[57] They beat up or literally threw off the trains anyone they found there using a Wobbly card without being a Wobbly. Joe finally becomes "a hobo and a Wobbly, one of the reckless rambling boys who despised the soft security and comfort of a dull-paced city existence."[58]

To understand the IWW story we should insert it into its historical context. In 1910, of ten million unskilled workers in the USA, three and a half million were migrants; the IWW grew fast in this country and in countries like Australia and New Zealand, because in all of them the freedoms of frontier life were being replaced by the disciplines of wages. The age of urbanization in America ran from 1870 on.[59] In that year, according to the Census Bureau, a quarter of the population lived in urban areas. By 1900, the proportion was two-fifths, and by 1920, one-half. In correspondence with that development went *trustification* in big business, the fastest growth period being 1897 to 1904. In 1904 J. P. Morgan bought out Carnegie to form U.S. Steel; then followed the formation of the corporation giants that are still familiar names: Rockefeller, Swift, Duke, Frick, Sears, and Montgomery Ward. By the end of 1904 there were 318 trusts, with more than seven billion dollars in capital.

In natural reaction, this was also the age of reform: first of populism, then of progressivism; then of socialism. "While it lasted, all manner of things seemed possible in America."[60] Renshaw says that it was by 1900 that progressivism, giving a voice to middle-class protest in the cities, had superseded populism, with its farmer constituency. The spokesmen for the progressives were the muckrakers, and a little later, Theodore Roosevelt. They wanted to restore economic individualism and political democracy.[61] By 1911 thirty-three cities had socialist governments, and socialism dominated several important unions.[62] The socialist sympathies of the nearby town of Haledon played a part in the Paterson strike, as we shall see.

The equivalent movement in the world of the arts and ideas often called itself a renaissance, as we have seen. The word was sometimes used to cover everything new that was happening in the country—everything that the writer approved. For instance, Percy MacKaye, founder of the pageant movement, claimed that his masques and pageants, by renewing the communal faith of citizens, could serve the general American renaissance. And Theodore Roosevelt, inspecting the Armory Show, was ready to welcome its experimentalism as a sign of a rebirth of energies, though on other grounds he disapproved it. But as his name reminds us, we are now thinking of the most official establishment; one of MacKaye's 1913 masques was performed in the presence of President Wilson, and members of his family took part; and to MacKaye's fiftieth birthday celebrations the secretary of state, the secretary of commerce (Herbert Hoover) and a Supreme Court justice sent messages of congratulation. This was

the official renaissance, and such sponsorship could smile on a lot
of things, but not on the Armory Show or the IWW. Even socialism
could be viewed as idealistic, and Victor Berger could be welcomed
as a member of Congress, but not Bill Haywood. The IWW was not
a part of the official renaissance.

For instance, on June 7, 1913, the day of the Pageant, John A.
Fitch wrote an article for *Survey* magazine, under the heading, "The
I.W.W., an Outlaw Organization." His point was that "Against this
organization are arrayed the forces of present day society. It is denounced by the press, thundered against by the pulpit, and anathe-
matized by the spokesmen of the business world."[63] Fitch ends with
an allusion to the persecution of the early Christians.[64] But he is
himself clearly shocked by many of the IWW's practices, especially
its recommendation of sabotage.

On the other hand, in the world of the arts and ideas, the renaissance was supposed to be unofficial; and a lot of people in the arts
found just what they wanted in the Armory Show, and a lot of people
in politics found just what they wanted in the Paterson Strike. In
some sense, what was at issue in 1913 was to decide, were these
events part of the American renaissance or not? Mabel Dodge and
her friends answered yes, they were the climax to it. Socialist
politics—and realistic painting—were insufficiently challenging. The
SPA's tactics, for instance, were gradualist and Fabian, and young
people looked for a more militant policy and image—looked to
the IWW.

This was not just a matter of militancy, but of a whole style,
affecting taste and aesthetics. In 1900 intellectual socialism was
under the influence of William Morris and Jane Addams and Howells.
The Chicago Arts and Crafts Exhibition in 1902 showed bookbinding
and handicrafts from Addams's Hull House.[65] Such arts and crafts
work was in some sense culturally conservative, however left-wing
and populist in its political sympathies: it was in the service of good
taste, beauty, and harmony. But over the next ten years the quite
different culture of the hobo intellectual came to power in the left
wing; Upton Sinclair's anthology, *The Cry for Justice*, ended with
extracts from Jack London. London and Reed apprenticed themselves
to Whitman rather than to Morris, and to foreign models like Maksim

Gorky and Pancho Villa. The cultural style of the Wobblies proper could be called anticultural and be said to have more in common with the frontiersmen and the hobos than with the socialists.

The most prominent leader of the SPA was Victor Berger, socialist mayor of Milwaukee from 1910, and later the first socialist member of Congress. He argued for a personal, not institutional, combination of union allegiance with party allegiance. This was what Haywood recommended, too (he was himself a member of the SPA from 1901 on), but for him the union would be dominant in those combinations, while for Berger it would be the opposite. Moreover, for Berger the union loyalty in question would be to the AFL, which he hoped to dominate. He distrusted the IWW, as people who set fire to wheat fields, derailed trains, broke machinery, killed policemen. Because of this conflict, Haywood was thrown out of the SPA in 1912 and in the presidential campaign that year campaigned for Debs.

The question of sabotage was a crucial one, which was discussed in graver tones than the other charges against the union. John Fitch, in the article mentioned, dismisses the charge of antipatriotism and disrespect for the flag brought against the IWW, but he says that sabotage would undermine the morals of the race, and in another place would undermine the health and well-being of the race. The religion of America, after all, taught production and construction as prime values; if the IWW was destructive, it was un-American.

After 1908, the IWW had a lot to say about the subject, but as Foner says, "The truth is, it was exceedingly difficult to determine exactly what the IWW meant by sabotage."[66] Émile Pouget's pamphlet *Sabotage* translated by Giovannitti, was on sale at the Paterson Pageant. Two of the most prominent Wobbly symbols were a hunched black cat, spitting and showing its claws, and a wooden shoe, often crushing a snake. But explicit statements were very cautious.

This was true of the wider subject of violence. "Like sabotage, violence was the subject of endless discussion and debate in IWW circles."[67] Haywood and Ettor were explicitly against it, Flynn and St. John were not. But there was inevitably a suggestion of prudence and public decorum about opposing violence; and whatever the leaders said, the union was associated with violence, by its own members as well as by its enemies, and to its advantage as well as to its disadvantage. It was a part of the frontier character, the populist and antiestablishment character, which distinguished it from rival organizations and attracted bolder and freer spirits, especially younger and unmarried men.

The Wobblies were in some sense intellectuals—if sometimes also anti-intellectuals. They liked to debate and confound professors.[68] They organized Propaganda Leagues and Industrial Education Clubs. There were many "cultural" activities by which they made themselves known to both prospective members and their liberal audience, activities like songs and jokes as well as marches and slogans, cartoons, and symbols.

Bill Haywood wrote a series of "Shots for the Workshop," one-line epigrams like "The manager's brains are under the workman's cap," or "To the working class there is no foreigner but the capitalist."[69] Haywood's language was often imaginative: he called the bankers of New York "the barbarous gold barons. They did not find the gold, they did not mine the gold, they did not mill the gold, but, by some weird alchemy, all the gold belongs to them."[70] His article in the Paterson Pageant program was called "Smoothing Out the Wrinkles in Silk."

The logo most IWW papers used had three stars (standing for education, emancipation, and organization) over a northern hemisphere, with the slogan An Injury to One Is an Injury to All. By 1911 the union was publishing six newspapers in five languages, and in 1912 there were thirteen. The two that lasted were *Solidarity* (1909–17) and *The Industrial Worker* (1909–13). In 1920 Paul Brissenden listed sixty periodicals with IWW sympathies.[71] *Wilshire's Monthly* had a circulation of four hundred thousand, and the weeklies, the *National Rip Saw* and *Appeal to Reason*, sold twenty thousand each—and when running a serial like Upton Sinclair's, that number would go up. They published pamphlets in editions of hundreds of thousands, on issues that went beyond politics in the narrowest sense, such as Flynn's lecture, "Small Families and Proletarian Necessity."

All these activities had an imaginative and symbolist character; and especially important was the symbolism of the flag. We have seen Haywood redrawing the American flag in his early days in Colorado, and the red flag was another of those symbols of international and revolutionary socialism which the IWW always used. The same symbolism was used by the other side. During the Lawrence strike the conservative Boston papers said "Old Glory was dragged on the ground as strikers retreated before the drawn bayonets of the militia."[72] The army and the flag were of course important symbols of patriotism, and the IWW—but not openly—contested patriotism as a bourgeois ideology. This symbolic conflict became especially acute at Paterson, because the silk mills *made* flags, including "Old Glory." The owners instituted a Flag Day in March, which was, according to the workers, a dismal failure; and when in April the AFL, with the owners' blessing, tried to intervene by sending two representatives of the United Textile Workers, John Golden and Sarah Conboy, to address the workers, they used the Stars and Stripes again. In a moment of confusion and shouting, Sarah Conboy seized the flag and waved it—according to one account, wrapped it around herself—but the workers responded by all flashing their red IWW membership cards, to make a red banner.

Two-color Wobbly "stickerettes" were glued to boxcars, flophouse walls, lamp posts, billboards, pitchforks, shovels, factory gates, jail-houses. Haywood suggested many of the slogans (Sit Down and Watch Your Pay Go Up) and Ralph Chaplin did many of the drawings, but their distribution was the work of the whole union.[73] There were IWW bands; one, organized in the Northwest by J. J. Walsh, wore red uniforms to parody the Salvation Army bands. (Walsh led the "overalls brigade" to Chicago for the 1908 convention at which de Leon was ejected.)

In the Wobbly halls, and even in the jungles (the patches of wasteland where hobos made their camp fires when no shelter was available) there was a culture with both moral and aesthetic aspects. A man's past was his own affair, and usually every race or nationality was equally welcomed. At least in theory, as we have seen, long epic poems were composed and recited on the spot. When the Wobbly martyr Joe Hill was awaiting execution in Salt Lake City (charged with murder) his last message to the people of Utah ended, "I have lived like an artist, and I shall die like an artist."[74]

Above all, there were the Wobbly songs, gathered into the *Little Red Songbook* (first published in 1909 for a nickel) or sold individually on song cards, which were extremely popular. The IWW was proud of its reputation as the union of songs and jokes which marked it off from the AFL. The first leaflet contained four songs, three of them parodies of Salvation Army hymns; then there was an edition with sixteen such parodies; and the final version had thirty-eight songs and the preamble to the IWW constitution, plus the "Red Flag," the "Marseillaise" and the "Internationale." The subtitle to the collection was *Songs to Fan the Flames of Discontent*. It was often called the Bible of the movement, and there were debates in the Wobbly papers in 1911 and 1912 about whether the songs were not more useful than the pamphlets; Joe Hill naturally argued for the songs.

His most famous song, "Casey Jones" (with the line, "You'll get pie in the sky when you die") was written in 1909 and parodied an original of 1907. He also wrote "Nearer My Job to Thee," and a version of "Ta-ra-ra-boom-de-ay" and "It's a Long Long Way Down to the Soup Line" ("Good-bye, good old pork chops / Farewell beefsteak rare . . ."). Other famous songs were by Covington Hall, Ralph Chaplin ("Solidarity Forever") and T-Bone Slim ("The Lumber Jack's Prayer": "I pray, dear Lord, for Jesus' sake / Give us this day a T-bone steak / Hallowed be thy holy name / But don't forget to send the same").

The songs that came out of the West and Northwest were primarily satirical, though of course there were solemn hymns like "Solidarity Forever." Another kind of poem and song, such as "Bread and Roses," expresses the eastern, immigrant, socialist side of the Wobbly sensibility. As was said before, it is significant that this is a song for women, while the others are for men. "Bread and Roses" was written by James Oppenheim (1882–1932), later editor of the literary magazine *Seven Arts*, but then a contributor to *The Industrial Pioneer* and *The One Big Union Monthly*. Poems of a similar kind were published in *The Masses* by, for instance, Louis Untermeyer and Rose Pastor Stokes. Oppenheim's poem was set to music by Caroline Kohlsaat, and so became a Wobbly song, also. Giovannitti also wrote an Italian version of the same song, "Pan e Rose." (His poetry, which got published in magazines like *The Atlantic Monthly*, was somewhat like Whitman's, somewhat like the expressionism of Leonid Andreev.) This sort of art corresponded better to the hopes of liberal or left-wing intellectuals like Percy MacKaye or Hutchins Hapgood: "Self-expression in industry and art among the masses may become a rich reality, spreading a human glow over the whole of humanity . . . from which we shall all be the gainers—in real life, in justice, in art, in love."[75] It also corresponds much more centrally to the paintings of the Eight.

However, the other, more sardonic element in Wobbly culture was perhaps the more important; it certainly challenged the intellectuals more, and was more congruent with later modernism, in forms like Brechtian drama. It was linked to adventure and action, rather than to social and political theory, and to violence rather than to orderly procedure. This was given voice above all by Haywood. Ed Boyce, Haywood's first friend and teacher in labor politics, became president of the WFM in 1896, when the union had languished for five years. By 1901 he had made it the most dynamic and radical union in the country, says Conlin.[76] It was socialist, aggressive in industrial action, and independent of the conservative labor movement of the East. Leading his followers out of the AFL in 1897, he said he was not a *trade* unionist, and that the men of the West were a hundred years ahead of those of the East.

He and his friends, including Haywood to begin with, saw the owners as intruders, and insisted on their own Americanness.[77] Haywood in his early days spoke of his "old American family." They referred to western precedent and the American myth; Haywood referred to John Brown, and Lincoln, and 1776. In the West, of course, until 1880 American racial stock (with the exception of the blacks) was predominantly English-Scots-Irish-German-Scandinavian.[78] It was after 1900 that the flood of immigrants from southern and eastern Europe began, constituting 70 percent of the total immigration for the decade 1900 to 1910. This was the challenge the IWW faced in Lawrence and Paterson: how to mobilize the Catholic peasants of southern Europe and the Jews of Poland and Russia. (The song "Do You Lika Missa Flynn?" sung in Paterson and during the Pageant itself, has that resonance: do you trust us English-speaking comrades?)

Boyce (and Haywood to begin with) approved of F. J. Turner's ideas about the frontier. They were empowered by that myth of moving west whenever city life became oppressive, of starting again in the infinite spaces where a man had to deal with nature, not with society. In historical fact, for every factory hand who had turned farmer between 1860 and 1900, twenty farmers had gone into the factories.[79] But such facts probably reinforced the pathos of the frontier myth. Even when the IWW began to work in Lawrence and Paterson, that myth probably worked on their side, endowing them with a promise of hope they did not need to articulate.

However, perhaps their appeal to intellectuals and artists, their sense of being mythical, worked to their long-term disadvantage. One feature of the organization was the mixed locals, which included members who were not industrial workers. These locals were intended to be only recruitment stations and propaganda centers, but they were stronger than the factory locals, says Margaret Gerteis, who speculates that this may have weakened the IWW as a union.[80] Perhaps there was too great a distance between the workplace and the public agitation; this, as we shall see, was probably true of the Paterson Pageant. Moreover, Wobblies were seen together with other left-wingers, socialists and anarchists, instead of having a clear profile of their own. So at least some of the members argued, in a debate in the Wobbly press in spring 1914.

To some degree, the success of the union created difficulties for it and accounted for the defeat at Paterson. Steve Golin, discussing "The Unity and Strategy of the Paterson Silk Manufacturers in the Great Strike," decides that the owners were strong because they were united, and this unity was not produced by any trust or by any large pool of capital, but by their joint fears of the power of the IWW.[81] And by May 1913 they had won the support of the Paterson press and clergy and small businessmen, when it came to closing down, for instance, the halls where the strikers held their meetings. They were, of course, in a stronger position than the Lawrence owners, because they had invested in mills elsewhere (notably in Pennsylvania) and so were not dependent exclusively on the Paterson operation.

The IWW was a masculine society. Joe Hill dedicated his "Rebel Girl" to Flynn—who took that as the title for her autobiography—but we have seen that women counted for little in the IWW. One woman, Laura Payne Emerson, wrote songs, but not the famous ones; Agnes Thekla Fair sold her own poems. More important, Mother Jones was a feminist in her way, and cared about the exploitation of children, even leading a crusade of children to talk to Theodore Roosevelt when he was president, but it seems to be generally agreed that she was peripheral to the movement as a whole. And this masculinism of the left was so like that of the right that it led to some curious ambiguities. The ideas of adventure and of male solidarity, so important to the IWW, had been claimed before by Kipling and Roosevelt; so that most of John Reed's verse, to the end of his life, sounds just like Kipling's.

One sign of that confusion is the popular poem, "The Cry of Toil" (also sung) which appeared in the *Industrial Union Bulletin* in 1908, attributed to Kipling. It was sometimes known by its first line, "We have fed you all for a thousand years." It was a popular Wobbly poem, and was published again in 1918 with the copyright belonging to Haywood, and now said to be written by "an unknown proletarian."[82] In 1929 it was put into Marcus Graham's *Anthology of Revolutionary Poetry* as a parody of Kipling. This uneasy shifting of categories signals a split between the anarchist and the socialist wings of the left. There was some feeling that a true socialist could not be an adventurer, nor vice versa: to take an example from the life of Marx, had Lassalle been a true socialist, and if not, was it not because he had been an adventurer?

But the IWW (and other people) apprehended and defined working-class culture as masculinist and adventurous. In *The Spirit of Labor*, Hutchins Hapgood reported on his study of the labor movement in Chicago, where "labor is most expressive, most violent, where the workingman abounds in his own sense . . . I felt a kind of class sweetness under their rough manners, and also a class rebelliousness."[83] He wrote a biography of an unidentified worker-leader called Anton (actually Anton Johannson), stressing the "rough sweet health of his personality."[84] (It is of course Whitman on whom Hutchins draws for this vocabulary, and for these perceptions that he is mediating to his middle-class audience.) Anton says about himself, "The men saw in me a peculiar, rough honesty, and workingmen like that. I know men, and felt instinctively that it was best to appeal mainly to the manhood in a man."[85] The whole book is a cult of manhood; Anton's wife cautions him not to "break loose," but we are told that she would not love him so much if he obeyed her.

Hapgood describes himself as, in contrast, someone who had "never worked with my hands in my life," so he is very deferential.[86] This was a general attitude, especially toward migrant workers or hobos. In *The Milk and Honey Route* (1931) Nels Anderson talks about what he calls Hobohemia, which he distinguishes from the older and less interesting Vagabondia. "Hobohemia is American. It is a kingdom of he-men and hard men. Women have never been suffered to enter. Boys are sometimes found there, but even boys, like the modern Eves, enter at their peril. That is why it remains the only earthly reminder of the Garden of Eden."[87] Hapgood talks about the *yeggs*, the most hardened hobos, who prefer boys to women, and against whom Anton had to defend himself as a young man.[88] They too are part of what he deferred to.

The prime example of what he—and Reed and the Village in general—admired was Bill Haywood. Their admiration for him was a cult of masculinity. They deferred, no doubt, to his size and strength, and perhaps to his sexual power and to his experience and his eminence as a leader, but we should acknowledge also an intellectual power which we can recognize in him as much as in well-known writers. In Haywood's description of Cripple Creek, for instance, we recognize a Wobbly or WFM prose, with its focus on both geology and industrialism, and its readiness for western jokes. "Here nature, the conjuror, had shaken up the porphyry dikes and into each split and seam had spurted up gold-bearing quartz or quartzite, which congealed. To the dismay of the mining experts, the same old nature wizard split the mother granite and filled its cracks and crevices with gold. This untold wealth remained hidden through all the ages until 1889, when a forlorn prospector, whose view of the scenery was obscured by the hind end of a jackass, dug with a dull pick into a streak of rich ore."[89]

A darker-hued version of the same rhetoric can be heard in this passage about Butte. "On approaching Butte I marvelled at the desolation of the country. There was no verdure of any kind; it had all been killed by the fumes and smoke of the piles of burning ore. The noxious gases came from the sulphur that was allowed to burn out of the ore before it was sent to the smelter. It was so poisonous that it not only killed trees, shrubs, grass, and flowers, but cats and dogs could not live in the city of Butte, and housewives complained that the fumes settling on the clothes rotted the fibre."[90]

Clearly Haywood was a remarkable writer and leader, who gave the idea of a Wobbly great dimensions, while remaining true to its traditional shape. Ralph Chaplin in his autobiography makes us feel the devotion he could command. For instance, Chaplin's mother, on the point of death, asked to be given a rebel funeral, meaning evergreen sprays and red carnations and a eulogy by Haywood. When she died, he came and spoke about her in what Chaplin calls the language of the West, which was also the language of literature. "Look at the hands of our people. They are hard and scarred and calloused from trying to make a dream come true."[91] It was the language of the West, of the Wobbly movement, because he spoke for all those others. The others were present when he spoke.

Chaplin's book expresses vividly the emotional faith of the movement. "We were expected to 'keep moving,' yet we couldn't move at all without breaking the law. And, every time we broke the law, the law tried to break us . . . We would stand together, fight for one another, steal for one another, and share our last crust with one another. . . . But not until the rebel songs of the IWW resounded from every threshing rig, every freight train, and not a few 'hoosegows' did the situation finally change."[92]

That was the pathos of the IWW movement, and the strikers of Paterson had their own equivalent for that. But the Pageant expressed that pathos in a particular artistic form. Nineteen thirteen was the year the American Pageant Association was founded, with an annual bulletin, a series of conferences, and an educational program. The first bulletin listed fifty pageants across the country, many of them historical, nostalgic, and picturesque, but some with a strong social conscience and purpose. These were usually instruments of pacification, aimed at immigrants, as Linda Nochlin says in her "Paterson Pageant."[93] In the 1913 bulletin, John Collier (Mabel Dodge's friend) said the new pageantry was the forerunner of a civic life based on common consciousness and brotherhood.

The central theorist of this movement was Percy MacKaye, who in 1915 published *The New Citizenship: A Civic Ritual Devised for Places of Public Meeting in America*. His interest went above all to *masques*, which were dramatized episodes within a pageant. Introducing his masque *Caliban* (1916) MacKaye said, "There is a growing but groping movement called 'pageantry,' that lets people take part in creating a popular art."[94] He had been working on it for ten years by 1916, and it was to be the expression of the people and by the people. He stressed the idea of poetry as spoken words, not written, and the role of the poet as citizen, as spokesman for the community. His largest achievement was the 1914 *Pageant and Masque of St. Louis*, where seventy-five hundred people performed the history of America to an audience estimated at half a million. A modest example of the same thing occurred on the same night as the Paterson Pageant, on Henry Street in New York, the work of Lillian Wald's Settlement House there. This was a simple procession of people dressed as, first Indians, then Dutch settlers, then English ones, and so on, down to the then-current tenants of Henry Street, described as 90 percent East European Jews. Settlement houses were, it seems, frequent instigators of pageants. This one being in some political sympathy with the Paterson Pageant (Lillian Wald was one of the signers of a petition to the president, asking for an investigation of the situation in Paterson), the comparison brings out the much more radical and aggressive character of Reed's work.

For instance, MacKaye was in alliance with Percival Chubb, who led the festival movement, dedicated to giving dignity to national holidays and symbols like the Fourth of July; the Paterson Strike and Pageant were quite hostile to national symbols, notably to the flag. MacKaye's work was establishmentarian in high-culture terms also: his Gloucester Pageant of 1910, watched by twenty-five thousand spectators, presented the people of Gloucester dressed as Chaucer's Canterbury Pilgrims. (The effect of the performance on the performers, according to MacKaye, was quite like the effect of the Paterson Pageant—it brought to birth a group spirit and solidarity.) Then he cited the universities both as future patrons for his "civic theaters" and as precedents, as far as public funding went. Thus his work was eminently respectable. One of his seven types of civic theaters was sociological theater, and the example of that was plays put on at Jane Addams's Hull House, the greatest of settlement houses. That shows the progressive side of the pageant movement. But there was nothing radical about it, in either political or aesthetic terms: two of those who took part in the early 1905 masque in Cornish, New Hampshire, were Maxfield Parrish and Kenyon Cox, two of the bêtes noires of the New York realists. That marks the playful and genteel character of the pageant movement, which Reed and Haywood transformed in their work.

The historical ideal behind MacKaye's work was Greek theater, which exerted a guiding influence on both society and the state in ancient Greece. It reconciled the traditions of art with those of democracy. He campaigned for state-endowed and public playhouses, to create an equivalent American drama of democracy, or fine art for the masses. In *The Playhouse and the Play* (1909), he says that the tendencies of art are idealistic, as are those of "our renascent republic."

This phrase signals MacKaye's accord with the widespread idea that an American renaissance was taking place, but his version of the idea was very closely linked to the educational establishment; in the same book he says that the highest schools of the country are already the seats of a modest but vital dramatic renascence, and he cites the work of George Peirce Baker at Harvard and William Lyon Phelps at Yale. He was also linked to the political establishment. As noted before, in 1913 his masque *Sanctuary* was performed in the presence of President Woodrow Wilson, and with the participation of members of Wilson's family; and in 1925, at a dinner in honor of his fiftieth birthday, messages came from the secretary of state, the secretary of commerce (Herbert Hoover) and a Supreme Court justice.

MacKaye belonged to a prominent family. His father, Steele MacKaye, had known William and Henry James when they were boys together, but he went on to become an actor and a man of the theater. He studied with a French voice teacher, Delsarte, between 1869 and 1872, and developed the latter's system—known as Delsartism—to cover bodily and facial expressions. This system was something Isadora Duncan studied as a girl, and her art developed from it. Gordon Craig said Delsarte's bust should stand in her temple of the dance, but Percy MacKaye said it should be his father's bust. There were many connections, in the world of dance and theater, between the MacKaye family and Craig and Duncan, and it is no surprise to find that Robert Edmond Jones, devoted to Craig, illustrated some of MacKaye's books.

MacKaye, though now largely forgotten as a poet, was highly thought of in his day. In the MacKaye symposium, Robert Frost said MacKaye had hastened the day when the American national life should cease to be raw.[95] Vachel Lindsay thanked MacKaye that "now at last we have an America—just beginning to bloom and sing . . . we are now moving toward the grand style, in all things—from skyscrapers to National Parks."[96] Lindsay and Sara Teasdale saw the pageant of St. Louis, and Teasdale said MacKaye had put poetry literally upon the lips of more Americans than any other poet.[97]

Part of MacKaye's doctrine of pageantry was the idea we meet in *The Independent*'s report on the Paterson Pageant: that the drama of the ancients had its origins beside the altars of their gods, and that modern drama began under the arches of medieval cathedrals. (It was the Puritans who had shut and locked the doors of the playhouse.) Therefore, of course, the pageant of American citizenship was the modern equivalent. He mentions Wagner's *Gesamtkunstwerk* as a recent model to follow, and asks us to see the evident superiority of *Siegfried* to Mozart's *Don Giovanni*. (This pattern of taste was followed out in the equivalent German movement of festivals, to be associated with the names of Dalcroze and Laban.)

MacKaye describes three kinds of theater as cultural rivals in 1913. There was the classical, and as he says segregated, drama, the current master of which was Ibsen; but his pessimistic message, MacKaye thought, was essentially European, deriving from conditions of over-population, while to the American millions, thank God, the wilderness was still an inspiration and a promise of opportunity. We had no need of Ibsen or his theater. There was vaudeville, the form of theater organized by and for the business community, but this was deplorable for its inorganic and fragmentary character and its neurasthenic or demented mood. And then there was pageantry, the drama of democracy.

These ideas connect with those of Gordon Craig, who said in 1907 that in his theater a new religion would be found, one that would not preach but would reveal the truth, reveal silently in movements and by visions. At least his cinquecento Florence pageant was to have no audience, only actors, according to Mabel Dodge; and that idea, of a performance aimed first at the participants (the opposite of vaudeville) was an important aspect of pageant doctrine. We know that Robert Edmond Jones was devoted to Craig's ideas (he also worked with MacKaye), and Mabel Dodge credits him with insisting on the roadway through the audience. Craig wanted very large buildings, like the amphitheaters in which Isadora Duncan danced, and that was what Jones found at his disposal in Madison Square Garden. But one would guess that the dominant ideas of the pageant must have been at least sanctioned by Bill Haywood and probably were born between him and John Reed.

Haywood must have known something about pageants. Hutchins Hapgood described in the *Globe* a dinner for Haywood, Lippmann, MacKaye, and Boyesen (a poet, teacher, radical, and farmer).[98] There were four other people present, unnamed, but we might guess that they included Mabel Dodge and John Reed. Hapgood presents Haywood as a natural poet whose eloquence could reach non–English-speaking audiences. He instinctively spoke to Italians differently from the way he spoke to Poles. He used a vocabulary of three hundred words, and his audience responded to him as instinctively as lovers respond to each other. According to Hapgood, Haywood was the center of the dinner party; the talk was about labor, poetry, and justice. Of them all it was Haywood who had a vision to express, he who was the poet, though others present had published verse—that is, MacKaye and Boyesen. And it seems clear that he had ideas about the function of art. "Haywood talked forcibly and feelingly against the poetry and the literature of isolation. Still more feelingly he spoke for the poetry of work."[99] Workers could still find beauty in their labor if they were but relieved of its stresses and strains. He could not understand, we are told, the aloof and conventional attitudes to poetry of MacKaye and Boyesen. He glowed, while they reasoned.

This use of the word *poetry* was familiar in 1913, though soon to be made illegitimate by modernist pundits like T. S. Eliot. Haywood apparently spoke of the solidarity of the working class (his IWW comrades Ettor and Giovannitti had just been released from their Lawrence sentences), and "He told how he got thirty-seven different nationalities to sing the same songs together. He commented on the wonder of that . . ."[100] International singing of that kind was put into the Paterson Pageant, and it may be that in these anecdotes we glimpse the consultation that went on between Reed and Haywood.

T H E
Show

. . . a creative lull occurs always when artists of a certain period are satisfied to pick up a predecessor's work where he dropped it.
—MARCEL DUCHAMP in Michel Sanouillet,
Salt Seller

Art is an end in itself and so opposed to life which is relations and necessity. . . . If there was no identity, no one could be governed. Governments are occupying, masterpieces are interesting.
—GERTRUDE STEIN, *Writings and Lectures*

We can never rise to be a great people until we bring art back as an inherent part of life. . . . Unless we have art in the house, we cannot learn its language.
—KATHERINE SOPHIE DREIER,
in *Western Art and the New Era*,
and in the Brooklyn Exhibition catalog

The idea that painting could dispense with symbols for known emotions, states of mind, or ideas caused an extraordinary liberation of form and created consciousness of states of being which escape words.
—VIRGINIA SPATE, *Orphism*

*F*rom the start the AAPS had an International Exhibition of Modern Art in view, so that we must dismiss the complaints by some participating American artists, taken up by some historians, that the Show had been intended to present *their* work but had been perverted by certain organizers into a showcase for the Europeans. In fact, seven hundred American works were shown, to five hundred European works. It is true that the leading organizers were more excited by the European entries, but then so was the audience.

They looked for a large exhibition hall, and at one point considered the Madison Square Garden, where the Paterson Pageant was to be played, but its rent was very high and would absorb all the takings (as the Pageant organizers were to discover). So they chose the Armory of the Sixty-ninth New York Regiment, "the Fighting Irish," at Lexington Avenue and Twenty-fifth and Twenty-sixth streets. They would redecorate the building, hiding its military character and creating the atmosphere of art instead, as the Pageant organizers would redecorate the Garden, hiding its establishment character and creating the atmosphere of protest. (The two buildings were in fact only a few blocks apart.) They agreed to pay five thousand dollars for a month, plus five hundred dollars for janitors. Davies procured the money—from where was never made known, but presumably from some of the wealthy women art lovers with whom he was supposed to have had influence. The AAPS signed the contract on May 25, 1912, and put down a deposit of fifteen hundred dollars, and got itself incorporated on July 1.[1]

During the summer of 1912 Davies read an account of an exhibition in Cologne, which was organized around a historical and explanatory account of modern art, such as he wished to give in his exhibition: the Internationale Ausstellung des Sonderbundes Westdeutsche Kunstfreunde und Künstler. He sent this account to his close associate, Walt Kuhn, suggesting that he might like to see the exhibition, and when the latter agreed and returned to New York posthaste, Davies organized his passage.

Kuhn got to the Cologne Exhibition on the day it closed, but was able to look at the paintings as they were taken down. They included 125 van Goghs, 26 Cézannes, 25 Gauguins, and so on. He made contact with owners, arranging to borrow some, and went on to The Hague, where he saw Odilon Redon's work, and finally to Paris.

There the Fauves had passed the peak of their fashion, and were being replaced by cubism, which then meant Picasso and Braque, but also Léger and Gris, and the Duchamp-Villon brothers. Also modern, but not so securely established, were those influenced by orphism and futurism, like Robert Delaunay and Marcel Duchamp. Walter Pach was Kuhn's main guide through the maze of schools and galleries and gossip. Their largest loan, of over a hundred pictures, came from the Galéries Émile Druet.

The Show catalog finally listed 1,270 items, but other things which arrived too late for the catalog were also on display. Most probably seventy-three Redons, thirty-eight Augustus Johns, fourteen Cézannes were shown, and lesser numbers of lesser celebrities.

In late October, Kuhn had wired that because of the wealth of material, Davies should join him in Paris to share the responsibility of choosing, so the latter dropped everything to get there in early November. They put in ten days of work in Paris and went on together to London, leaving Pach in charge of things in France. In London they attended Roger Fry's Second Postimpressionist Exhibition at the Grafton Gallery and picked up some more Matisses. (Because of the Steins' good relations with Matisse, they already had a fine selection of his work.) They were not impressed with the English painters; they could not take Vanessa Bell and Duncan Grant seriously as cubists, and they more or less ignored German and Italian painting. The futurists were unrepresented, perhaps because they insisted on being exhibited as a group, and of the Germans there were only Kandinsky and Kirchner. The international, or non-American, aspect of the Show was to be overwhelmingly French.

Kuhn and Davies sailed from Liverpool to New York on November 21, still with a great deal to do. They had to divide up the Armory space, build the actual gallery rooms, group and hang the exhibits, get up the catalog, launch the publicity, invite the guests, and so on. All twenty-five members of the AAPS worked on these projects, though some of them did so with growing misgivings as the excitement focused more and more exclusively upon the French artists. Inside the Armory they put up eighteen octagonal rooms with twelve-foot outside walls covered in fireproof burlap and greenery, ten-foot inside walls, and a dome of yellow cloth streamers, for a total cost of three thousand dollars. The Sixty-ninth Regimental Band was to play in the gallery. Visitors were to move from the entrance either down the straight-ahead center room and then to left and then right, or vice versa. The history of modern art was represented by the exhibits of the four rooms in the central line, after which one turned right to rooms of American painting and one of English, Irish, and German, or left to the sequence of French painting, which culminated in the cubists.

The style of the redecoration was very sober (the principal color came from the evergreen sprays) as compared with either that of the Pageant (which splashed scarlet everywhere) or that of Diaghilev's exhibition of Russian paintings in Paris (which was boldly theatrical in style). Davies clearly aimed at making modern art respectable by aligning it with the art of the past (establishing its lineage, its legitimacy) and by aligning it with that most respectable of revolutions, the American. The logo of the Show was the Massachusetts Tree of Liberty, and the catalog was educational. Branches of pine trees were displayed, carrying out the Tree of Liberty motif, and the slogan was The New Spirit.

Davies seems to have chosen his committees with political skill. For instance, he kept Henri off the domestic committee, which chose American works for display, and put Glackens in that chair, because of the Eight, Glackens was the most modernist in his taste, and so most in sympathy with Davies's feeling, which was that, for instance, American sculpture was very out of date. (It was still public-building sculpture, while the French sculptors had largely broken with that tradition.) Thus the committee accepted nothing by Daniel Chester French, and only one piece each from Janet Scudder and Anna Coleman Ladd. (The sculptor Gutzon Borglum, vice president of the AAPS, resigned just before the Show opened.)

Walter Pach and Frederick J. Gregg, a journalist, made honorary members of the AAPS, were paid twelve hundred dollars each for publicity work, and they were, by general agreement, very successful. Henry May says the Show was "a masterpiece of carefully planned showmanship." Brown says it was undoubtedly the best-publicized art show in American history: "The drum-beating was almost worthy of a Barnum . . ." and he speaks of "the circus atmosphere."[2] Alfred Stieglitz, in a letter of April 30, 1914, called the Show "a sensational success, possibly primarily a success of sensation."[3] The first order of catalogs was for fifty thousand copies and cost forty-four hundred dollars. The four pamphlets came out in editions of five thousand (besides the one by Fauré on Cézanne, there were two pieces by Pach, on Odilon Redon and Duchamp-Villon, and some extracts from Gauguin's *Noa-Noa*) and a series of fifty-seven half-tone picture postcards.

The twenty-five members of the AAPS were all men, but the list of honorary vice presidents began with Mrs. Gardner, Mrs. Dodge, and Mrs. Davidge; followed by nine men, including Sir Hugh Lane, Professor Joel Spingarn, Alfred Stieglitz, Augustus John, Monet, Renoir, and Redon. Mrs. Davidge ran the Coventry Studios, with financial help from Mrs. Whitney; she also protected various men of talent, like Edwin Arlington Robinson. She played—less brilliantly—the role Mabel Dodge was to play; there were of course several such patrons.

The special issue of the magazine *Arts and Decoration* which prepared the public for the Show included a historical chart of modern art, by Davies. Using three categories, classical, romantic, and realistic, he sorted out the bewildering variety of recent schools into a comprehensible pattern. The romantics included not only Delacroix and Daumier, but Renoir and Redon, van Gogh and Gauguin; the classicals included the postimpressionists, and above all the cubists. This was a powerful piece of propaganda for the cubists, for this was the moment (in literature, the moment of T. S. Eliot and T. E. Hume) when the idea of the classical was exciting the avant-garde. Especially in France and England, the realistic and the romantic were being left behind with the nineteenth century. The twentieth was announced to be the century of the classical.

The Show opened on February 17, with thousands of invited guests and a speech by John Quinn. He said it was a red-letter day in history, and one that would be remembered forever. Later to be famous in literary history for his protection of Eliot and Joyce, Quinn has been said to represent the new kind of art patron—patronizing modern art—which replaced the J. P. Morgan type, the patron of traditional art. Quinn was a lawyer who had been interested in politics, but turned away from it in disgust in 1912, feeling betrayed by his leader, William Jennings Bryan. He hoped that he would find in art what had failed him in politics—men of principle.[4] (We glimpse there the moral and spiritual challenge which modern art offered to politics.) He bought modern paintings at the Show and played a prominent public part at its opening and closing.

The Armory was open from 10:00 A.M. to 10:00 P.M., except on Sundays, when it opened at two. On weekday mornings it cost a dollar to go in; at other times, twenty-five cents. Photographs of the street outside show the curbs lined with expensive automobiles. Brown estimates that about ninety thousand attended, the majority in the second two weeks. The feeling of a success was unmistakable toward the end, and on the closing day, March 15, the Sixty-ninth Regiment's fife and drum corps played, and members of the regiment, together with members of the AAPS, guests, guards, guides, ticket sellers, followed the painter Daniel Putnam Brinley in a snake dance through the rooms.

If we now turn our attention to the pictures on display, we can discern some contrastive patterns. For instance, John Sloan's *Sunday, Women Drying Their Hair* (1912) makes a sharp contrast with Marcel Duchamp's *Nude Descending a Staircase* of the same year. This was a contrast between New York realism, which had been the avant-garde of American art, and the School of Paris. One big difference, of course, lay in the latter's repudiation of recognizableness, its blatant devotion to abstract values, pictorial and analytical. Sloan's

175

women are completely and immediately recognizable as women of a certain physical type and as belonging to certain social and geo- graphical and age groups; their being together, and the painter's seeing them together, is an event, and the time and place of the event could not be clearer. We know the women's bodies, and what they make of them, as individuals and as a group, whereas Duchamp's nude is abstracted from time and space and sex and even physique; the image is robotic, both in movement and in color. The painter insists on how far he is from flesh and blood; there are curving lines of force around the figure, some of them dotted lines, to tell us this is a diagram. Talking about the picture, Duchamp cited studies of movement by Marey, Muybridge, and Eakins, but his picture differs from theirs by its partly ludicrous effect—as if a single-file procession had been abruptly halted and those behind were bumping into those in front. The effect is ironic and analytic and so, as Duchamp says, more cubist than futurist.

Of course the same contrast would not emerge so vividly if we aligned Sloan with some older French paintings at the Show, like Daumier's *Third Class Carriage* (n.d.) or Cézanne's *Femme au Cha- pelet* (1898). But it holds good for most modern French paintings there, like Picasso's *Femme au Pot de Moutarde* (1910), and van Gogh's *Montagnes à Saint Remy*, in which we recognize values quite different from the humanism of American realist painting—a spiritual intensity derived from a formal intensity. Of course there are excep- tions: Munch and Redon have a different kind of intensity, as much a matter of content as of form. But if one tries to explain the strong impact of novelty which the European painters had on the American audience, one must surely point to a difference of this kind.

The rhetoric of the Show itself revolved around life values. The preface to the catalog, written by Gregg, said, "Art is a sign of life. There can be no life without danger, as there can be no development without change. To be afraid of what is different or unfamiliar is to be afraid of life. And to be afraid of life is to be afraid of truth, and to be a champion of superstition . . . ."[5] But this rhetoric did not apply well to the most modernist among the paintings, which it tended to assimilate to the old-fashioned realism of the Eight. Arthur J. Eddy appealed more to the new art in his book, *Cubists and Post-Impres-*

sionists, of 1914, saying that the art of the future would be more spiritual; the keynote of the modern movement in art was "the expression of the *inner self*, as distinguished from the representation of the outer world."[6] This obviously linked up with the ideas of Kandinsky's essay, and with many of those who frequented 291. It was close to the theories with which Katherine Dreier defended modern or abstract art in the 1920s and 1930s. You can also see this idea reflected in the complaints of John Sloan and Maurice Sterne against the introspective character of the new art. Sterne, for instance, saw two weaknesses as causing the "present universal chaos"—the first was Picasso's passion for innovation, and the second was the emphasis on self-revelation, on "turning in, away from nature."[7]

Other pictures in the style of the Eight were Eugene Miller's Tolstoyan subjects: *Hunger under a Bridge* and *Convicts and Guard*. Among the American modernists (mostly Stieglitz's protégés), Dasburg had three pictures and one sculpture, and Katherine Dreier had one picture. (Dreier was a rival rather than a disciple of Stieglitz, but she had read Kandinsky.) Dove, Demuth, and Weber were not represented, though a few months later Weber was given the first one-man museum show for a native modernist, by the Newark Museum. Stuart Davis's *Babe la Tour* was a commedia painting, and his *Dance* and *Servant Girls* resembled Toulouse-Lautrec. Bellows showed some pictures of horses and of circuses.

Henri, like Sloan, painted a lot of big women (for instance, *The Gypsy*), and Abraham Walkowitz did five thousand drawings of Isadora Duncan. Works of this kind, when painted and looked at with intense feeling, are icons of a cult of *magna mater*, which had been widely revived among artists at the end of the nineteenth century; you could find it in the works of Ferdinand Hodler in Switzerland, Augustus John in England, and D. H. Lawrence in literature. This is strikingly absent from the works of the School of Paris; if we look at Picasso's portraits of women, from Fernande to Gertrude Stein, we find very little of that feeling—not to mention the more striking case of Duchamp. His *Bride Stripped Bare by Her Bachelors, Even* is in origin an ironic mockery of that cult. Clearly, Duchamp knew something of that cult, was interested in it, but his mockery relies on a different, narrower, negative tradition, strongest in Paris, which includes Jarry and Villiers de l'Ile Adam. (His bride floats over his bachelors in the same transcendent horizontality as Molly Bloom does in *Ulysses*, and Joyce has much the same relation as Duchamp to that cult.)

This mockery of the human, and especially the female, nude was deeply offensive to the American art-loving public, even that part of it with no knowledge of the magna mater cult. Beautiful paintings of female nudes—seen, often, simply as objects to be owned by powerful men (quite the reverse of the magna mater cult)—were an essential, perhaps the essential, part of the traditional world of nineteenth-century art. It was a battle waged on behalf of beauty against the philistine world which was still suspicious of art and nervous of nudity and sex. Kenyon Cox, for instance, a principal enemy of the Show, had been a champion of artistic freedom in this matter of nudes, in his day; the modernists', for instance Matisse's, sadistic deformation of the Female Form Divine, as it was often called, was just what infuriated him. As Brown says, "Years of concerted effort on the part of the artistic community to establish the notion in the Puritan mind that depiction of nudity had sanction because the human body was the work of God had left its mark."[8] The modernists were no longer interested in extending God's handiwork to include sex; they were nearer to seeking to contract God's handiwork to the vanishing point, but more exactly they declined to discuss Him.

There was dissent inside the AAPS before the Show opened. On its very eve Gutzon Borglum resigned, and sent an emotional letter to the press. (He was famous for colossal mountainside monuments, and sculptures of Indian scouts—quite the reverse of modern art.) Leon Dabo left for Europe just before the opening; according to Myers, he said, "This man Davies has started something. I'm afraid it may be more of a calamity than a blessing, though it's a damn good show."[9] The calamity was of course the way the American artists were cast in the shade; and many things, some accidental, conspired to give that effect. Some artists who obviously deserved to be shown were not: Max Weber refused to send in the two pictures he was invited to; he had wanted to show eight. If he had done so, the American section would not have looked so unlike the European. Roger Fry showed eleven Webers at the Grafton Group Show the same year in London—one of them the futurist *New York 1913*.

But it was some of those who did show and who were deeply involved in the organization who were most aggrieved by the result. Myers treated the Show as a cultural tragedy: "The American art world in the years immediately preceding 1913 was a landscape before an impending storm. . . . the stage was well set for the greatest French invasion that was ever to descend upon us."[10] The Show had taken up a whole year of his energies, and he protested the injustice of excluding such lions of the American past as, for instance, William Merritt Chase, in favor of French upstarts. "Here was young America innocently advocating a French propaganda." He blamed Davies more than anyone else and saw his fault as a failure in democratic and patriotic vitality.

Davies, he said, had fallen victim to a pessimistic philosophy, which was un-American. ". . . recognized and applauded by a wealthy world at his feet, but with no love for his fellow Americans, he let the foreign lure rape him."[11] The last phrase also hints at a theme that runs under many of these complaints—a failure in virility: Davies was in life the favorite of wealthy women, and in art the painter of epicene dreams. Such rhetoric of course worked to the advantage of the New York realists, who seemed so masculine. Guy Pène du Bois said, "When Robert Henri, and Life, strode into Chase's school, in 1899, it [Life] strode into America—but only on a visit."[12] Life soon lost out again, to the forces embodied in the French paintings, the emasculating virus they carried. "Man, in other words, has ceased to take pride in man."[13] That is why modern art could not be part of the official American renaissance and why Theodore Roosevelt confidently recommended the American paintings over the French; but of course it was the latter which were to prove the stronger in the conflict.

Some of the official comment on the Show was very disapproving and very close to official comments on the IWW. *The New York Times* said, "It should be borne in mind that this movement is surely a part of the general movement, discernible to all of the world, to disrupt, degrade, if not destroy, not only art but literature and society too

. . . the Cubists and the Futurists are cousins to anarchists in politics . . . and all would-be destroyers who with the pretense of trying to regenerate the world are really trying to block progress in every direction."[14] Speaking for art criticism, Kenyon Cox said the real meaning of the cubist movement was the total destruction of the art of painting.[15]

However, more of the press comments were quite genially philistine and consisted of jokes about the paintings' unintelligibility and the (probably fraudulent) obscurity of all modern art—often with a reference to Gertrude Stein's writings. Thus a poem in the *Chicago Tribune* on February 8, 1913, ran:

> *I called the canvas Cow with Cud,*
> *And hung it on the line,*
> *Although to me 'twas vague as mud,*
> *'Twas clear to Gertrude Stein.*

And at the Show's dinner for the press, Walt Kuhn read out a burlesque on Stein. As we have seen, it was easy for many Americans to suspect her (and Duchamp) of cheating the public, and yet to like and admire them for it; that was part of the American attitude to art, and it made the path of modernism in America smoother than it would otherwise have been.

The processes of writing history induce us to treat these negative comments on the new art as mere signs of failure on the writers' part—moral, intellectual, or aesthetic failure to meet the painters' challenge. That has certainly been the case with most histories of the Armory Show, which have treated the new art as simply art—Duchamp as simply the twentieth-century Leonardo—and lay all the onus on the audience to approach the new paintings as closely and lovingly as the old familiar ones. If, however, we assume that the new work *was* different—which the artists certainly said it was—and could not be approached in the same way, then we will pay more sympathetic attention to those who denounced it. Those who welcomed and protected it are really less interesting, from our point of view, than the hostile critics who recognized the dangerousness which the artists had tried to build into their work.

One of the hottest critics, as we shall see, was Kenyon Cox. He saw in the new paintings the result of a lack of discipline and an exaltation of the individual, which had begun with Whistler and Manet. He saw even Cézanne as suffering from being cut off from tradition. It is easy for us now to see how Cox overlooked the group character of modernism, the extent to which all these painters watched each other's work and shared a common, if inarticulate, purpose. But he was not wrong to see that purpose, individual or group, as marked by a stronger will to rebel against bourgeois taste (against the social contract) than the purposes of earlier artists. The modernists wanted to break the habits of sensibility that chained art to its social function of pleasing, diverting, consoling the ruling class, and that wish drove them to a new and deeper alienation. That was a very significant change, and if we have learned to overlook it we are blinder than Cox, not more insightful.

As far as individual artists went, the savagest attacks were made on Matisse, for paintings which were found to be ugly, childish, absurd, and indecent—decadent distortions of color and drawing.[16] Cubism caused much less offense, no doubt because of its analytical and classical character, i.e., the subdued colors and intricate patterns. Of those considered cubists, Picabia was more attacked than Picasso. (He was in New York and present at the Show and gave interviews to the press, in which he said provocative things.) Duchamp and Brancusi were also much laughed at. The description of *Nude Descending a Staircase* as an explosion in a shingle factory was much repeated, and was attributed to both Julian Street and Joel Spingarn. For many years Duchamp was known widely and only as the painter of that picture.

The great commercial and critical success of the Show was Odilon Redon, which vindicated the risk Davies and Kuhn had taken in bringing so many of his pictures to America. (He sold thirteen paintings and pastels, plus twenty prints.) Van Gogh, Gauguin, and especially Cézanne also won recognition as important artists; they became, almost overnight, comprehensible enough for connoisseurs to be comfortable with the high reputations they came with. Among the Americans, Chanler and Sousa-Cardoza also won praise, but these of course were decisions which later art history did not endorse in the same way. And being successful in this sense of winning something like a consensus of approval was not, in the world of modern art, any more important than being notorious; the world of modern art, in that way, was like the world of entertainment, so that despite being attacked, Stein, Duchamp, and Brancusi were just as true beneficiaries of the Show as those who were praised.

Pach on the other hand, like Davies, tried to explain this new art, and to move from controversy to consensus. He wanted to make it respectable, relegating to unimportance those traits of Picasso and Duchamp (among others) which were in one way or another deconstructive. He defended the Show in an article entitled "The Cubist Room" in *For and Against* in 1913, by comparing movements of taste in the arts of political movements like the abolitionists. Despite our being heirs of the latter movement, he pointed out, we still respect George Washington, even though he was a slaveowner. And so, when we accept modern art, we are still able to love Leonardo. Thus art lovers should realize that they were not being asked to renounce all the past achievements of art in order to appreciate the new painters. He also explained cubism as an attempt to bring the graphic arts to the level of purity which man had already achieved in the more abstract arts of music and architecture.[17] Painters, Pach said, now need an art of expression instead of an art of imitation.

This sort of argument was common in the age of modernism, though there was a good deal of confusion or disagreement about which arts were more abstract or pure than others. Gertrude Stein, as we know, argued that she was using words as abstractly as the cubists used paint, so that painting was purer than literature. The nearest thing to consensus was the idea that music was the most abstract and pure.

Prominent among the attackers was the muralist and art critic, Kenyon Cox. His teacher in France had been the academic realist Gérôme, who as recently as 1893 had tried to prevent France from accepting a set of sixty-five impressionist paintings for official display, on moral grounds. "For the Government to accept such filth, there would have to be great moral slackening."[18] Gérôme and Cabanel had disapproved of Corot and Millet. But Cox, though labeled a pink and white idiot by George Luks, and much despised among advanced artists in 1913, had been advanced himself in the 1880s, as we saw.

The Armory of the 69th New York Regiment, the "Fighting Irish," located on Lexington Avenue between 25th and 26th streets. *Walt Kuhn Papers, Archives of American Art, Smithsonian Institution.*

(Far left): Walt Kuhn and Arthur B. Davies divided the interior of the Armory into 18 octagonal rooms which they draped with burlap and evergreen sprays, while they suspended bold, yellow cloth streamers from the ceiling. *Walt Kuhn Papers, Archives of American Art, Smithsonian Institution.*

(Left): Marcel Duchamp (1887–1968). *Nude Descending a Staircase, No. 2*, 1912. Oil on canvas, 58 × 35 inches. *Philadelphia Museum of Art; Louise and Walter Arensberg Collection.*

Paul Gauguin (1848–1903). Postcard reproduction of *Faa-Iheihe*, 1898. Original, oil on canvas, 21¼ × 66¾ inches; Tate Gallery, London. *Walt Kuhn Papers, Archives of American Art, Smithsonian Institution.*

Madison Square Garden by McKim, Mead, and White. The Garden was erected in 1887; it contained the only amphitheater in the city, and its tower—the second tallest in the city—was decorated with Spanish Renaissance motifs and fleurs-de-lys, popular in the Renaissance as emblems of the joy of life.
BBC Hulton Picture Library.

(Above left): **Program cover for the Paterson Strike Pageant.** *Tamiment Library, New York University, New York City.*

(Above): **Elizabeth Gurley Flynn at a Paterson rally in 1913. At the age of 15, in January 1906, Flynn addressed the local Socialist Club on "What Socialism Can Do for Women" and attacked marriage, quoting from Paine and Gorky, from Marat and Mirabeau. Theodore Dreiser, then editor of** *Broadway Magazine,* **christened her the "East Side Joan of Arc."** *Tamiment Library, New York University, New York City.*

(Left): **Carlo Tresca. Max Eastman described him as "the most pugnaciously hell-raising male rebel I could find in the United States." During his career as labor activist, Tresca was arrested 37 times for blasphemy, sedition, criminal obscenity, conspiracy, and murder; and was shot at, bombed, kidnapped by fascists and had his throat cut. At Paterson alone, he was arrested seven times, tried three times, and held on $30,000 bail.** *UPI/Bettmann Newsphotos.*

Reality versus dramatization: *(above)* Frank Tannenbaum addresses a crowd of unemployed strikers in Union Square, New York City, 1913. *UPI/Bettmann Newsphotos.* While *(below)*, striking workers enact "Picketing the Mills," a scene from the Paterson Strike Pageant. *Tamiment Library, New York University, New York City.*

(Left): **Mabel Dodge during her stay in Florence, Villa Curonia. In 1912, Dodge returned to America to establish her salon at 23 Fifth Avenue:** "When I came to New York to live last winter, it seemed to me that there were a great many interesting men and women, all thinking and doing different things, but there didn't seem to be any *centralization*, any place where all *sorts* of people could meet under one roof and talk freely on all subjects." *BBC Hulton Picture Library.*

(Bottom left): **John Reed in 1920, the year of his death. The poet Harry Kemp described Reed upon his arrival in New York in 1911 thus:** "The huge, genial broad-faced youth presented the hulking appearance of a full-grown bear, yet still somehow, in spite of its growth, a powerful cub that life had not yet licked into shape." *UPI/Bettmann Newsphotos.*

(Bottom right): **William "Big Bill" Haywood during the Paterson Strike, 1913.** *McClure's Magazine* offered this portrait of Haywood: "Take a character like this, hard, tough, warped, immensely resistant, and give him a final touch of idealism, a Jesuitic zeal that carries the man beyond himself, and you have a leader who, like Haywood, will bend his people to his beliefs." *Culver Pictures, Inc.*

(*Above*): During the miners' strikes of 1901–1903, Bill Haywood organized smelters and mill workers around Denver to demand an eight-hour working day. He revealed his talent for propaganda with the poster, "Is Colorado in America?," which led to his arrest for desecrating the American flag.

Two icons to the radicals of 1913: *(above right)* Isadora Duncan in "Aulis," and *(below)* Pancho Villa galloping across Mexico. Duncan represented a cultural goddess to the readers of *The Masses*: "Isadora, the embodiment of undisciplined rich upswelling life and the wonder of life. The vestal who has served Dionysos." Villa succeeded Haywood as John Reed's archetypal hero of masculine radicalism and was exalted in Reed's *Insurgent Mexico. BBC Hulton Picture Library.*

But now, writing under the title, "The 'Modern' Spirit in Art" in *Harper's Weekly*, March 15, 1913 (he also wrote for *Century* magazine and for *Scribner's*), he protested that he had made every effort to like the Show: he had reminded himself how mistakenly Gérôme and Cabanel had condemned impressionism, and he had recalled that conservatism was common to men of middle age: he had determined not to be afraid of the new. But "This thing is not amusing; it is heart-rending and sickening."[19] If these painters represent our time, it means that we are going mad. He passes over the American artists, except for Marsden Hartley, in order to concentrate his fire on the cubists. They are destroying the art of painting, and what they are putting in its place is revolting and defiling. A lack of discipline and exaltation of the individual have been destructive forces since the 1860s, beginning with Whistler and Manet. Now we see the result: Gauguin is a decorator tainted with insanity; Rodin and Matisse are worse; in the former's later work we see inordinate self-esteem and immoderate self-exploitation, while from the latter's canvases stares out leering effrontery.[20] He, Cox, still believes there are laws in art, as there are commandments in morals.

Most art critics were unfriendly; for instance, Frank Jewett Mather in *The Nation*, who called Matisse's art essentially epileptic. And besides these psychiatric and medical diagnoses, there were also political ones. The day after the Show closed, the *Times* came out with its charge of anarchism, and *Art and Progress* agreed. Elliott Daingerfield called modernism "the chatter of anarchistic monkeys," and Cox and Mather both used the word *anarchism*. *The Independent* for April 1913 compared the new art to syndicalism, and Royal Cortissoz (his admiration went to Sargent and Boldini) spoke of Ellis Island art, to associate the new painting with both immigrants and bomb-throwing terrorists (such as the IWW).[21] This conservative language was not confined to the right, however. Some people on the left also read the signs of decadence in cubism and futurism. For instance, Louis Fraina, to be one of the founders of the Communist Party of the USA, wrote "The Social Significance of Futurism" for *The New Review* in December 1913.[22] He saw both new schools of art as expressing a destructive cultural urge conditioned by the times. "They represent capitalism dominant [cubism] and capitalism ascending [futurism] . . . Their aggressive and brutal power are identical with those of our machine civilization, like the sky-scraper: no socialist could support them, because they try to mechanize man."[23] This argument was a natural ally of that change of opinion which was identifying life values (and therefore cultural values) with nature and against the city. It is significant that it was associated with socialism. It had considerable success with critics for the next two generations, but among artists themselves there was more readiness to exploit the aggressive and brutal powers of the city and the machine.

Among the Show's allies and advertisers, Stieglitz wrote in the New York *American* for January 26 before the Show opened, "The dry bones of a dead art are rattling as they never rattled before . . . This glorious affair is coming off during the month of February . . . They're breathing the breath of life into an art that is long since dead."[24] Joel Spingarn, professor of philosophy at Columbia, wrote in the *Evening Post* on February 25, "The opening night of the International Exhibition seemed to me one of the most exciting adventures I have ever experienced . . . though it needs repeating in every generation, madness and courage are the very life of all art."[25] The Show's champions naturally wanted to claim both to be mad and inspired and to be soberly traditional and classical.

Hapgood wrote about it for the *Globe* with such enthusiasm that his editor put his review on the front page. He treated the exhibition, he said later, "as I would a great fire, an earthquake, or a political revolution; as a series of shattering events—shattering for the purpose of re-creation. The excitement of physical happenings was in the article, no esthetic criticism . . . I wrote that the thing that stood out boldly was the vitality of the exhibition as a whole . . . Life was there rather than art."[26] This was life values in the most literal sense; an artist had told him that the Show had made him want to live for another fifty years.

Like so many others, Hapgood pointed to Gertrude Stein as the American and literary apologist and equivalent for the cubist painters. "There is an American woman now living in Paris, who is, I think, the only American living who is trying to do in writing what Picasso and Matisse are trying to do in plastic art." (After the Paterson

Pageant, he wrote about Mabel Dodge in similar tones and terms: "There is a woman in New York who is a promoter of the spirit.")[27]

Hapgood also drew a comparison between this artistic radicalism and the kind he had seen in contemporary labor. Looking back, in his autobiography, he saw that, "Much of the expression of those explosive days was the same, whether in art, literature, labor expansion, or sexual experience, a moving and shaking time."[28]

The organizers of the Show talked about it in the same rhetoric of the American renaissance. The preface to the catalog, by Gregg, suggested that American artists would now find out how far they had fallen behind, and would meet the "forms that have manifested themselves on the other side of the Atlantic. Art is a sign of life . . . This exhibition is an indication that the A.A.P.S. is against cowardice even when it takes the form of amiable self-satisfaction . . ." and so on. Thus the Show, and modern art as a whole, were recruited as parts of the moral renaissance of America.

Perhaps the most significant judgment on the Show—because the most normative—came from someone who was not an art critic but who was a leader of the American renaissance, Theodore Roosevelt. As Henry May says, "The greatest spokesman of practical idealism in America in 1912, overwhelmingly the most interesting figure to people and press, was . . . Theodore Roosevelt . . . his freely expressed views on art and science and religion were still authoritative for many, and they were invariably moral."[29]

He came to inspect the Show on March 4, the day after his old rival, Taft, had had to leave the White House, and he was in a happy mood. Shown around by Davies, he had plenty to say. When Davies justified modern painters by saying that traditional ones also built up their figures from geometrical constructions, he replied, "I daresay the Venus had a skeleton inside her, and that is the place to keep it."[30]

His essay appeared in *Outlook* on March 22, entitled "A Layman's View of an Art Exhibition." His tone was, however, less that of the layman than that of the president, the leader of the nation. He described the Show as noteworthy and a work of real value because it showed "our people" the art forces which of late have been at work in Europe. However, he could not share the AAPS's view of the extremists on exhibit.

Of course, he agreed, there can be no life without change (Roosevelt was an adept at this rhetoric, which he had long ago made his own) but change can be a sign of death and retrogression also. Probably we should not take most of these pictures seriously, probably we should treat them like the mermaids at a P. T. Barnum show. (We should appreciate the cheek with which we have been fooled, and pay the price of admission ungrudgingly.) If we are to take them seriously, the extremists, the lunatic fringe, deserve no praise— except insofar as they help to break old fetters of habit and conformity. Cubist pictures are for those who like the colored pictures in the Sunday papers, and his Navajo rug is a better work of art than Duchamp's *Nude Descending a Staircase*. Much of it reminded one of cave paintings (this hinted at cultural regression, and therefore at decadence). However, he concluded, there is nothing commonplace in the exhibition. "There was not a touch of simpering, self-satisfied conventionality anywhere in the exhibition."[31] This both reassured the readers about their leader's kindliness and showed them how to use the American renaissance rhetoric of adventure, manliness, and morality against modern art.

Those readers, the followers of Roosevelt, included artists as well as philistines. When du Bois expounded Henri's idea of art, which depended on manliness, he said, "The man the artist was to begin by being had a remarkably close resemblance to an American, or to the American ideal of an American," and he invoked Roosevelt as an example.[32] Henri of course therefore saw the danger of the Armory Show. He saw that the "great men" of the exhibition were "preoccupied by artifice," but they were considered greater than the American painters, because of "the colonial spirit of dependence."[33] More moderately but similarly, Sloan said in 1946, "I am all for the study of cubism . . . But the danger in too much abstract work today is that so much of it is *heartless* . . . It is going from the abstract, to the abstruse, to the absurd."[34]

The resistance of such artists always expressed itself in terms of Americanism or masculinism, often with politically conservative allusions. Myers said, "Davies had unlocked the door to foreign art and thrown the key away. Our land of opportunity was thrown wide open to foreign art, unrestricted and triumphant; more than ever before, our great country had become a colony; more than ever before, we had become provincials . . . The great French moderns revealed themselves in all their pristine glory; and while the American artists were finally shown, in this whirling medley of art on parade, they had to take it on the chin."[35]

Du Bois said that since the Show, Americans have not known what art is or should be. They have lost touch with the basic truth. "An artist must be a man first. He must stand on his own feet, see with his own eyes, the brave eyes of bold manhood, and report his findings in the straightforward unfinicky manner of the male."[36]

What were the results and consequences of the Armory Show? First of all, its continuations in other cities, the International Exhibitions of Modern Art in Chicago and Boston. Six hundred thirty-four of the items shown at the Armory were exhibited again at the Art Institute in Chicago between March 24 and April 16, and were seen by about two hundred thousand visitors. The response included more hostility and ridicule than in New York; a senator was sent by the Vice Commission to study in particular Duchamp's *Nude* and a painting called *Prostitution* to see if they were obscene, and there were many jokes about a Matisse figure that had only four toes on one foot. There were even attempts to burn Matisse (and Brancusi and Walter Pach) in effigy, attempts allegedly inspired by faculty at the Institute. Then April 28 to May 19, 244 items, all of them European, were shown at Copley Hall, Boston. Only 12,600 paid to enter there, and the event was not a success, either financially or in terms of the interest stirred up.

Then mock Armory shows were popular for several months, satisfying the American appetite for mockery and for ideas of fraud and hoax. There was, for instance, an Academy of Misapplied Arts, sponsored by the Lighthouse for the blind, which attracted five thousand visitors over two weeks, got a good press, and ended with a successful auction of the paintings exhibited.[37] There were also serious cubist exhibitions, which followed immediately after the Armory Show, though on a much smaller scale. In May 1913 ten cubist paintings were put on view in Gimbel's store in Milwaukee, having been bought in Paris by the Gimbel Brothers; shown again later that year in Cleveland, Pittsburgh, New York, Philadelphia, and in April 1914, again in Milwaukee. These were paintings by Gleizes, Metzinger, Villon, Léger, etc., and were received quite without controversy. Then in Pittsburgh in December 1913 there was an American cubists and postimpressionists show of forty pictures chosen by Davies.[38] Much later there were revivals of the Show at the Cincinnati Art Museum in 1944; at Amherst College in 1958; and at the Munson, Williams, Proctor Institute in 1963.

As for the financial results of the Show, 174 of the items exhibited were sold (123 of these came from abroad) plus 90 prints that had not been on display.[39] The sales produced $44,148, of which $30,491 was paid for imported works. Davies and Stieglitz led the buying on February 20. Davies bought a Duchamp-Villon terra-cotta, a Villon *Arbres en Fleur*, and a Manolo statue—all for $648; Stieglitz paid $500 for the Kandinsky *Improvisation*. On the twenty-second the collectors Bliss and Quinn bought, guided by the advice of Davies and Kuhn. Duchamp's *Nude* was bought unseen for $324 by a San Francisco dealer, Fred C. Torrey (or, according to another account, $348), and the Metropolitan Museum bought Cézanne's *Colline des Pauvres* for $6,700 (the first purchase of a Cézanne by an American museum). Thus the new art began to penetrate inside homes and galleries.

The important collectors affected by the Show included John Quinn, Walter Arensberg, Arthur J. Eddy, Lillie P. Bliss, Katherine Dreier, and Albert Barnes, and their collections ultimately formed the basis of the artworks of the great museums of today. Bliss's career as a collector began at the Show, where she bought, among other things, two Redons. (Her twenty-six Cézannes became the nucleus of the Museum of Modern Art.) Quinn spent $5,800 on Redon, Derain, Duchamp-Villon, Villon, and others. The next biggest buyer was Eddy, whose collection became the nucleus of the Chicago Art Institute, so far as modern art went. He bought two Duchamps, a Villon, a Picabia, and others. New galleries also came into existence because of the Show: in December 1913, the Daniel Gallery, to be a home for avant-garde art for the next fifteen years; in February 1914, the Bourgeois Gallery, for which Pach arranged shows; in March, the

Carroll Gallery, of which Quinn acted as the angel. Thus the new taste was institutionalized—and older forms of taste lost their basis and support.

As for the Show's effect on individual painters, one can make another list: before 1913 Joseph Stella, Arthur C. Dove, Kuhn, and Epstein—and among younger painters, Dasburg and Davis—had all been realists, in one sense or another, and after the Show they were modernists. Stella is an especially interesting case. He arrived in this country in 1896, an educated man, and so did not have the typical immigrant experiences. He executed several commissions for *Survey* magazine on themes relating to immigration and labor; also in 1905 he did drawings of Ellis Island immigrants for *Outlook* and illustrations for the realist and radical writer Ernest Poole. In August 1913, the *International Socialist Review*, for which Bill Haywood wrote, put on its cover a drawing of his which had been in *Survey* four years before, but gave it a quite new significance: in *Survey*, captioned *In the Church of the Double Cross*, it showed a young immigrant singing a hymn; on the *Review* cover, with the magazine's subtitle "The Fighting . . . Working Class," he seemed to be shouting defiance. But by then Stella was no longer a realist artist. His *Battle of Lights, Coney Island* of 1913 is often called *the* American futurist painting, and during the war he prepared such similar works as *Brooklyn Bridge* and in the 1920s, *New York Interpreted*. He had found in modern painting a cultural imperative that satisfied him better than his social sympathies.

Sloan, Glackens, Shinn, and Luks—all the New York realists— were affected. Sloan's case can be taken as exemplary. In *Gist of Art* he talks about the effect Picasso had on him. "When I saw his work in the Armory Show, along with that of Cézanne and the other great ultra-moderns, it opened my eyes to a fresh way of seeing the art of all time. I lost some of the 'blinders' of prejudice about subject-matters which had made me pass by a lot of important things with conspicuous religious subject matter. Henri had stressed the painting of contemporary life, perhaps so much that some of us didn't realize how many Renaissance and Romanesque paintings or sculptures were really based on the contemporary scene of those times."[40] He mentions Giotto and Carpaccio in particular, but of course it was moderns like

Renoir who had more immediate effect on him. "I learned from the Armory Show to have a more conscious interest in the problems of plastic realization . . . I have tried to assimilate ideas from study of the ultra-modern movement, while continuing to teach the importance of humanism."[41] That was of course the challenge—how to continue to serve humanist values while exploring the new imperatives of modernism.

For Sloan, "The Armory Show was a great awakening and perhaps an irritating factor."[42] He turned from painting life to painting art. Contemporaneously, though perhaps coincidentally, he seems to have lost faith in direct political action. He declared that, for instance, *The Masses* should be a magazine of social satire rather than party propaganda. He kept, of course, his devotion to Gene Debs—"one of the most Christ-like men I had ever met . . . He would share his clothes or his last crust of bread with any man who was poorer than himself."[43] And Debs returned the feeling; in his cell at Fort Leavenworth he kept a Sloan drawing. But Debs's day was done, as was the IWW's a few years after the Armory Show; and Sloan turned toward "plastic values"—though Milton Brown feels that later phase of his work was never as satisfactory.

As for the institutional effects of the exhibition, nine of the twenty-five members of the AAPS resigned in 1914 over the treasurer's report on the Show; given in April, the report showed very small profits. The leaders of the revolt were Henri and Sloan, Luks, Bellows, and Myers. Most of them resigned on May 18, Myers a little later. Du Bois wrote to the *Tribune*, saying that the accounts had been cooked, but when they were finally fully rendered in August 1916, they seemed to be straight enough. There had been very complicated dealings with Customs over the works imported for the Show and then exported again afterward. And then twelve thousand catalogs and sixty thousand postcards, and other such things, had to be disposed of. But the Society had its last meeting in February 1916, and its only achievement had been the Show.

However, a new orthodoxy had been established, as Pach says, one hostile to Sargent and Daniel Chester French at home; and to Gérôme and Bouguereau in France. The new heroes were Cézanne and van Gogh, and the future belonged to Picasso and Duchamp.

Pach compares the latter with Rimbaud. It was Duchamp's ambition to "cross the line that marks the separation between painting done from nature and painting whose forms are neither imitated nor remembered nor yet adapted; for once a man was going to create in his own image, which is to say, that of the mind. Heretofore such a privilege had been that of the gods alone."[44] Such language was not Duchamp's own; indeed such inflated rhetoric about the value of art was something he ruthlessly punctured, and yet that spiritual ambition was his. He just expressed it more negatively, not by exalting art so much as by diminishing everything else.

In *The Modern Spirit* Brown says that Fauvism and futurism had little appeal in America, and cubism was very influential because of its rationalism.[45] The rationalism and the spiritual ambition together constituted the character of cubism and made it reassuring to culture critics, however enigmatic the actual paintings were. Thus cubism became the dominant modernist school, outside America as well as inside. In other ways, as we know, cubism was rather retrogressive, and futurism and dada were more adventurous. But elements of those movements were in the Show in the work of Duchamp and Picabia, and in some sense under the general heading of modern art.

T H E
Pageant

7

Even during the Revolution Hamilton had been impressed by the site of the Great Falls of the Passaic. His fertile imagination envisaged a great manufacturing center, a great Federal City, to supply the needs of the country.
    —WILLIAM CARLOS WILLIAMS, *Paterson*

Hamilton organized a company to hold the land thereabouts, with dams and sluices, the origin today of the vilest sluicehole in Christendom, the Passaic River; impossible to remove the nuisance, so tight had he, Hamilton, sewed up his privileges unto kingdomcome. . . .
                —WILLIAM CARLOS WILLIAMS,
                        In the American Grain

Onward Christian Soldiers

Onward Christian Soldiers
March into the War
Slay your Christian Brothers
As you've done before.
Plutocratic masters
Bid you face the foe
Men who never harmed you
Men you'll never know.
                        —ANONYMOUS

*T*he Paterson Strike Pageant took place in the "dingy arena" of the Madison Square Garden on June 7, 1913.[1] About 1,500 strikers had assembled at Turn Hall, Paterson, at 8:00 A.M. that morning, and at 9:00 were rehearsed by Reed, who afterward led them through the town to the music of a lively band to the railway station. There at 10:45, 1,147 of the strikers boarded a special train of thirteen coaches which took them from Paterson to Hoboken, while another 800 marched behind Carlo Tresca to Union Square to rejoin the trainload and other silk industry strikers from New York City and elsewhere. (Money for the Pageant had been raised among the workers of New York City, largely by the efforts of John C. Steiger, himself a silk worker.)[2] They marched up Christopher Street and Fifth Avenue with a band, singing the "Marseillaise" and the "Internationale," and led by an eighteen-year-old worker called Hannah Silverman.

The first the strikers had heard about a pageant had been from Bill Haywood on May 16. Three days later he presented Reed to them as the man who would direct it, and Reed asked them to suggest the strike scenes they should represent.[3] This was less than three weeks before the event. Rehearsals began at Turn Hall, in Paterson, the Monday before the Pageant. They practiced their songs, with Reed back in his Harvard role as cheerleader, at the Haledon meeting on Sunday, May 25.

There were naturally many changes of plan along the way. As first announced, two hundred workers were to take part, and they would walk the twenty-three miles from Paterson to Madison Square Garden.[4] As late as May 31, *Survey* announced that the third episode would be "Forty Pickets before an Irresponsible Judge"—which was not put on—and, because the police forbade the firing of a gun on stage, the actual shooting of Modestino could not be represented. (Vincenzo Modesto, or Modestino, had been killed, accidentally, by a police bullet in the course of clashes between them and the strikers.) In a copy of the scenario in Reed's papers, two episodes are described that were never enacted. One was the trial of the pickets, and the other was the failed appeal to the flag of the AFL envoys, John Golden and Sarah Conboy.

The committee organizing the Pageant more than once debated dropping the whole idea as too unwieldy—first during the first week of rehearsals, and again during the second week, only ten days before the announced date. They also had financial anxieties. The original scheme had been to present the Pageant for two or three successive nights, but they found the cost of renting the Garden prohibitive. Reed said the rent was $1,000 a night, while building the stage cost $600, and the scenery $750.

It was apparently the enthusiasm of strikers' representatives at the committee's meeting which made them go ahead; these representatives of the 10,000 striking silk workers of New York City volunteered to raise more money to meet the production costs. (The scenery included, besides the two-hundred-foot backdrop of a mill, painted by John Sloan, wings consisting of smaller representations of a dozen mills.) The project seems to have grown in size continually: later three hundred strikers were to have performed, and on June 2 the Central Strike Committee announced that five hundred had now been assigned parts, and appealed for more volunteers; and finally about twelve hundred did take part. (According to one report from an unsympathetic source only six hundred appeared on stage, and the others never left the basement of the Garden.)

A letter by Edward Eyre Hunt, a friend of Reed, dated June 12, says that a week before (presumably a week before the Pageant) the executive committee had voted unanimously to give up the project because costs were mounting, newspapers were boycotting them, and the IWW itself seemed lukewarm; but then the striking silk workers of New York City vowed to raise as much as five thousand dollars more and to put the Pageant on themselves, if the "highbrows" couldn't.[5]

The letter also describes committee meetings at a dowdy uptown apartment with a coughing child. Haywood sat with his arm around a slatternly, hard-faced girl—he always embraced the women of his clan as he talked to them. At a center table sat the delicate blond F. Sumner Boyd, acting as chairman. The stately Mabel Dodge apparently spoke through an intermediary. Margaret Sanger's husband had long black hair, as disordered as his wits. And sweet, old-fashioned Jessie Ashley was deaf and reedy-voiced. (Also present were Hapgood, Giovannitti, Ernest Poole, and other left-wing intellectuals.) In this scene, presumably close to reality, Mabel Dodge volunteers one thousand dollars which is needed.

Rehearsals had been held in the union hall in Paterson with John Reed in charge, directing things with a megaphone. He asked the strikers how the events they were reliving had felt and took suggestions from them about how they dragged their feet approaching the mill in the mornings, but it seems that his main assistants were Greenwich Village friends like Hutchins Hapgood, Jessie Ashley, Alexander Berkman, Bobby Jones, John Sloan, and above all Mabel Dodge. Altogether, Golin reports, some eighty or ninety Villagers worked on the Pageant, including, as well as those already mentioned, Inez Haynes Gillmore, William English Walling, Rose Pastor Stokes, and people with theatrical experience, like Ernest Poole, Eddy Hunt, and Thompson Buchanan. The committee—just who its members were varies in different accounts—met often in the Sangers' uptown apartment.

The march along Fifth Avenue and to the Garden was a part of the Pageant. The history of the Garden emblematized that of New York, of America in its finance-capitalist phase. The site had belonged to a Vanderbilt, and it was Carnegie and Morgan who developed it and gave the contract to McKim, Mead, and White. Barnum had used the site between its being a railway station and being developed.

In 1913 it was a magnificent Renaissance building, in cream-colored brick and terra-cotta trim and with arcades copied from Italy on both the street level and the roof garden. On top of the tower stood a sculpture of Diana by Saint-Gaudens. As you entered there was a theater on your left and a restaurant on your right, above the restaurant a ballroom and concert hall, above that a cafe and roof garden. (It has been described as a "wildly eclectic pleasure palace on an un-precedented scale.")[6] The amphitheater itself was 188 feet by 304 feet, with a roof of exposed steel and glass, measuring 167 feet by 277 feet. It was used for political conventions, but also for every kind of sports event—the stage being designed to adapt to many purposes and functions, to become a boxing ring, a racetrack, a theater. This is what made it so suitable to the Pageant. But it must also have seemed to the twelve hundred marching toward and inside it that June 7 like an official building they were occupying, and halfway to the White House or Congress.

When the marchers arrived at the Garden, they were given one last rehearsal—it began at 2 P.M.—and then ate a meal supplied by New York sympathizers. Reed and Hunt conducted the rehearsal with megaphones, and there were journalists and photographers there. There was a good deal of Wobbly printed matter already piled up there, notably the program pamphlet edited by F. Sumner Boyd. (There was also a poem entitled "Bill Haywood," by Tom Flynn, Gurley's father, and a red-bound translation of Émile Pouget's *Sabotage*, translated by Giovannitti.) The cover of the program, also scarlet, was a drawing by Bobby Jones which became a famous Wobbly symbol: a muscular young worker climbing up, over, and out of a factory and toward the reader—one hand and one foot emerging from the frame.

Tom Flynn's poem had six stanzas, both connecting Haywood to his rough labor background, and defiantly claiming for him the civilized gifts of eloquence and poetry.

> *He wonders where you got it, Bill*
> *Your clear and ready speech,*
> *Was it down in the depths of the dripping mines,*
> *Where the straining timbers screech?*
> *Or was it the roar of the fire-hung blast,*
> *As it tore men's lives away,*
> *That taught you to think as a man should think,*
> *And say what a man should say.*

Haywood's eloquence is quite distinct from ordinary literary kinds.

We want men who are used to toil,
Not dreamers of idle dreams
Nor the politician's compromise
Nor the "intellectual's" schemes.
We want men who'll look death in the eye
When the hireling shoots to kill
And that's why we want such men as
    you,
Our lion-hearted Bill.

It seems that Tom Flynn felt the same sort of manly love for Bill Haywood as John Reed did. (Reed led the strikers in a song he had composed, "The Haywood Thrill.") Perhaps Gurley Flynn shared some of Mabel Dodge's reservations.

The actual program took up only three pages of thirty-one. The pamphlet presented the demands which the strikers were making— for an eight-hour working day, and other things—and began with a six-page essay on "The General Strike in the Silk Industry" by Boyd. He said, "The pageant represents a battle between the working class and the capitalist class, conducted by the IWW . . . It is a conflict between two social forces . . ." There were also short essays, often reprinted from *Solidarity* or similar sources, by Ewald Koettgen, Phillips Russell, Bill Haywood, and two by Gurley Flynn. Some were quite technical discussions of the new looms and their productivity; others were more political and inflammatory, on contract slavery or owner sabotage.

After the rehearsal, John Reed was, according to Hunt and Dodge, on the verge of collapse from tension and exhaustion. ("I knew he couldn't have done it without me. I felt that I was behind him, pouring all the power of the universe through myself to him.")[7] But he re-covered by 8:00, and they reassembled for the performance at 8:30 —it did not actually begin until 9:00—with the dread letters IWW spelled out in red lights on all four sides of the tower, visible to all Manhattan. According to Mabel Dodge, this device had been kept a secret, and the authorities could not find out how to turn the lights off until too late. Thus the union flaunted its presence in one of the famous new buildings of Manhattan. They had taken over, for one night, one of the palaces of the ruling class. Sheriff Julius Harburger, a prominent representative of law and order and always ready with a quotable phrase, denounced the performance to the press: he said it contained "sedition, treasonable utterances, un-American doctrines, advocating sabotage . . . inflammatory, hysterical, unsound doctrines"[8] and assured them that if one word of disrespect to the flag was spoken during the Pageant, he would stop the show so quickly it would take their breath away.[9]

There was a line for tickets which at one point stretched for twenty-eight blocks. Box seats cost from twenty to thirty dollars, but a large part of the audience entered for twenty-five cents, or free, by showing their "little red cards" at the door. There was a total audience of over fifteen thousand, a thousand of whom had to stand. Eight hundred strikers had walked from Paterson to attend.[10] Hunt says the air was electric, and the galleries were crowded by 8:00. There were big red banners everywhere.

What they saw when they got inside was a huge stage at the Fourth Avenue end of the hall, and across it hung the two-hundred-foot drop picturing the dismal front of a Paterson silk mill, with lights blazing through the "windows" and an entrance thirty men could go through abreast. The auditorium was decorated with IWW banners, featuring the color red, and the program sellers wore red bows in their hair if they were girls, red bow ties if they were men; there were red carnations, and the children present wore the same color. One banner did not originate with the IWW, at least not with the leadership. No God, No Master hung from the top gallery on the Twenty-seventh Street side, but as soon as it was pointed out to Patrick Quinlan, one of the organizers, he climbed up and tore it down. That was an anarchist slogan which had caused the IWW a lot of trouble in Lawrence because it provoked the clergy especially against them. It was understood that this banner was another attempt to discredit them.

Right through the seating, from the stage out to the entrance to the Garden, stretched a roadway. Mabel Dodge says that Jones had insisted on making the Pageant into a Gordon Craig affair, which meant inducing audience participation by marching the performers along this roadway and through the middle of the audience. And in fact the audience on June 7 did join in the strikers' singing, and their cheering of the Wobbly speakers, and their booing of the police.

In the scenario in the John Reed papers, this roadway is not referred to. Strikers enter and exit to right or left of the stage. But across the scenario is scrawled (among other things) the word *Craig*; so it may be that at a discussion of the scenario Craig's authority was invoked for making this change—which was a major one, in terms of the Pageant's effectiveness, to judge by the comments of those who were there.

The Pageant's theme was officially said to have been taken from a remark by one of the women strikers: "We were frightened when we went in, but we were singing when we came out," which refers most clearly to the first scene or episode.[11] There were six of them. In the first, a throng of workers, with their coat collars turned up to suggest a winter morning, assembled outside the factory and gloomily went inside to work. Some carried lunch pails, same dragged umbrellas apparently. The sound of the looms was heard. The program legend read, "The mills alive—the workers dead." And then from inside came the sound of shouting, the cry to stop work and strike, and out onto the stage burst the workers, now intoxicated with sudden freedom. "The workers begin to think," according to the program. The account in *The Independent* runs, "Down from the stage and the entire length of the main aisle the workers march, cheered all the way by the sympathetic audience of 15,000, working men and their families."

The second episode was entitled, "The mills dead—the workers alive" and showed a line of quiet, determined pickets patroling the entrance to the deserted mill. But when they halted the few scabs who appeared, the police rushed up and a scuffle began, and a general clubbing ended in arrests. Gurley had warned the organizers never to depict the workers being violent, and by at least one account there was some slapstick in this episode because of the bamboo nightsticks wielded by the police. Then the police marched their captives down the long aisle again, while the audience hissed and booed.

The third episode began with funeral music (the "Dead March" in *Saul*) and a procession carrying the coffin of Vincenzo Modestino.

Rebel funerals, and especially those of martyred workers, were important Wobbly rituals, and Haywood and Flynn personally had persuaded Mrs. Modesto to let them make a dramatic spectacle out of this one—first of all in Paterson, on April 19, attended by fifteen thousand mourners, and now again on stage. Mrs. Modesto, the widow, was not in the audience, but the dead man's mother and his three children sat in a box, all wearing black. At the head of the line advancing through the audience came a police officer, again greeted with hisses, and then the coffin, carried by strikers, and then the whole thousand and more. On the stage they gathered around the coffin, covering it with the carnations they each of them threw ("the crimson symbols of the workers' blood") and then listening to speeches by Haywood and Tresca, speeches which they had actually made at the actual funeral. Haywood vowed by the blood of the slain man to protect the widow and children, and Tresca, speaking in Italian, promised blood for blood, *sangue per sangue*.

The fourth episode was heralded by cries of "Musica!, Musica!" and centered upon the singing, in various languages,—English, German, Italian—of songs which had grown out of the Strike. Toto Ferrazano, one of the strike personalities, led the audience in, for instance, "Do You Lika Missa Flynn?" He had composed several of the strikers' songs. Of course they also sang the international anthems of revolution, the "Marseillaise" and the "Internationale." The IWW had made the latter its own, with the refrain,

> 'Tis the final conflict,
> Let each stand in his place,
> The Industrial Union
> Shall be the human race.

There were Italian and German choral groups.

At some point during the performance, Haywood addressed an appeal to the audience for funds to support the Strike. He described the IWW as a "militant, fighting organization," and said three hundred of the performers had spent time in the terrible Bastille of the Paterson jail. Allegedly some seven or eight thousand dollars were subscribed.

The next episode represented both May Day 1913 in Paterson and the day when the children were sent away from their homes to foster parents in New York. (Hutchins Hapgood and his wife took in some of those children.) It began with a May Day parade through the audience and up on to the stage. On the stage they listened to a speech by Gurley Flynn, who according to newspaper reports, entrusted the children, "many dressed in flaming red," to their foster mothers, so that they might have "the roses put in their cheeks, and class solidarity in their hearts." (Flynn had refused a stage career, in order to speak her own piece; here she had both at once.)

Last came a strike meeting with speeches by the strike leaders, set in the Turn Hall in Paterson. (There was no change of scenery to support these changes of imaginative location. The appeal was directly to the audience's imagination.) The strikers debated the issue and voted for an eight-hour working day, and said the program, "No court can declare the law thus made unconstitutional."

The performance over, the strikers set off for home, but the special train did not reach Paterson until 2:00 A.M. They had done what they set out to do that morning. They had cast a new truth and a strong demand in the teeth of Manhattan: a truth of class conflict and a demand for radical change, which contradicted the pleasant half-truths of the politicians, theaters, and newspapers of the establishment.

Judging by John Reed's article in the June *Masses*, and by his autobiographical writings, the main idea of the Pageant was his. The theatrical styling may have been Jones's, but that article by Reed, "War in Paterson," begins with a description of the mills and the picket lines strikingly like that presented in the first two episodes of the Pageant. And his vision of politics in general was theatrical. He describes Haywood surrounded by the Paterson strikers thus: "Surrounded by a dense crowd of short, dark-faced men, Bill Haywood towered in the center of the room. His big hand made simple gestures as he explained something to them. His massive, rugged face, seamed and scarred like a mountain, and as calm, radiated strength."[12] And in *The Adventures of a Young Man*, he explains that Haywood and Tresca attracted him because "I liked their understanding of the workers, their revolutionary thought, the boldness of their dream, the way immense crowds of people took fire and came alive under their leadership. . . . In the jail I talked with exultant men who had blithely denied the lawless brutality of the city government, and gone to prison laughing and singing."[13] This was the language of a national cheer-leader, of an audience leader, a master of ceremonies on the grandest scale. The Pageant was a direct theatrical equivalent of Reed's language.

But its theatrical style was far from being merely personal to Jones; it was recognized by a sizable segment of the audience as an important part of the event. *The Independent* saw the Pageant as returning to the origins of drama. The reporter pointed out that there was no plot, as there was not in the Elizabethan history plays; there was no curtain—just John Reed, standing in front of the crowd with his megaphone; and so the Garden was like a pre-Elizabethan inn-yard. Of course the most important thing was that, "It was not a pageant of the past; but of the present—a new thing in our drama," but still it was a pageant.

The same magazine commented, "It is an unequalled device for clutching the emotion of an audience—this parade of the actors through the center of the crowd." It cited the dramatic liturgy of the Roman Church, out of which English drama derived, the processional in the Episcopal, and even the familiar wedding march. In New York theaters it had been seen only rarely—last season in Max Reinhardt's "Sumurun," and in one or two other cases, but "never with more effect than in this performance, where actors and audience were of one class and one hope."

Such a response testifies to the reporter's educated understanding of the pageant genre. So did Hutchins Hapgood's review in the *Globe*. But he also stressed the value of the form's transparency, that it was the self-recorded life of the strikers. "The art of it was unconscious, and especially lay in the suggestion for the future. People interested in the possibilities of a vital and popular art, and in constructive pageantry, would learn much from it." Because it turned the lives of masses of men, a phalanx of life, into a spectacle. The preliminary training or rehearsal for the performance was the Strike itself—the strikers' gradual self-understanding acquired at union meetings constituted three and a half months of unconscious rehearsal. "Life passed over insensibly into a certain, simple form of art . . . That is the great thing about it, the almost unprecedented thing; it is that that is inspiring and hopeful . . ."[14]

We have already discussed the form in which Reed cast the experience of the Paterson Strike. But of course that experience itself was very different from the content of most pageants, and it was very transparently presented; Modestino's funeral, for instance, had been dramatized primarily on the burial grounds in Paterson when fifteen thousand people attended it; what was shown on June 7 was simply a repetition. And the spirit was different from that of MacKaye's pageants; in terms of spirit, the Paterson Pageant belonged, or aspired to belong, less to MacKaye's genre and more to the series of radical theatrical events that ran from the David pageants of the French Revolution to the anniversary representation of the storming of the Winter Palace in St. Petersburg after the 1917 Revolution.

The immediate responses to the event of June 7 can roughly be divided between those concerned with its artistic character, which were enthusiastic, and those concerned with its political effect, which were not. This division (not wholly consistent) can be detected in the newspaper reports, for instance. The theater reviews were favorable, the editorials were admonitory or minatory. *The Independent* was very appreciative of the pageant's artistic effect, but the previous month it had editorially warned its readers against sympathizing with the strikers. And *The New York Times* said, "Under the direction of a destructive organization opposed in spirit and antagonistic in action to all the forces which have upbuilded this republic, a series of pictures in action were shown with the design of stimulating mad passion against law and order and promulgating a gospel of discontent . . . IWW leaders have at heart no more sympathy with laborers than they have with Judges and Government officers . . . The motive was to inspire hatred, to induce violence."[15] They recognized the intention to make a revolution.

Perhaps the most interesting response was that of the *St Louis Mirror*, which was taken up and developed by *Current Opinion*. They said that the key to the "puzzling rise" of the IWW was America's hostility to emotion. (As the argument proceeds, it becomes clear that we can translate *emotion* as *imagination*.) The union is succeeding, we are told, because it "calls to battle those who are rusting for lack of conflict. It appeals irresistibly to the love of adventure and romance."[16] The pageant was a burst of romanticism, and the leaders —especially Haywood—are known to be "emotional": Ettor reads Shelley, Tresca Browning, and Flynn Maeterlinck, while Giovannitti is a poet himself. Someone on the other side with equal emotion, an imaginative judge or chief of police, they said, would make short work of the IWW; but one would guess that the only individual they could have named as equal to the task was Theodore Roosevelt. In similar vein, the New York *Tribune* wrote, "The IWW has not been highly regarded hereabouts as an organization endowed with brains or imagination . . . [but] this stamps its leaders as agitators of large resources and original talent."[17] This is perhaps the response that Haywood at least had been most hoping for.

Katharine Lord had invoked the theory of pageants in her earlier account of a woman's suffrage pageant at the Metropolitan Opera House, in the *New York Evening Post*, under the title of "The Pageant of an Idea," and this was recalled when reviewers wrote about the Paterson Pageant. The earlier event, she felt, had been too exclusively symbolic, with not enough action to enforce the idea, and she brought out the important criterion that a true pageant has to have a profound effect upon its performers before it can have that effect on the audience. (In this it is the opposite of vaudeville, where the performers calculate their effects on the audience. The same difference can be found between modern dance and classical ballet; modern dance, both in America and Germany, developed in parallel relation to pageantry.)

Survey for June 1913 remarked that the star speakers (Flynn, Haywood, Tresca) had been less effective and vigorous than the mass of strikers, and that the latter had escaped all staginess because they had refused to be theatrically "produced."[18] This comment, like *The Independent*'s, was clearly sympathetic to the event and responsive to the idea of a pageant. And other papers said it was spectacular, unforgettable, and a new art form. (In Paterson itself the morning paper called it a laughable farce, at the expense of the workers, but the evening paper was quite favorable.)

Susan Glaspell and George Cram Cook, the founders of the Provincetown Players, attended the performance and sat up late to discuss it afterward. Writing in 1927 she calls it "the first labor play," and says Reed "put into it the energy of a great desire, and in their [the strikers'] feeling of his oneness with them they forgot they were on stage." She and Cook were soon to bring the Provincetown Players to Greenwich Village as the Poets' Playhouse. Reed (and Dodge) were also involved with the Players, and it was Reed who encouraged Cook to risk creating a playhouse in New York, when Glaspell was full of doubts. They were, she says, men of faith. "Jig [Cook] spoke of the deep and original creative feeling that is found in some American men."[19] She thinks, she says, of Moscow and Delphi: meaning that Moscow was where Reed died pursuing his political dream, and Delphi was where Cook's life ended, also in 1920. Cook too had left New York and gone to Greece, and was there trying to establish a new theater by reviving the old Greek drama.

The Provincetown Players were an important force for renewal in the New York theater for the next decade and more. They launched the career of Eugene O'Neill, among others. Theirs was a somewhat different kind of theater from the Pageant—closer to MacKaye's "segregated, European drama"—but Cook's later dream was quite similar. He believed that "If there is nothing to take the place of the common religious purpose and passion of the primitive group, out of which the Dionysian group was born, no new vital drama can arise in any people."[20] Reed had told them about a miracle play he'd seen in Mexico, performed every year in the same village.[21] It was the quest for such a theater which led Cook to Greece. Glaspell's biography of him is entitled *The Road to the Temple*, and the idea of a theater as a temple was important to Laban and Craig and, for that matter, Isadora Duncan. A pageant was a performance in a secularized and politicized temple.

Craig was an influence upon the Paterson Pageant via Bobby Jones (and Mabel Dodge). Nineteen thirteen was the year when fifteen students joined Craig at the Arena Goldoni, a neoclassical amphitheater on the outskirts of Florence, where he intended to create the theater of the future (a significantly Wagnerian phrase), a temple sacred in character and uplifting in its effect on the national life. His school was to study voice (but to abstract it into sound), scene (but translated into light), and action (but transformed into motion). These were all ways to redirect theater away from naturalistic representations of bourgeois society and manners toward a freer, grander expression of ideas, as a pageant also was. Those ideas reached the Pageant via Jones and Dodge, and perhaps via Sloan and Jack Yeats.

When we turn to the politically minded, we get a different account. We have already seen that the newspaper editorials were inclined to be severe, but more interesting is the judgment of those involved, notably people in the IWW In her autobiography, *Rebel Girl*, Gurley Flynn calls the Pageant "a unique form of proletarian art,"[22] but she also speaks, though more discreetly, of its bad effects. She thought that the work for the Pageant had hurt the Strike. First of all, it caused jealousy among the workers as to who would be chosen to take part, and then it distracted attention from the Strike, so that the first scabs got into the mills during the Pageant rehearsals, when the picket lines were neglected.[23] Mary Heaton Vorse says that Flynn "Always believed that the pageant had much to do with the failure of the strike. She felt that this disillusionment [with the poor financial results] together with diverting the workers' minds from the actual struggle to the pictured struggle, was fatal."[24]

Margaret Sanger, as we shall see, attacked the Wobblies from an anarchist point of view in 1914, and the anarchists (writing in *Mother Earth* and in *The Social War*) were hostile to the Pageant. Artistically, they found the performance too locally photographic, while politically they found it insufficiently militant and revolutionary. From the opposite political wing, the AFL attacked it as childish and gave hints about the mysterious disappearance of the expected profits.[25]

Such judgments, and especially Flynn's, were of course influenced by the strike leaders' relations to each other, and to the strikers themselves. Bill Haywood, whose attention was anyway divided between Paterson and Akron, where a rubber strike was taking place, seems to have given most of his energies to the general publicity for and dramatization of the Strike. (At least some of the newspapers gave them less attention, and less favorable attention, than they had during the Lawrence strike—this was true of *The New York Times*, for instance—and they badly needed outside contributions to help the families of the unemployed.) And in this work he found his main assistant in John Reed, who in his turn mobilized his Greenwich Village friends, as we have seen. Lippmann, Eastman, Sanger, Rodman, and Kemp made several pilgrimages to Paterson during the Strike and were busy with the Pageant.

Haywood, moreover, spent a lot of his time being sick. He suffered from an ulcerated stomach, and is said to have lost eighty pounds during the period of the Strike. He could not retain his food. But his attention was also distracted by Greenwich Village—or so at least people supposed. While in his dealings with the Paterson strikers, he leaned heavily on Tresca—who could of course speak to them in Italian—he spent a lot of time with the artists and intellectuals in New York. He lived with more than one Village woman—first with a schoolteacher called Shostac, and then with the rich feminist lawyer, Jessie Ashley. He wrote poetry, visited Henri's studio and Stieglitz's gallery, and as we know appeared at Mabel Dodge's Evenings.

Dodge reports both Hapgood and Steffens as saying that, after attending her salon, Haywood "never made a convincing attack on capitalism."[26] Indeed, she felt that he failed to make himself effective in the salon itself. When asked to explain the differences between the IWW, anarchism, and socialism, he talked "as though he was wading blindfold through sand. It was in vain that Walter Lippmann tried to draw him out—his heavy cheeks sagged lower."[27] This is certainly not the account either Eastman or Van Vechten gives of Haywood's performance in the debate with the artists, and it may be that we should discount Dodge's report. Quite apart from her frequent tendency to malicious exaggeration, she was clearly just then engaged in a struggle for the loyalty of John Reed, in which her opponent was Haywood. Reed seems to have been in love with the image of manhood projected by Haywood.

Dodge was turning away from her political interests, which were not natural to her, in the sense that they were never so strong in earlier or later phases of her life. As she herself says, "I was passing out of the radical group into the artist group by that time."[28] Moreover, the idea of life values was at that time taking a radical feminist turn, as we have seen. In *Venture*, Eastman presents her as turning away from politics toward sorcery; that may be mildly caricatural, but the lines he gives her are quite plausible—and quite feminist: "These cocksure sarcastic brains! What do they know about the world? Just typical male egotism, that's all science is. Hard as nails, both of them, Dr. Moses and Karl Marx."

In her own account of Haywood, in *Movers and Shakers*, she mocks him as an Eminent Man, and clearly betrays hostility to masculine modes of action, like politics, in the name of feminine modes, like love and art. Haywood, she says, had "the regular 'public man' look that is produced by a satisfied need to shine in a crowd, no matter what ideas are the vehicle of this urgency."[29] She is scornful of the Village women who clustered about him excitedly, treating him as an oracle and an idol. She describes him as a large, soft, overripe Buddha, with the smile of an Eminent Man; and when she describes Lippmann also as a kind of Buddha, we realize that her iconoclasm is provoked by the whole field of political power. Her way of assessing and analyzing such men is quite like D. H. Lawrence's way of treating political leaders in, for instance, *Kangaroo*. She may be in part imitating Lawrence, but the main reason the same ways of writing come naturally to both is surely because they share the same erotic or life values.

But these reflections have carried us across the line that separates the immediate reactions to the performance of June 7 from our next topic, the more long-range consequences of the Pageant.

Immediately after the Pageant, some of those most deeply concerned in it disappeared from New York and from Paterson. Mabel Dodge and John Reed set sail for Paris and Florence on June 19 to stay at the Villa Curonia. They were beginning their love affair, which they had postponed consummating during the work on the Pageant. With them went Mabel's son and Carl Van Vechten, the novelist, and Bobby Jones, who was determined to study with Craig in Florence. The experience of designing the Pageant had made him decide to make theater design his lifework. When Craig refused to take him on as a pupil (apparently because of some earlier quarrel between

Craig and Dodge), he made his way to Germany, to work with Max Reinhardt. Reinhardt's *The Miracle*, a production which made use of some of Craig's ideas, and had a great success in London in 1912.

John Reed says that after the Pageant his nerves went to pieces.[30] The Strike was lost and "the leaders, too, broke down under the long strain of the fight. The IWW itself seemed smashed—indeed, it has never recovered its old prestige." Reed certainly did not forget Bill Haywood. He planned to write a play about him, and in a letter to Lippmann of September 18 we find him worrying about the outcome of the Paterson Strike. But for the summer of 1913 he was preoccupied with Mabel and Europe, and when he got back to America he was sent to report on Pancho Villa and the Mexican Revolution.

This sudden disappearance must have reinforced suspicions among the strikers of some inauthenticity in the commitment of their Village friends. Bobby Jones, for instance, had drawn that cover for the Pageant poster, on which the young worker figure was an emblem of virility, but he himself was anything but that. Muriel Draper, in *Music at Midnight*, tells of her meeting with him at the Villa Curonia immediately after the Pageant. When her party arrived, Jones had gone to bed, but she ran into his bedroom to have a gossip, and he got out of bed to show some lengths of beautiful material he had just bought, and they fell to draping them over her. This was a far cry from the IWW, and indeed a betrayal of its macho ethos.

Meanwhile, back in New York, Jessie Ashley and F. Sumner Boyd drew up a financial report on the Pageant and announced a deficit of $1,996. The expenses were $7,632, the receipts $7,645, with bills and loans of $2,009, and cash in hand of $13.[31] Apparently ten thousand of the fifteen thousand programs were never sold, except as wastepaper. And the strikers' relief fund got only $384, with about the same amount going to repay loans from the New York silk workers. (Mabel Dodge, John Reed, Bill and Margaret Sanger, Upton Sinclair, and Jessie Ashley converted their loans into gifts.)[32] All this probably came as no surprise to the committee, but apparently the strikers had—understandably enough—equated publicity with profit, and thought they were earning a fortune for the strike funds.

There was apparently some suspicion that the funds had been misappropriated by the leaders—like the suspicions about the AAPS funds. John Steiger, the New York silk worker, was one who spread such rumors. They focused on Haywood in particular, because of a rather mysterious pattern of vacations during that summer and early fall. He stayed on in Greenwich Village, living with Jessie Ashley, through August; then he went to Provincetown, staying with Mary Heaton Vorse, and we find a headline in the *Boston Post*, on September 29, 1913: "Haywood Resting in Provincetown"; and then he went to Paris, again with Ashley. It was this trip, announced as funded by "a friend" and necessary for his health, which aroused most comment.

The Strike came to an inglorious end. In mid-July the bosses offered to negotiate shop by shop, and this induced some of the skilled workers to settle. When the strike committee agreed to allow this, the IWW, alarmed, insisted on a referendum, by which the plan was rejected. (The IWW usually confined itself to advice and stayed out of power struggles with the local committee, but this was obviously a crisis.) The socialist silk weavers withdrew from the strike committee. In June the New York socialist paper, *The Call*, had said that the Paterson Strike was not, as the IWW wished to imply, a revolution, but only a strike—something to be compared with the work of the AFL. The IWW called this article a bullet in Paterson's back.[33] Joseph Ettor complained that the Socialists had never really supported the Wobblies, and "The crime against the Paterson workers was not committed in Paterson but in New York on the lower East Side."[34] This was typical of various internecine quarrels on the left which broke out, once it became likely that the strike would be lost. And in 1914 Margaret Sanger wrote "The Paterson Strike" for *The Revolutionary Almanac*, an anarchist paper edited by Hippolyte Havel. She attacked the Wobblies for their policy of nonviolence, for the length of the strike, for the failure to confront the authorities over free speech and sabotage, and for the alliance with the socialists— especially at Haledon. In her autobiography, Sanger says the Italians were not behind Haywood, whose pacific policies betrayed them; he was, they said, a sick man, and getting soft; even in the Pageant, conviction was lacking.[35]

By July 29 most employees were back at work; twenty-five hundred went elsewhere, two thousand more were blacklisted by Paterson employers. The wages lost in the strike were estimated at $5,500,000, and the owners were supposed to have lost an equivalent amount. Landlords lost two to five months' rent, and special police cost the town ten thousand dollars. There were fifteen hundred arrests and five deaths. Paterson was never again a prosperous textile center.

Gurley Flynn gave a talk entitled "The Truth about Paterson" before the New York Civic Forum. She said the strike failed because the ribbon weavers were conservative and because the Pageant was distracting, though "a beautiful example of realistic art." *Outlook* magazine reported her as saying that contributions to the strike fund had been coming in at the rate of two hundred dollars a week until the quarrels attracted bad publicity.

She herself was involved in those quarrels. By June she had been publicly at odds with some of the local leaders of the strike. Adolph Lessig had stirred up anger by threatening to cut off the town's electrical power, just when she was trying to conciliate the middle class. She accused him of working for the companies. He and Ewald Koettgen tried to settle behind the IWW's back. She also quarreled with Patrick Quinlan, who proposed a rent strike.[36] But her analysis of the main sequence of events has been accepted by most historians.

Steve Golin, however, insists that the purpose of the Pageant was always to publicize the Strike, and that it should not be judged by the money taken in for tickets.[37] He says that late in June the strikers' relief fund did begin to grow, as a result of outside contributions and in response to the Pageant, but he does not give us enough evidence to judge how important that was. But he makes a case that this publicity was needed because of a generally unfavorable attitude in the press, and because of the toughness of the owners' resistance.

It also seems to be true that this project was especially Bill Haywood's, among the leaders. He was an imaginative man, and one, moreover, at a high point in his career, when he may have been seeing himself as a national political figure. He was certainly in touch with a new circle of admirers, the people of Greenwich Village. Above all, one might guess, the admiration of John Reed may have intoxicated him. Reed was after all a remarkably gifted man and favorite son of the Village, and he was finding in Haywood a model of heroic manliness. All this would help explain why Haywood could feel—

despite the negative judgments of Flynn and others—that the Pageant was the greatest personal triumph of his career, as Ralph Chaplin says he did.[38] Indeed, Golin argues that Haywood was right, and that the Pageant was a new cultural form, created equally by workers and intellectuals, and ideally suited to the needs of industrial action.[39]

The Federal Industrial Relations Commission, chaired by Frank Walsh, was occasioned by this strike and others. John Collier, who worked on it, asked Mabel Dodge to persuade radicals to testify, and she wrote to thirty of her friends, including Haywood, Hapgood, Goldman, Steffens, and Lippmann. Haywood would, but for sickness, have testified together with W. E. B. Du Bois and Paul Kennaday. In fact, he appeared on May 12–13, 1915, in Washington. His main enemy on the commission was a California merchant, Harris Weinstock. Haywood was very effective in speaking for the IWW, describing various strikes, defending the union against charges of violence and unscrupulousness, and turning accusations of sabotage against the employers, as in the matter of their dynamiting of silk.

The Masses and the *International Socialist Review* stayed loyal to the IWW, but as Steve Golin says, "After Paterson, they [the Wobblies] were never able to regain the initiative in organizing factory workers. All histories of the IWW agree that the organization suffered. Its invasion of the East, after the spectacular initial victory at Lawrence, was turned back in the war of attrition at Paterson."[40] And the quarrel between Flynn and Haywood, which developed in 1915 and 1916 and effectively ended her career in the IWW, began over the Pageant, according to Golin. Flynn would never have agreed, of course, that the Pageant was Haywood's great achievement. She was, in any case, a less imaginative mind.

In 1918, when the IWW leaders were indicted by the government on various charges, she wrote to President Wilson, saying that she had had bitter disagreements with the leadership in 1916 and had ceased to work with them and the government agreed, so she was exempted from the trial which sent Haywood to jail. That split began in the course of the Strike because, Golin suggests, of some jealousy on her part over the publicity Haywood got and the welcome given him by Greenwich Village.

Apparently there was talk of repeating the Pageant, and Reed and

Grace Potter (who wrote enthusiastically about it) wanted workers all over the country to devise such plays and to bring the best of them to New York for a festival every May Day. But that plan got lost. And whereas Haywood—just after the event—told the strikers it had been the biggest thing the IWW had ever attempted,[41] Flynn said rather sarcastically that David Belasco would no doubt sign them all on, and she later charged the event with various evil effects. It is perhaps significant that she charged it above all with generating jealousy—it left twenty-four thousand jealous people behind[42]—and that she laid the blame on the intellectuals. It may be that she herself was jealous and that the intellectuals were the objects of that jealousy.

Ironically, the IWW was more successful in organizing in Paterson after the Strike than in Lawrence because it was harder for the owners to blacklist in Paterson. But the union's membership numbers changed in proportion to the criticism. The IWW had made great gains between August 1912 and August 1913, but it began to lose in the fall of 1913, especially in the East. Moreover, though there were some gains in the West and Midwest in 1915 and 1916 because of the war boom in the economy, the upswing proved temporary, and the IWW never recovered.

T H E
Check:
1913-1920

8

*In the early days before World War I, when
Bohemianism and radicalism met, the role of
the intellectual as social critic was largely un-
questioned . . . the assumption reigned in Bohemia that modern political, scientific, and artistic
discoveries were all revolutionary. . . . The war
burned away the optimistic clouds.*
    —JAMES B. GILBERT, *Writers and Partisans*

*We both went to the Paterson Strike around the
first War and worked in the Pageant. She went
regularly to feed John Reed in jail and I listened
to Big Bill Haywood, Gurley Flynn, and the rest
of the big hearts and helping hands in Union
Hall. And look at the damned thing now.*
    —WILLIAM CARLOS WILLIAMS, *Paterson III*

*The Bride is the (involuntary) representation of
the only Myth-Idea of the modern world: Criticism . . . from the 17th century onward our
world has had no Ideas, in the sense in which
Christianity had ideas during its time of apogee.
What we have, especially from Kant on, is Criticism.*
    —OCTAVIO PAZ, *Marcel Duchamp*

*T*he bad feelings left over at the end of the Paterson Strike, and those left over at the dissolution of the AAPS, gave a check to the optimism and idealism of 1913. And that was reinforced by several other developments over the next few years, which will be the subject matter of this chapter.

The twin events of 1913 constituted a climax and a turning point, after which the energies which had been mounting began to decline, and the paths which had been converging began to diverge. But this was not immediately obvious, for of course the leaders of the IWW and the painters of the AAPS continued their lives and their work after 1913 with a strong sense of sequence, as did those Greenwich Village men and women I have described as their audience.

For instance, when John Reed and Mabel Dodge came back from Europe, he got an assignment he welcomed—to cover the civil war in Mexico, a revolt led by Pancho Villa and others against Porfirio Díaz, for *The Metropolitan*—and he left New York in great excitement, much to Mabel Dodge's distress and displeasure. She in fact left her home to follow him, caught up with him, and stayed with him all the way to the Mexican border. On the journey, Reed wrote to a friend about her: "I think she expects to find General Villa a sort of male Gertrude Stein, or at least a Mexican Stieglitz."[1]

This suggestion that she refused to recognize political and military realities, and imposed art and personality categories upon them, was shrewd enough. But it would be just as true to say that she rightly saw that Villa was *not* Stein, that his world was quite *unlike* Stieglitz's, and that it was a place where her values could not prevail. She was upset to see Reed passing out of her reach, into a world of men—of war, of politics, of history, of violence.

For when Reed reached Villa, on December 26, 1913, what did he find? "The most natural human being I ever saw—natural in the sense of being nearest to a wild animal . . . Hands, arms, trunk moved with the swiftness and sureness of a coyote. . ."[2] His eyes were those of a man who could kill. This gives an entirely different sense to Mabel Dodge's concept of nature. Her cult of nature was incompatible with one that took Villa as an exemplum.

Villa gave Reed a privileged place in his entourage, and Reed rode beside the Mexican soldiers and was deeply thrilled to be able to win their acceptance. "I made good with these wild fighting men, and with myself. I loved the men and I loved the life."[3] He paid Villa himself a devout and enthusiastic attention, as a bigger and better Haywood, a master of manliness—a wild animal but also a hero and man of destiny. It seems likely that Villa took the place of Haywood in Reed's imagination, or at least that Reed associated him with the Wobblies. He tells his readers that Villa's rule in his parts of Mexico was like what that of the Wobblies might be, and that Villa was a hearty man like Haywood—familiar with violence, a passionate gambler, and with an even more macho record with women. And in Mexico there was no one like Mabel Dodge to deflate and debunk such a figure for Reed. Perhaps Reed was relieved to be set free from her feminine irony. In some of D. H. Lawrence's stories about Dodge, written in the 1920s, he expresses a resentment at her and her irony which Reed may also have felt. For instance, he imagines her put into the power of a Villa-like character in "None of That" and into the power of an Indian tribe in "The Woman Who Rode Away."

Reed's writing about Mexico, which is very vivid, is also very Kiplingesque, as was recognized at the time. The advertisement put out by The Metropolitan said, "John Reed in Mexico. Word pictures of war by an American Kipling. . . . What Stephen Crane and Richard Harding Davis did for the Spanish-American War in 1898, John Reed, twenty-six years old, has done for Mexico." These phrases are the insignia of the life of men, away from which Mabel Dodge had been trying to lure Reed; adventure, characteristically upper-class adventure, was embodied by Kipling in literature and by Theodore

Roosevelt in politics. Reed was clearly disillusioned with Roosevelt in strictly political terms, but as an adventurer the ex-president still commanded his mind. In Eastman's novel about Reed, he is depicted as calling Roosevelt "the livest kid on earth," and that suggests the sort of allegiance he felt to the older man.

But despite all such continuities, it seems that the spirit of 1913 began to die already in 1914. At least, the blame for its death was again and again attached to the war. Hapgood dated the beginning of his long period of depression to that moment. "The hope and buoyant faith, which had been mine during my work on the *Globe* and at the time of Mabel's salon, had changed in a few brief years or even months into something almost incomprehensibly different . . . I was rudderless, like the rest of the world."[4] He even declared "We were the Cause of the War: the violence and inconsistency of our emotions, the impotence of our ideas . . ."[5] And this idea is also expressed in Mabel Dodge's memoirs—that her own lust for power in those years corresponded to that of the great powers.

Lincoln Steffens was luckier. He found something to do in Mexico, like Reed; he too reported the revolution there, and he too went to Russia. Of course, these two men, who found themselves in 1914 and 1917, were more in sympathy with the world of men than Hapgood and Dodge. John Reed invited Hapgood to go to Russia with him, and was annoyed when Hapgood had family reasons for declining. But Reed and Steffens too had to change, had to exchange some of that hope and buoyant faith in order to deal with the world after 1913.

One sign of the change in Reed comes in a curious phrase in his report on the party conventions in *The Masses* in August 1916. His main purpose is to attack Theodore Roosevelt for betraying the Progressives. (Roosevelt had delayed his decision about whether to run as their candidate until the convention nominated him, and then he declined.) The article ends, "And as for democracy, we can only hope that some day it will cease to put its trust in men."[6] What can *men* mean? The context implies that it means the willful personalism associated with Roosevelt. And what was there for Reed to turn to away from men, the object of his cult for so many years? Subsequent events suggest that it was the impersonalness of Lenin and his *im-personal* willfulness, embodied in systematic analysis and programmatic action. Reed and Steffens went to Russia, and the latter came back declaring, "I have been over into the future, and it works." This sense of the future was quite a long way from Greenwich Village and the spirit of 1913.

The IWW continued its work, but gradually turned away from the eastern cities, back toward the West as its major field of action. In 1914 some of the members founded an Agricultural Workers' Organization in Kansas City, which became the largest single union of all those under the Wobbly umbrella. The IWW was still strong in the West. And the same year a university sociologist called Carleton Parker interviewed eight hundred migrant workers in California, in some sense randomly, and reported that half of them knew the Wobbly songs and some of the Wobbly ideas, and were attracted to them. He also found that 80 percent of those he interviewed were under forty, which gave some statistical corroboration to what many people had long assumed impressionistically.

At a late 1913 meeting Haywood had persuaded the membership to centralize the control of the organization, putting power into the hands of the national leaders at the expense of local groups. This was something he had wanted for some time, and the union's defeat at Paterson made it seem more urgent. In September 1914, moreover, he took over the post of secretary-treasurer from Vincent St. John. (The latter had come to doubt the efficacy of combining revolutionary work with that of a labor union.) In 1916 Haywood's taking of power into his own hands and centralizing everything in Chicago led to conflicts between him and other colleagues, notably Flynn, Tresca, and Ettor.

In that year Flynn went back to the Mesabi Range, where she had organized the miners before. It was good union country, with lots of Finnish socialists and a long tradition of striking. In June that year another strike broke out in Aurora, Colorado, where those involved had been brought in by the owners, as scabs, in 1907. After a killing, Tresca led the strikers in a vow of *sangue per sangue*, and he was arrested as a result. That was when Flynn arrived, and Mary Heaton Vorse came to join her. As a result of Flynn's negotiations with the legal authorities, Tresca and his companions were freed in a deal by which three Montenegrin workers pleaded guilty, and drew heavy sentences of up to twenty years. Haywood, speaking for the IWW, disapproved. Flynn said the deal had gone wrong; Haywood said she should not have made any such deal. They also quarreled over his keeping control of all IWW resources in Chicago, including the strike funds, and refusing to go to the strike area himself.

Besides those internal conflicts, the union had to worry about national events, and indeed international ones, with the outbreak of war in Europe in 1914. Gradually, and then suddenly, the national atmosphere became very unfriendly. In 1917 Idaho and Minnesota passed laws against the IWW, and by 1920 twenty-three states had followed suit. Joe Hill had been arrested and charged with murder in Utah in 1914, and despite all the union's efforts, was to die in 1915.

The war was an enormous event, the effects of which stretched everywhere and can be analyzed into infinity. From our point of view, its significance was the way it both injured the spirit of 1913 and promoted the two spiritual projects of modernism and revolution. The damage done to what I have called the spirit of 1913 was fatal. That is why I have called this chapter "The Check"; the atmosphere of hope and confidence which so many people in New York in 1913 had been creating for each other began to blow apart, and not perhaps until the late 1960s was there any equivalent.

But in certain ways the war intensified the appeal of modernism and revolution, above all by fatally injuring the plausibility of the bourgeois state and its ideology. Most simply, one can point to the Russian Revolution of 1917 as a great burst of socialist action, offering incalculable inspiration and encouragement to sympathizers all over the world; and to the dada movement which began in central Europe at much the same time, being transformed into surrealism in France, and stimulating artists all over the white world to hope that they could both practice their art and simultaneously defy the civilization that oppressed them. Both these events derived from, or were triggered by, the Great War.

Both events brought with them disillusioning consequences, of course. The post-1917 history of Bolshevik rule in Russia is one of the bitterest human legends for those who believed in revolution as a spiritual project. And dada and surrealism proved very narrow in their appeal, turned inward on their participating groups, and largely negative or destructive. The energies that went into these actions were not the happy, hopeful, optimistic moods of 1913, but rather something more grim and desperate. Nevertheless, both were bursts of energy, and many acts of heroism, individual and group, and many works of art resulted. The great spiritual projects had their affirmative effects: they accomplished themselves in brilliant feats which drew others on to invest their own energies in comparable work.

But before we discuss the war and its effects, we should continue the sketch of the prewar history of the group we are concerned with. The three years of war in Europe spread a gas of war fever over the whole world which had its effect in America, so that before the outbreak of war in 1917, perhaps even before 1914, these people were already moving in the directions they finally took.

Thus the New York painters' work was obviously stimulated by the events of 1913. John Sloan said that after the Armory Show he began to compose with plastic motives instead of narrative ones and that he learned the importance of color from Renoir and van Gogh.[7] Sloan accepted modernism, understanding it in a rather symbolist or spiritual way. "The ultra-modern movement," he said, "is a medicine for the disease of imitating appearances. It is a return to the root principle of art: that art is a result of an interest in Things, not effects . . . the use of symbols, graphic devices for things."

In 1916 he led a revolt of the artists at *The Masses*, partly in the name of artistic freedom and against the editors' ideological control. Art Young, who was on the editors' side, said Sloan and his friends thought they advanced the revolution just by putting an ashcan into their pictures.[8] It is hard to know whether to ascribe this change also to the influence of the Armory Show: Sloan was perhaps always ready to rebel against ideological control. He said an artist is the only person who has a right to be independent. In 1916 he began to teach at the Art Students League, and in 1917 helped found the Society of Independent Artists.

Max Weber, on the other hand, soon reacted against the Armory Show influence. He explained the abrupt end to his cubist and futurist experiments by saying, "In my early days I discovered the geometry in the work of God; now I feel the need to return to the works of God themselves."[9] He had emphasized the height of skyscrapers, the speed of traffic, the growth of the city in pictures like *New York, 1913*. But by 1918 he was turning back to Lower East Side subjects and to expressionist styles. This involved him in a revolt against both technique and technology. "Technique has to some a devilish fascination that makes their work a machine. But the wonder and blessing of the spirit is that it can manifest itself best through the simplest means and that it knows of no technique."[10] His stress falls on the spirit again, as it had in early discussions at 291. "Art does not lie in its means; it lies in its mission, in its purpose, in its message, in its prophecy."[11] One might say he was a Taos painter ("Must I not stand under a dome of silence to see?")[12] who refused to go to Taos; in his crabbed and negative and dedicated career, Weber can sometimes seem an American Cézanne.

Marcel Duchamp was the purest example of the artist who would not go to Taos. His America was New York, the city of modernism. He had no interest in life values, and so there was no sympathy between him and Mabel Dodge or even Stieglitz. The latter considered Duchamp a charlatan, or so Duchamp tells us in Cabanne's *Dialogues*.[13] In return, he called Stieglitz a moralizing Socrates.[14] For his first years in New York, he worked on his *Large Glass*, a work in oils, varnish, lead foil and lead wire, silvering, and dust, for about two hours a day; he concentrated for a year on the top half, and then on the bottom half. By 1923 he was bored with it and stopped work.

He also worked on his readymades, notably the snow shovel he entitled *In Advance of a Broken Arm* and a comb on which he inscribed *Two or Three Drops of Height Have Nothing to Do with Savagery*. The titles, while in some sense nonsensical, are of course an essential part of the whole; Duchamp was always a verbal and conceptual artist. In 1918 he painted *Tu m'*, a ten-foot by two-foot inventory of his ideas up to then, which he gave to his friend and patron, Katherine Dreier. This involved some trompe l'oeil games: a bottle brush projects through an illusory rent in the canvas, which is secured by three real safety pins. Such games were of the essence of his work. Others included paying his dentist with a painted check, acting a nude Adam in a ballet, painting a mustache on the Mona Lisa, and creating a second identity for himself as a woman called Rrose Sélavy.

Interviewed in 1915, he praised New York for so quickly demol-
ishing its old buildings, saying that the dead should not be allowed
to be stronger than the living.[15] He now scorned cubism; he and
Picabia both declared it a word without a meaning. They had passed
on to other ideas, although—as part of the break—they did not name
those ideas as new isms. The naming of schools was left to the
scholars—and to American painters.

The modernist stimulus had various results on American artists,
but perhaps the most important was one we can label American
futurism. Francis Picabia opened a show of paintings at 291 two days
after the Armory Show closed. (Stieglitz bought some of the pictures
for himself, as an investment.) Picabia, and later Duchamp and other
French painters, began to tell Americans that their cities, and especially New York, were cubist or futurist experiences, with their
glass and steel skyscrapers, their rectangular street plans, and their
constant rebuilding; and that they needed to be represented in terms
of speed, force, and fantasy—terms unlike those used in traditional
European art.

Le Corbusier, in the preface to his *Toward a New Architecture*,
said that American factories and grain elevators were "The magnificent First Fruits of the New Age. The American Engineers overwhelm
with their calculations our expiring architecture."[16] In the *New York
American*, Picabia called New York a great cubist or futurist opera,
and he turned to painting fantasy machines, with fantasy titles like
A Little Solitude in the Midst of Suns. Albert Gleizes, when he arrived
in 1915, told reporters that the men who designed the Brooklyn Bridge
were geniuses as great as those who built Notre Dame de Paris—but
of course it was architecture of an opposite *kind*.[17] Two of the
paintings—both bought by Stieglitz—were titled *New York, 1913*,
and the same title was used by Max Weber for one of his pictures;
and Joseph Stella's studies of the Brooklyn Bridge and Coney Island
belong to this genre.

This kind of art was to be taken up by many gifted American
painters over the next thirty or forty years; it was perhaps the most
attractive, or the easiest, way to combine the modern European forms
and ideas about art, with native subject matter. It blended with native
literary traditions, like Whitman's verse and Dreiser's fiction about

city life—and indeed with the traditions of other nineteenth-century city novelists, like Dickens, Dostoyevsky, and Balzac. This was the kind of vitalism which turned the city into a great animal, subject to attack in these years from another and somewhat opposite kind of vitalism which identified the life force with Nature and Woman and saw the City and the Machine as forms of death. This second kind of erotic vitalism or *Lebensphilosophie* (we can illustrate it simply by citing the name of D. H. Lawrence) grew in power when the horrors of the First World War made all technology seem a machinery of death. And this is what was to inspire the artists of Taos.

Somewhat similar to futurism was precisionism, similar in its focus on mechanisms, but opposite in its static character. "Precisionism," says Brown, "resulted from the domestication of cubism, coalescing with mechanism—an esthetic equivalent of machine production."[18] Lewis Mumford wrote in 1934, "Face to face with these new machines and instruments, with their hard surfaces, their rigid volumes, their stark shapes, a fresh kind of perception and pleasure emerges: to interpret this order becomes one of the new tasks of the arts."[19] Among the painters tackling this problem, Man Ray, Gerald Murphy, and Louis Lozowick are usually listed. But the most typical precisionist was Charles Sheeler, who in 1927 took photographs of Ford's automobile plant at River Rouge (the first to produce complete automobiles on the assembly line) from which he then painted.

Associated with both these schools were various kinds of what we might call dadaism. Ray made his *Object to Be Destroyed* in 1923. Then there were the abstract portraits, like von Freytag-Loringhoven's *Portrait of Marcel Duchamp*, composed of gears, and so on; Sheeler's self-portrait as a telephone, of 1923; and Picabia's self-portrait as a car horn, of the same year. The painting of portraits, so long one of the central art forms, was suddenly relegated to the wasteland or the suburbs—to nonartists. What were now called portraits (in literature, too, in Gertrude Stein's work) were mockeries of that genre, so long the pride of the Renaissance tradition. Picabia and Duchamp were leading spirits; de Zayas praised Picabia as the only artist visiting America who had, like Cortés, burned the ships that linked him back to Europe.

There was more of dandyism in this work than in, say, precisionism or futurism. Charles Demuth (the closest to Duchamp) was unique among Americans in his combination of the attraction to industrial landscape with a sensibility of dandyism. He did not make that endorsement of life values typical of the Stieglitz school. From 1914 on he was often compared with Marin, because of the debt both owed to French painting, but Marin was no dandy, and Demuth, as Henry McBride said, never reacted against science and technology in the name of life, as Marin did. Replying to a 1929 questionnaire, asked what he looked forward to, Demuth said *the past*, and his friendships and enthusiasms were for aesthete-dandies like Duchamp, Gertrude Stein, and so on. He lived in what he called the province, but went often to Greenwich Village and stayed at the Brevoort and painted, for instance, the Hell Hole and vaudeville performers.

Duchamp went with Demuth to the Hell Hole and such places. (He is depicted there in one of the latter's pictures.) He wrote about their friendship that Demuth "had a curious smile reflecting an incessant curiosity for every manifestation life offered. An artist worthy of the name [This is very high praise from Duchamp] . . . worshipping his inner self without the usual eagerness to be right. Today art is no more the crop of private soils, and Demuth is among the first to have planted the good seed in America."[20] As is often the case with Duchamp, the last sentence is as misleading as the preceding one is illuminating. Though art may be in some sense more "democratic" as a result of his and Demuth's influence, that democratization is only a matter of breaking certain links between the artist class and bourgeois taste (and those links have been changed rather than broken). And certainly art is no less private, rather more private, for their work.

This was still Greenwich Village but there was a difference from the heroic age of 1913. What defines that difference? The answer is suggested by an anecdote told by Art Young. Gertrude Drick Smith, an art student with John Sloan, organized a picnic on the top of the Washington Square Arch, on January 23, 1917. Smith was a Village character; she had named herself Woe in order to be able to introduce herself with the formula "Woe is me." She played the violin and painted, and was a companion of Jack Yeats and written about by James Oppenheim. She had found a blind and unlocked door to the arch stairs, and she invited five friends to join her there on top for a New Year's party. There were Chinese lanterns and a bonfire, and each guest was given a toy pistol to fire, as she read out a Declaration of Independence of Greenwich Village from the rest of the United States. The Villagers wanted to have nothing more to do with the rest of the country—nothing more to do with war and politics and history.

This sweet and sour little performance answered to something deep in the mood of the Villagers, and remained in people's memories. Edmund Wilson, for instance, when he wrote his play about the Provincetown Players, *This Room and This Gin and These Sandwiches*, tells a version of this story. But what makes it appropriate to our study at this point is that two of the guests were John Sloan and Marcel Duchamp—so profoundly different from each other. They shared the impulse to back away from the world of power, and to practice art as a means to that end. But whereas Sloan supplemented that impulse with socialist convictions, and made his painting into a way to reestablish links with ordinary people, Duchamp supplemented it with a radical critique of all politics and all moral seriousness. He was committed to modernism in art, at the expense of all possible allies as well as alternatives. The ceremony on the arch symbolizes for us a handing over of the keys of the Village—and of the kingdom of art—from Sloan and realism to Duchamp and dada.

There were of course strong reactions against the spirit of modernism in art—as against the spirit of system in politics. Humanism did not die in 1913. Hapgood wrote, "It is a very striking thing, in both Leo and Gertrude Stein, that they are capable of absolute esthetic and moral condemnation of human beings, and are also incapable of close human association."[21] Hapgood himself of course stood for an idea of art (and every other value) which was inseparable from the supreme value of human warmth and compassion and enjoyment. "There is only one way in which I have full self-esteem—in *liking* so much, seeing so much as beautiful, dignified, and good."[22] This is what he and his friends—including so fickle a philosopher as Mabel Dodge—found in their erotic values. The same judgment is made in Max Eastman's comments on bolshevism. *The Masses*, he says, was "a too laughing and singing institution" to convince a Russian Bolshevik.[23] And he is sure that John Reed died absolutely disgusted with the men of system he had to deal with in Russia, like Radek and Zinoviev.[24] Of course Hapgood and Eastman were not alone in these judgments; during the long lives as writers ahead of them after 1913, they stood closer to "average" opinion than did, say, Gurley Flynn or Stein and Duchamp; but still the latter were the leaders of thought, and the former were—after 1913—reactionary.

To impose some order on this crowded field of events and ideas, it seems profitable to divide them up between results of the Great War, which were felt by everyone; results of the Bolshevik Revolution, felt mostly by the politically minded; and results of the latter's nearest equivalent in art, the dada movement, interesting mostly to the art world. It may also help clarify the general drift in our two fields if we introduce two new figures: Dorothy Day, the greatest religious radical in the American Catholic Church in this century, and William Carlos Williams, the modernist poet and New Jersey doctor. They had no relations with each other, and only an ideological connection with the group we are discussing (the connection put forward in this book) but they were in some sense truer heirs of the spirit of 1913 than those who actually participated in the events of that year, but went on to other ideas.

Dorothy Day, the radical daughter of a Chicago sportswriter, arrived in New York in 1916, at the age of nineteen. She began to write for the socialist paper, *The Call*, her first articles being reports on her own attempts to live on the weekly income which the police claimed was enough to support life in the city. She also wrote reports on, for instance, Margaret Sanger's sister, Ethel, after she had gone on a hunger strike in prison. This combination of radical politics with ascetic interests prefigures the ascetic piety she was later famous for. She earned money also as an artists' model; it was even rumored, wrongly, that she had been the nude descending the staircase.[25]

She already admired the Wobbly leaders when she arrived in New York, having read labor publications at college and back in Chicago as early as 1913. The most effective speaker she heard, she said, was Elizabeth Gurley Flynn. "Wherever she spoke, the audience wept heartily and gave heartily to the cause. The night I heard her . . . I gave everything I had in my pocket, not even saving out carfare, so that I had to borrow the fare back to the office, and go without lunches for some days afterwards."[26] Art Young saw Day at the Greenwich Village bar, the Hell Hole. He mentions her in his autobiography as D, "the tall girl writer who went after local color by associating with a gang of roughs, called the Hudson Dusters."[27]

In May 1917 she was hired to be the assistant editor of *The Masses*, for which Young drew, and she was in charge of the magazine for three months while the editors were away; so that she put together the issues which induced the authorities to prosecute it for making antiwar propaganda. The editors were put on trial, and the magazine was suppressed under the 1917 Espionage Act. In some ways Day's weekly, *The Catholic Worker*, which began in 1933, continued the work of *The Masses*—and more exactly, it continued the work of some of the Wobbly weeklies.

But her work incorporated a profoundly conservative impulse also, since it was done within and in the name of the Roman Catholic Church. Day did not cease to be a radical or to fight for the working class, but it nevertheless made a difference that she did so within the confines of a traditional theology and church structure. In terms of that enlightenment intellectual history of the West to which the socialist revolution belongs, she was reactionary. She also differed from her IWW forebears by embracing peace and accepting only nonviolent modes of action.

William Carlos Williams, born in 1883, who was to make himself the poet of Paterson, attended the Armory Show and was strongly influenced by it. "There was at that time a great surge of interest in the arts generally before the First World War. New York was seething with it. . . . It came to a head for us in the famous 'Armory Show' of 1913. I went to it and gasped along with the rest. [He was especially struck by Marcel Duchamp's work, the *Nude Descending a Staircase*] . . . But I do remember how I laughed out loud when first I saw it, happily, with relief."[28]

Williams knew John Reed on Fourteenth Street, but he was not politically minded, and the more significant relationships for him were with artists, and especially painters. Some early lines on the Paterson Strike show how conservative, indeed crude, his class sensibility was.

Heavy drink where the low, sloping foreheads
The flat skulls and the unkempt black or blond hair
The ugly legs of the young girls, pistons
Too powerful for delicacy.
The women's wrists, the men's arms, red . . .[29]

He preferred the Arensberg circle, into which Duchamp moved when he arrived in New York in 1915, and where he became a dominant figure. Williams was on one occasion snubbed by Duchamp, "something that filled me with humiliation so that I can never forget it . . . I realized then and there that there wasn't a possibility of my ever saying anything to anyone in that gang from that moment to eternity . . . I bumped through these periods like a yokel, narrow-eyed, feeling my own inadequacies, but burning with the lust to write."[30] He in fact stayed friends with several American modernists like Marsden Hartley and Charles Demuth, and, in literature, with Ezra Pound and Gertrude Stein; but the figure of Duchamp remained very challenging to him. He was awed by the latter's creativity, but frightened by his apparent disrespect for art.[31] Williams earned his living as a doctor, and that experience—in Rutherford, a town near and like Paterson—colored and focused his vision as a poet. He therefore continued (but transformed) the work of the realist painters, as Day continued (and transformed) the work of the political radicals.

Robert Coady, a New York art dealer, in 1917 produced a magazine, *The Soil*, which praised technology, vaudeville, movies, sports as American. Williams liked this magazine, which expressed many of his own Americanist views, but complained that it slighted the values of art. Both this and Williams's own magazine, *Contact*, attacked Duchamp and his friends. (Even more vigorously, *Contact* attacked Williams's archenemy, the modernist poet, T. S. Eliot.) Coady said an ideal American art would be "young, robust, energetic, naive, immature, daring, and big-spirited."[32] He cited the Panama Canal, the East River, Jack Johnson the boxer, and Annette Kellerman the swimmer, as examples. Loeb's *Broom* also followed *Seven Arts* in relating American technology with spiritual values. *Broom* and Munson's *Secession* both began in 1922. All these voices, of which Williams came to be the representative, reacted against the "pure" modernism of Duchamp and Eliot, back toward John Reed and the spirit of 1913.

But we must pay attention primarily to the vicissitudes of the participants in the Armory Show and the Paterson Pageant under the impact of world tragedy.

The Effects of the 1914–1918 War

The outbreak of war in Europe came as a shock to the IWW leadership. They had not expected it and did not know how to deal with it. Haywood said it left him speechless. "When the war broke out I was struck dumb. For weeks I could scarcely talk."[33] (In 1913 he had said, "The world is turning against war.") The war brought many problems to the left in general, perhaps especially to the socialists, because many of them were of German extraction, but also to all the organizations that had seen patriotism as a form of bourgeois-state mystification, deserving always to be downplayed. The IWW declared that, ". . . of all the idiotic and perverted ideas accepted by workers from the class that lives on their misery, patriotism is the worst."[34] In the Paterson Strike, as we saw, the symbolism of the Stars and Stripes belonged to the owners, and the counterimage that belonged to the workers was the international Red Flag.

The same was true of the writers for *The Masses*. They tried to fend off the power of the war by declaring it uninteresting. Hapgood wrote an article, "War is a Bore," and Reed another in which he said that the conflict in Europe was not *our* war. This was entitled "The Traders' War" and appeared in *The Masses*, in September 1914. It ended, "But we must not let ourselves be duped by this edifying buncombe about liberalism going forth to Holy War against Tyranny. This is not Our War." The quarrel between England, France, and Russia and the Central Powers was quite unlike the exciting and romantic war he had reported from Mexico. The war in Europe was both sordid and appalling, both enormous and merely capitalist.

But Reed was, after all, famous as a war reporter, and to most American readers, apparently, the war *was* exciting, and the left was dragged from its moorings in the wake of a national enthusiasm. (It is interesting to note Lippmann's enthusiasm for Reed's war journalism in 1914—an enthusiasm with a note of relief: Reed had tried to follow *The Masses'* politics, but "his real chance came when *The Metropolitan* magazine sent him to Mexico.")[35] Art Young said, "After the declaration of war by the United States [in 1917] I felt that there was no hope for the human race . . . He saw even socialist friends going war-mad . . . Everybody's brains were snapping."[36] Mabel Dodge wrote a long essay titled "The Secret of War," of which part was published in *The Masses* in 1914, saying there was no sign of suffering, or even division, in wartime Paris. The syndicalists were working for the government, sending the workers to fight for the great humanitarian cause. She described the difference between the man in uniform and the man out of it as spiritual. "Some chemicalization has taken place. He [the man in uniform] is transformed by it. He is perhaps not more alive but he is differently alive than he was before. Somehow he is quickened." And the secret of war is that *"Men like fighting. That is the force behind the war . . . We have been saying for a long time that war isn't civilized. We should have realized perhaps that civilization isn't human. Perhaps peace itself isn't human. Not in the same way as men are human."*[37]

She concluded with another truth, "just as deep and just as profound." "Women don't like war." But these were not truths that anyone in America was likely to admit as that country drew closer to participating, and Dodge, like the leaders of the left, was increasingly isolated. Young, for instance, having been involved in *The Masses* trial in 1917, found it difficult to sell his artwork; he survived largely by publishing in a Yiddish-language journal edited by Jacob Marinoff. Other figures on the left had to resort to other such expedients. And it was not only the left wing that was affected. Nineteen seventeen felt like a full stop for instance to Stieglitz, to Willard Huntington Wright (who edited the pro-German *New York Evening Mail*) and to Randolph Bourne, who was investigated by the police. Dreiser and Mencken were both branded as Germans. The *New Republic* was the only intellectual weekly which was in favor of America's entering the war.

Another effect of the war, or of its concomitants, was a move out of New York and toward—in the most important case—Taos, New Mexico. This is the dispersal to be discussed in the next chapter.

Mabel Dodge moved out of her Fifth Avenue home in 1916, going first to Croton-on-Hudson, where she had found a home for the dance school of Isadora and Elizabeth Duncan. Max Eastman and Floyd Dell followed her example. In her house lived Bobby Jones and Bayard Boyesen, and at times Reed and Maurice Sterne, who was to be her next husband.

She at first planned to move from New York to Paris, to promote modern art there, but then she met Sterne at a ballet rehearsal. She found him, she says, overripe, but with more dignity in his over-ripeness than Reed had in his greenness. She was pointing to a difference between European and American styles of manliness, but also between the world of the artist, in which women were prominent and primary, and the world of politics and history. Sterne was then a highly regarded painter, and had a lot of success with women, but he was also the victim of deep depressions and anxieties. He was a Russian Jew by birth, who arrived in this country at the age of eleven, and his childhood had been overshadowed by threats of anti-Semitic violence, often by the Cossacks themselves.

"What I liked about him was his handsome look of suffering. A dark torture ennobled him and added a great deal of dignity to that countenance, that would in later years become decidedly patriarchal. He was positively enveloped in a cloud of secrecy and caution. The man might have been in a jungle, so watchful was he . . ."[38]

Sterne was indeed a man bruised by early experiences of political and religious persecution. His older brother was sought by the Russian police while a student, and escaping only just in time, made his way to this country. Maurice and his mother sailed from Russia in 1889, and he studied at the National Academy of Design while working in a Third Avenue bar.

This history left him victim to periods of dejection and pessimism, and with various neuroses: he was unable to use the New York subway for a long time, unable to make decisions, unwilling to fight back against direct aggression. His mother seems to have exhorted him to be manly—for instance, to slap Mabel back if she hit him.[39] And no doubt because of this record of being dominated, he was ready to exploit protectors and evade responsibility. He was, for instance, ruthless with women. "My love affairs never lasted very long, not because I grew tired of my partners, but because I dreaded becoming too involved."[40] But he had a keen honesty, as these sentences suggest. Talking of his conversations with celebrities, he says, "After these interviews, I would remember little that the famous person had said, but every one of my own clever replies."[41] Mabel Dodge seems to have seen him from the start as raw material for her to mold (as well as an exotic type and a striking talent). She amazed him, he said: "For the first time in my life I could relax, rest my will, and do what someone else decided was best."[42]

His Jewishness was important to Mabel Dodge. She thought that he did not belong in the world of men; that he was at home only in his mother's crowded flat, "where she, wearing the hot black wig of Yiddish widowhood, cooked for him the foods of his childhood."[43] He belonged to the private life, not the public, and that was the direction in which she was turning in the face of the war. Though their relations were unhappy from the start—he was a practiced Don Juan, and she was very jealous—she felt she could transform him. She saw what he might be, what he ought to be; for instance, he ought to be a sculptor and not a painter. They married on August 17, 1917, and she sent him away the same day to Wyoming to paint that landscape.

A few weeks later he moved down to New Mexico, which she had heard about, and where she was to join him at the end of the year. She had seen pictures of Taos by Eanger Irving Couse and Mary Austin, had lectured on the Indians of the Southwest in Greenwich Village and attended the salon at 23 Fifth Avenue. This too was an experience she designed to do Sterne good. Before she herself left Croton to join him, she wrote, "You must feel the same affiliation with the Indians as you did with the East. [He had spent time in India and Bali.] They *are* the same blood and the same culture—totally unmixed with our known civilization."[44] But it was she herself who was to feel this profound affinity, and to make Taos a center for people who wanted to escape "white culture." (Taos had been "discovered" for painters in 1898, by Bert Phillips and Ernest Blumenschein, but they were traditionalists in art. It was Mabel Dodge who brought the modernists there.)

Even in Taos, the effects of the war atmosphere were felt. She summoned Andrew Dasburg and Robert Edmond Jones to join her there. Dasburg and Sterne, because of their German names, were suspected of being spies and agitators, and she was said to be trying to stir up disaffection among the Indians. In an absurd espionage plot, her cook, because he was called Seebach, was abducted and held hostage for a time. Similarly in Cleveland, John Reed's luggage was searched; and in New York, Willard Huntington Wright, a critic who expounded the new art theories, was persecuted by the police for his pacifist writings. (The persecution upset him so much he turned to writing detective stories instead of art criticism, under the name of S. S. Van Dine.) Alfred Stieglitz was forced to cease publication of *Camera Work* in 1917, and his protégé, Marius de Zayas, had to close his Modern Gallery in 1918.

What happened at Taos, at Mabel Dodge's behest, is a major example of the dispersal, and so must be described in the next chapter. But we may suggest here the different ways it affected different individuals—the way some were "selected by it" and some were not. The effect on Dasburg of the Taos experience was significant in his development as a painter. "Living and travelling in the dramatic mountains and valleys of the country fortified Dasburg's resolve to give up abstract art as an expressive vehicle."[45] Similarly Marin— later—responded to both the landscape and local culture, and is said to have been like D. H. Lawrence in his intuitive understanding of the Indian perspective. Stuart Davis, on the other hand, found nothing to paint in Taos and went back north to continue his studies of an eggbeating machine. Davis was more purely the modernist, and Taos was dedicated to an opposite enterprise. Max Eastman calls Davis "the most unbrotherly-hearted, unclass-conscious, arch-Bohemian, modernistical art-rebel" of the editors of *The Masses*.[46] Eastman tells of an encounter between Davis and Gene Debs, when the latter, assuming sympathy in the other man, grasped his hand as he poured out his political enthusiasm to him. Davis was stiffly silent, but when Debs left and his magnetic presence was removed, said, "Jesus, that man is alive!" (Duchamp would have been no more sympathetic politically, and might have been more sardonic in his comment.)

Marcel Duchamp was exempted from military service in France, but he felt himself under the pressure of military patriotism. According to some accounts, he was insulted on the streets of Paris by enthusiasts who wanted to see every young Frenchman sent to the front.[47] This inspired a bitterness in him against his countrymen, which lasted many years. And when Walter Pach suggested that he should move to America, where so many admired his painting, he accepted.[48] Indeed, before coming, he sent seven works to two exhibitions of French art at the Carroll Gallery, of which John Quinn bought three.

He was a great success socially in New York, being taken immediately into the circle of artists and intellectuals around Walter Arensberg, which included Wallace Stevens, William Carlos Williams, Marsden Hartley, Joseph Stella, and Charles Demuth. These people met regularly at the Arensberg apartment on Sixty-seventh Street, where Duchamp had a studio. Their evenings often ended with games of chess.

Duchamp was transformed here, according to people who had known him in France, like the Picabias. He became the center of everyone's attention because of his spontaneous high spirits, his handsomeness, and his piercing insights.[49] He earned a living by teaching French at two dollars an hour to a few favored pupils, like the Stettheimer sisters, eccentric amateurs of the arts. For a man of his temperament, with its anarchistic and nihilistic strains, exile and war at a distance could be favorable life conditions.

He has been said to have come to America as a missionary of insolence, a dandy; indeed Moira Roth suggests that he combined that role with that of femme fatale—an allusion to his alter ego, Rrose Sélavy.[50] The two roles of course combine distancing, mystery, and moral indifference; and the transvestism was another way Duchamp set out to disturb men of ordinary sensibility; his mocking revision of the Mona Lisa is, as Roth says, "disturbingly androgynous."[51] But what is most interesting about Duchamp is perhaps something almost opposite to these gestures of naughtiness—his alliance with Katherine Dreier.

One consequence of Duchamp's coming to this country was that he became the friend of this woman, so strikingly unlike him in style. Her family had been public servants and humanitarians in Germany,

long before they settled in Brooklyn. They were progressives: they
believed in and worked for the rights of women, children, and servants. The mother founded the German House for the Recreation of
Women and Children in 1908, and Katherine Dreier was its treasurer.
Of the four sisters, Mary and Margaret found careers in the women's
trade union movement, Katherine and Dorothea became painters.
They took lessons from Walter Shirlaw, and Katherine Dreier said
he taught her the connections between beauty, rhythm, and vitality,
and so prepared her to read Kandinsky and to make "the leap into
the great new expression in art."[52] She read Kandinsky in 1912, the
year she also went to the Cologne Exhibition and was overwhelmed
by the display of van Goghs.

She understood art in the terms given her by Kandinsky, and those
that she learned from Ruskin and Morris while living in London, and
above all those of theosophy. This new art was, for her, "a global
outpouring of repressed spirituality."[53] This was a far cry from Duchamp's usual way of talking about modernism, and some ludicrous
incongruities resulted. But a long-lasting relationship grew up between them, no doubt initially her work. When he went to Argentina
in 1918, she followed him, and for five months studied that country's
institutions of social welfare. Her book was called *Five Months in the
Argentine: From a Woman's Point of View*.

The nature of the link between them is perhaps suggested by her
letter of 1917 (apropos of his *Fountain*), in which she says that
American painters had "a certain brusqueness, a certain boldness,
a certain wholesome virility," but little spiritual quality.[54] Duchamp
was a delicate and graceful presence, by all accounts, and that can
be felt in his work. A different kind of link was that she loved
cryptography and the occult, and he loved teasing hidden (often
vulgar) meanings out of words and objects. But above all, "By pooling
their respective talents, these two forceful and self-willed individuals
accomplished more for the cause of modern art in America during
the 1920s than any of their contemporaries."[55] (One can agree to this
while pointing out that his will and forcefulness were much more
oblique and perverse than hers, and their cooperation remains a
paradox.) When he sent her the photograph of the woman he was to

marry (very briefly) in 1927, Dreier replied, "I know that if she becomes too powerful that out of self-protection you will vanish as you always have."[56]

It seems clear that he spoke to her of his career as a spiritual project, and in fairly conventional terms. In 1929 she tried to get him to join her in various modern art projects, but he refused, saying, "Don't see any pessimism in my decisions. They are only a way towards beatitude. Your life has been and is connected with the actions and reactions of so many people that you can hardly approve of my choice between a snale (sic) and a butterfly for a disguise. Please understand, I am trying for a minimum of action, gradually."[57]

As for the Wobblies after 1914, the leaders were arrested. In Chicago, on the eighth floor of the Department of Justice building, on September 5, 1917, there was a briefing session for six FBI agents, six detectives from the Chicago police, and seven members of the American Protective League—civilian businessmen who volunteered to help round up draft dodgers and dissenters. They were instructed in a search they were to conduct of the IWW headquarters at 1001 West Madison Street. Parallel operations were carried out the same day in San Francisco, Seattle, Portland, Pittsburgh, Cleveland, Detroit, Salt Lake City, Minneapolis, and Los Angeles. In Chicago the detectives spent three days packing up all the things they impounded, which weighed five tons. The newspapers reported that the IWW had plotted to paralyze work at army cantonments, having been funded by rich radicals.

Haywood asked Clarence Darrow to defend him, as he had before, but Darrow was busy with war work. On September 28 a grand jury returned an indictment against 166 Wobblies, under the title, *The United States* v. *William D. Haywood et al.* They were officially arrested that day, and opposite where they were given bail a cinema was playing *The Menace of the IWW* and *The Red Viper*. On September 30 Carl Sandburg, then a reporter for the *Chicago Daily News*, came to interview Haywood. "Haywood takes it easy. He discusses the alleged 10,000 crimes with the massive leisure of Hippo Vaughn pitching a shoutout. It was the voice of a man who sleeps well, digests what he eats, and requires neither sedates to soothe him, nor stimulants to stir him up." This was not of course true; Haywood suffered from an ulcerated stomach, as we know; but massive serenity was part of his image and part of his propaganda. It weighed heavily in his favor with the American public.

The Effects of the Russian Revolution

On our other two groups the revolution of 1917 took effect slowly and indirectly, but the IWW suffered sharply. Even in their case, however, the effect was continuous with that of the war. They had been accused first of being German sympathizers, then of being pacifists, and then of being Russian sympathizers; the common denominator to all the charges was that they were unpatriotic. The trial began April 1, 1918, and lasted five months—it was the longest criminal trial up to that date. John Reed, back from Russia, reported it. He described the defendants as "the boys who do the strong work of the world . . . One hundred and one *men*—lumberjacks, harvest hands, miners, editors."[58] The judge had "the face of Andrew Jackson three years dead."

Reed said he saw a likeness between the defendants and the executive committee of the Soviets, and could imagine them trying the judge as a counterrevolutionary. The hero of his story was of course Bill Haywood: "There goes Bill Haywood, with his black stetson above a face like a scarred mountain."[59] Haywood's three days of testimony were generally considered one of his finest performances, intellectually as well as emotionally; he was able to make the IWW concepts clear and at the same time familiar, with examples from American history; distinguishing between political and direct action, for instance, he described the Constitution as an example of the first, and the American Revolution itself as the second.

Haywood had expected to be acquitted, and had told all those accused to surrender and undergo trial, so there would be no charges left against them. Flynn and Tresca had disagreed with this strategy, and their distrust was justified, for he and his companions were found guilty. They were of course released on high bail, during appeals, but the feeling of the country was bitterly against them.

On Lincoln's birthday, 1919, fifty-four foreign-born Wobblies were deported. There were other trials in other parts of the country: in California 500 Wobblies were arrested between 1919 and 1924. In 1919 the Palmer Raids began, and 250 people were deported. Altogether 10,000 were arrested in the Red Scare.

In October 1920, when their last appeals had failed, Haywood and nine others decided not to report back to Fort Leavenworth. He was smuggled onto a ship and sailed for Russia. Passing the Statue of Liberty, "Saluting the old hag with her uplifted torch, I said: 'Goodbye, you've had your back turned on me too long. I am now going to the land of freedom.' "[60] This had serious consequences; his bail was of course forfeited, and one of his bondsmen, an old comrade called Mary Marcy took her life in despair. The IWW attorney, Otto Christessen, said Haywood had committed political hara-kiri. Clarence Darrow, who had subscribed one thousand dollars bail money, and had got another fifteen hundred dollars from a friend, said he was glad to see Haywood go.

Gurley Flynn, one of the few Wobbly leaders left in freedom, turned her energies to labor defense. In the atmosphere of grim repression, there was great need of this. In 1918 she founded the Workers' Defense Fund (which later brought Sacco and Vanzetti to general attention). She was affiliated with the National Civil Liberties Union, later the ACLU, of which she was a founder member. The IWW itself was shattered; some Wobblies drifted into the AFL: for instance, Justus Ebert, William E. Trautmann, and Giovannitti. Others, like Tresca, reverted to anarchism. But it was the Communist party, founded in 1919 by John Reed and others, which was the main heir of the old organization; it inherited William Z. Foster, Charles Ashleigh, Earl Browder, Jim Cannon—and ultimately, Gurley Flynn. The project of revolution went ahead, like that of modernism; but Moscow was the locus of the first, while New York was the locus of the second.

Reed had gone to Petrograd in September 1917 and reported on the events of the Revolution. The manuscript of *Ten Days That Shook the World* was with his publisher by mid-January 1919, and the book was read with enthusiasm by the Wobblies in jail—and by other old comrades in the same situation, like Emma Goldman. Reed had now found in Lenin a man of destiny beyond the scope of both Haywood and Villa, and in the Revolution an event large enough to save him from the conscious romanticism which had afflicted him before. He was now a full citizen of the world of men.

Of course many of his old friends in Greenwich Village were skeptical or disapproving. Mabel Dodge said his going to Russia was for "Adventure again, and perhaps a chance to lose himself in a great upheaval."[61] Max Eastman thought the Revolution had made him a "rather stern-mouthed earnest saint."[62] He found Reed "too bitter—too harsh—too damned adult."[63] Steffens said he had lost his smile, become "hard, intolerant, ruthless, clinched for the fight."[64]

Other people followed his example. Steffens himself made his own trip to Russia, and came back declaring that he had seen the future and it worked. Reed saw Emma Goldman in Moscow before he died. In England people like Shaw, Wells, and Sidney and Beatrice Webb made the same pilgrimage. Mary Heaton Vorse, after her visit to Moscow, where she saw Haywood, talked of the experience to John Collier, who wrote, "You told of Lenin, moving a pillar of cloud / And of cold fire, on towards Galilee."[65]

In October 1919 Reed went back to Sweden and got himself smuggled into Finland, and at the end of that year, crossed again into Russia. In February 1920 he prepared to leave, charged to return to America, to merge the IWW with the American Communist party. He was carrying a bagful of 102 diamonds, worth fourteen thousand dollars, and fifteen hundred dollars in cash. The diamonds were rumored to be Russian crown jewels, and to be intended to pay off Haywood's bail. But Reed was arrested at the last moment before his ship was to sail from Finland, and he was sent back to Russia. There he fell ill and died, on October 17, 1920.

The Dada Movement

The world revolution in the world of art that corresponded to the Bolshevik revolution in the realm of politics was called dada. The two were frequently compared at the time—for instance, by Duchamp's friend, Katherine Dreier—and though the two events were profoundly different, the use of the same word or concept for both is

243

more than a pun. Both intended to shatter the self-confidence of bourgeois culture so completely that it could never be repaired. Perhaps we may say that they succeeded, as far as high culture went.

Dada in fact began in Zurich in 1916, and was soon echoed in Berlin and Paris. When the Cabaret Voltaire opened in Zurich, on February 5, 1916, Hugo Ball, one of its leading spirits, said, "Our cabaret is a gesture. Every word spoken or sung here says at least one thing, that these humiliating times have not succeeded in wresting any respect from us."[66] Dada was a denial of respect and propriety even as those qualities are expressed in conventional modes of protest—which were felt to be contaminated by the system they protested against, because they protested within it as well as against it. Looking back, another pioneer of dada, Richard Huelsenbeck, wrote, "All of us were enemies of the old, rationalistic, bourgeois art, which we regarded as symptomatic of a culture about to crumble with the War. We loathed every form of an art that merely imitated nature and we admired, instead, the Cubists and Picasso."[67] (Cubism, however, could be considered conservative, as we have seen, and it was rather the bewildering variety and mutativeness of Picasso's art that they admired—the aspect in which Duchamp was his heir.) Hans Arp said that he and his wife renounced painting in oils at that time because, "we wanted to avoid any reminder of the paintings which seemed to us to be characteristic of a pretentious, self-satisfied world."[68]

Dada can be defined in a number of ways, and in some versions includes an artist like Kurt Schwitters, who made collages out of throwaways and wrote poems such as one that consisted exclusively of the letter W, and built a crazy house, called Merzbau. But this is not aggressively *anti*art, as is the truest dada, to be found in Tristan Tzara and Duchamp. Tzara said in his 1922 lecture on dada, "Art is not the most precious manifestation of life. Art has not the celestial and universal value that people like to attribute to it."[69] And Duchamp was to carry this recoil from art even further.

Surprisingly enough, 291 was quite receptive to dada. De Zayas brought out a proto-dada magazine, *291*, in twelve issues in 1915 and 1916. This was announced as both a magazine of satire and as representing modern French art. Picabia's machines were a prominent feature, but so were poems about women or claiming to express womanhood, for instance, de Zayas's *Femme*; Picabia's drawing, *Voil' Elle*; Meyer's *Woman*, and a visual poem by him and de Zayas, "Mental Reactions." Thematically, this will remind us of Duchamp (his magazine, *New York Dada*, included a Rube Goldberg machine, and his *Large Glass* is about Woman) and of the tradition he drew on—the tradition of *machines célibataires* and the misogynistic poems of Laforgue and Eliot.

The dominant tendency of the taste of the Arensberg group was toward dada, says Homer.[70] Arensberg, Duchamp, Stevens, Van Vechten, Kreymborg formed a coterie which loved Gertrude Stein and the French symbolists, says Wertheim. They founded various little magazines, like *Rogue* in 1915, and *Others*, which ran from July 1915 to May 1919, with a circulation of about three hundred. William Carlos Williams published in the latter.

In 1917 the Society of Independent Artists was founded by Walter Pach, Duchamp, and Picabia. The first president was Glackens, but Sloan was on the hanging committee, and he became president the following year and remained so till 1944. There were exhibitions with no jury, no prizes, and the artists listed in alphabetical order, to eliminate preferential treatment. The first, held at the Grand Central Palace, with twenty-five hundred works by thirteen hundred artists, was a great success. Williams read his futurist poem, "Overture to a Dance of Locomotives," and made the exhibition a symbolic event in his prologue to *Kora in Hell*. This was the organizational equivalent to those futurist paintings discussed before.

It was to this show that Duchamp sent in his upside-down urinal, signed R. Mutt. When it was not displayed, he resigned from the society in protest, because it was failing to live up to its creed of experiment and freedom. He was right, of course, but the committee perhaps recognized his challenge to art for what it was—the first in an infinite series, which in fact continued the rest of his life. Charles Demuth, always one of Duchamp's admirers, wrote a Gertrude Stein-like poem, "For Richard Mutt," for the dada magazine, *The Blind Man*, in 1917.

Duchamp can be said to have begun to produce *readymades* as early as 1913 (the upstanding bicycle wheel, and the retouched advertising picture, *Pharmacie*). They were given that name in 1915, and are a kind of dada, because they challenge the concept and status of art so directly.[71] Breton described them as "manufactured objects promoted to the dignity of art by the artist's will,"[72] which is accurate except that it misses the equivocation in *promoted* and the irony in *the artist's will*.

Jean Clair has contrasted the entry of Duchamp's *Fountain* into the art museum world with that of the Elgin marbles, a hundred years before. The Greek marbles, originally religious in their function, were transformed in the British Museum into "sacred" art. As Malraux said, *"L'âme du Musée imaginaire est la métamorphose des Dieux en sculptures quand ils ont perdu leur sacre."*[73] But Duchamp's readymades exploded that privileged aesthetic space, and he and his followers (in various arts, including music and dance) escaped the museum.

Clair sees a close connection between Duchamp's work on *The Large Glass*, which occupied him in the first years after he arrived in this country, and a literary work of science fiction, *Voyage au pays du quatrième dimension*. This story, by Gaston de Pawlowsky, was serialized in the magazine he edited, *Comoedia*, between 1907 and 1914 and issued as a book in 1923. Duchamp and Pawlowsky have in common a challenge they offer to the observer's point of view, and they replace science's axiomatics of the real with an axiomatics of the possible. Like Duchamp, Pawlowsky anthropomorphizes machines and loves the deformations of space created by fast movement. Above all, *The Large Glass* is the same kind of artwork as Pawlowsky's story: *"Manifeste anti-naturaliste, ce livre est un roman de l'Idée,"* says Pawlowsky ("An anti-naturalist manifesto, this book is a novel of ideas.")[74]

Michel Carrouges has made an interpretation of *The Large Glass* in connection with Kafka's "The Penal Colony," and various other works, by Jarry, Roussel, and Villiers de l'Ile Adam, in all of which machines intrude upon the processes of life. Carrouges says the twentieth century must reverse the tendency of thought since the Enlightenment. *"À la critique rationnaliste des mythes doit succéder la critique mythologique de la raison et des mythes."*[75] He found major support for his theory in Duchamp's work, for the main message of *The Large Glass* for him is *"C'est le grand minuit de la négation de la femme, et de l'athéisme, le coeur de la nuit du vendredi saint."*[76]

246

This interpretation has a lot of truth to it, but it pays no attention to the purely playful, meta-ironic aspect of Duchamp's mind—the dada aspect.

Katherine Dreier helped to found the Society for Independent Artists in 1917 and mixed with the modernists of the Arensberg circle. She was out of place there; heavy-footed in those nimble gatherings, says Aline Saarinen; an iceberg who wouldn't melt, says Henri-Pierre Roché. But she could not be displaced, partly because she became a friend and patron of Duchamp for the thirty-five years up to her death. Bohan suggests that her boldness and irrationality appealed to Duchamp, as a real-life dada concealed within a pompous haute-bourgeoise personality. When Man Ray gave a dada lecture on dada, she rose majestically at the end and joined him at the podium to say that she would now speak seriously about modern art. Ray simply resented her, but Duchamp may well have felt that that was the perfect gesture.

The pair they made together cannot but remind us of the Marx Brothers films; Dreier was as ebullient and embarrassing as Margaret Dumont; she was also as indestructible and so Groucho/Duchamp could safely betray her and high seriousness again and again. The two needed each other, because he needed a world which took art seriously as much as she needed his irreverent originality. Having voted against his *Fountain*, she wrote him that he must not resign from the society because his rare strength of character and spiritual sensitiveness were crucial if a more spiritual art were to establish itself in America.[77] This odd mixture of perceptiveness and imperceptiveness is to be found throughout her dealings with him. She explained his readymade snow shovel, for instance, as Duchamp's choice of the most perfect snow shovel in existence—which is, of course, far from Duchamp's intentions. (He told Cabanne, "The choice of readymades is based on visual indifference and a total absence of good and bad taste."[78] So that in her *Western Art and the New Era* we find her calling dadaists the bolsheviks of art, but saying that they have their constructive side, and have opened the eyes of many to beauty which otherwise might have passed unseen. The history of dada—the history of modernism as a whole—contains many such episodes, in which incompatible attitudes to art are tangled together.

Marsden Hartley, on the other hand, wrote an essay, "The Importance of Being Dada,"[79] which defined dada simply as showing the humor in existence.[80] The artist has insisted too much on his sufferings and his habits.[81] "Life as we know it is an essentially comic issue . . . reduce the size of the 'A' in art, to meet the size of the rest of the letters in one's speech . . . deliver art from the clutches of its idolators." Take away art's pricelessness and "make of it a new and engaging diversion, pastime, even dissipation, if you will."[82] This is, as Hartley's title implies, a rather Oscar Wilde and nineties version of dada; it ignores its energy of revolt as well as its strains of ugliness and insult, but it suggests the way dada was accommodated so that it could become part of the New York art scene, part of the project of modernism.

T H E
Dispersal

9

Margaret, all my dreams are coming true. My work is being fulfilled. Millions of workers are seeing the light. We have lived to see the breaking of the glorious Red Dawn.

> —BILL HAYWOOD, in 1918, as a prisoner in Fort Leavenworth, to Margaret Sanger

Art and Machinery

MARCEL DUCHAMP: *The only works of art that America has given are her plumbing and her bridges.*

FRANCIS PICABIA: *I have enlisted the machinery of the modern world, and introduced it into my studio. . . . I mean simply to work on and on until I attain the pinnacle of mechanical symbolism.*

Art and Nature

MAX WEBER: *When nature is reborn in us, it calls itself art.*

DOUANIER ROUSSEAU: *Don't forget Nature! (This was Rousseau's cry of farewell to Weber, as the latter's train pulled out of the Paris station, taking him home to practice art after his apprenticeship in France.)*

■

W e can see the later lives of these people and ideas in the form of a dispersal away from the focal point of New York in 1913. By 1920 the Wobblies had been crippled by government persecution, as we have seen, and its leaders turned to other organizations and ideas, and some of them to other places. Literal deportation occurred to many, and voluntary exile to others. John Reed died in Moscow and was buried in Red Square; the same thing happened to Bill Haywood within the decade, and to Gurley Flynn much later.

And if Moscow was one literal and symbolic destination, attracting the left, another was Taos, New Mexico, attracting some of the painters. That was where Mabel Dodge spent the rest of her life after 1920, and it was also a home to painters like John Sloan and Andrew Dasburg, and later, Georgia O'Keeffe. Through Mabel Dodge's agency, D. H. Lawrence also came there and joined in the work of studying the life of the Pueblo Indians, and recommending it to the rest of the world via the means of art. This was a lifework very unlike what was going on in Moscow, but both groups were trying to form an image of the good life that would save humanity from the evils of industrial capitalism and the bourgeois state.

Both groups lived far, geographically and in other ways, from the mainstreams of American life. And both followed models of work which veered away from the direct and simple activism of 1913.

Thus far this idea seems to apply neatly and symmetrically to the groups we have been studying: the IWW's heirs in the Communist party and elsewhere continued the project of revolution, and Duchamp, Man Ray, Picabia continued that of modernism. But in fact our group of painters split in two after 1913, dividing itself between those who went to the Southwest and those who stayed in New York. (The move away from New York is the important thing: Taos is simply the most important of a number of attractive landscapes, all representing nature.)

The painters of Taos did *not* continue the project of modernism: their life values of unconscious health, personal and cultural, were quite unlike those of Duchamp and his friends. They set to work rerooting themselves in a nonwhite culture and an untamed landscape—seeking to reappropriate them through art, though also through other means. (They themselves might have preferred to say that they were letting that landscape and culture reappropriate *them*.) Their work remained modern, since they were alert to contemporary art and indeed contemporary history—they felt themselves to be at the leading edge of contemporary consciousness—but it was not modernist. They did not, for instance, incorporate into their work the sardonic destructiveness of modern civilization, or its signs of bodiless abstraction.

This leads on to the paradox that the other painters, some of them in 1913 part of the same group, were *not* dispersed from New York. Duchamp of course came and went, and spent time in Paris, as did his friends; but that merely means that New York signals the habit of moving to and from other places, especially other capital cities. The group stayed where it was, with New York still its center, and even institutionalized itself and came to success there. The capital city of twentieth-century capitalism provided a friendly enough environment for their work. Calvin Tomkins, a writer for *The New Yorker* magazine, published two books about Duchamp in the 1960s aimed at a large general audience, and there are several other testimonies to his (and the other modernists') fascination for a large public. The paradox is that this, the one survival of the enthusiasms of 1913, the one not driven away from New York, was in spirit the one already dispersed—the one least rooted in a social time and place, least responsive to the joint social enterprises around it.

. . .

But let us first turn to the true heirs of the 1913 spirit, in its broadly human engagement, Dorothy Day and William Carlos Williams: those who stayed where they were, both literally and figuratively. They stayed in New York or New Jersey, and found their work there, in the streets and homes and shelters for the homeless. They stayed loyal to the engagement our main subjects repudiated; they insisted on combining a spiritual project, in art or politics, with ordinary, local, or traditional commitments—either combining the practice of art with action in service of their fellow men, or combining the agitation for political change with preservation of traditional religious forms and ceremonies.

In New York after 1918 Dorothy Day got to know Eugene O'Neill and other figures from the 1913 generation—O'Neill had been a friend of John Reed and Mabel Dodge, Andrew Dasburg, and Mary Heaton Vorse, and so on. Day's own generation of friends included Katherine Anne Porter, Malcolm Cowley, and Mike Gold, the communist and proletarian writer whom she was engaged to marry in 1918. She followed the practice of the Village in the matter of free sexuality, and had more than one abortion. In 1918 she moved in with Lionel Moise, a newspaperman ten years older than she, who had worked for the *Kansas City Star*, the *Chicago Tribune*, the *San Francisco Tribune*, and the *Los Angeles Express*. He had an IWW-like range of experience, as roustabout, seaman, and lumberjack, and loved animals and quoting Shakespeare. He had a reputation for being attractive to women but treating them badly; in that too he could be compared with Haywood and other Wobbly heroes.

By an odd coincidence, Ernest Hemingway worked with Moise in 1916, and was much struck by him—Moise was one of Hemingway's life-models. Thus we can see in these episodes of Day's life both a parallel to Flynn's relations with IWW men and a parallel to the literary tradition of America: Hemingway was a later version of Jack London and John Reed, and the women were both attracted to and suffered from that strain of macho egotism which recurred in the national character and literature.

In 1922 Day was arrested in an IWW boardinghouse in Chicago, and step by step she was drawn into her career of labor protest and then Catholic labor protest. After publishing a novel, *The Eleventh Virgin*, in 1924, she met a man she loved, Forster Batterham, and when she found herself pregnant by him, determined to bear the child (even at the expense of the man's love) and bring it up in the faith and order of the Church. It is not clear how seriously she had ever thought of herself as a literary artist, but obviously she gave up that career as she gave up various freedoms (or what are usually felt to be freedoms) at this point. She became in fact a remarkable writer, in her weekly essays for *The Catholic Worker*, but this was not modernist writing, and Day refused the option of modernism as a whole. For her, the spiritual project was the political one, blended into traditional religion.

William Carlos Williams, on the other hand, blended modernism with something like its opposite: with an "Americanist" populism. Neither he nor Day was wholly loyal to the original project. Day was not a revolutionary, and Williams was not a modernist poet (in this author's judgment). Both had other aims at heart, which they could not pursue without altering the direction in which the main ideas lay. This pattern of compromise is neither good nor bad in itself: Day seems the more interesting and impressive for the compromises she made, Williams the less. Other people will come to different judgments. For the moment the argument is only that they can be seen in these comparable terms.

Williams rejected the "pure" modernism of T. S. Eliot in order to stay an American poet. "When the *Dial* brought out 'The Waste Land' all our hilarity ended. It wiped out our world as if an atom bomb had been dropped upon it . . . To me especially it struck like a sardonic bullet. [Here the feeling is close to what he expresses about Duchamp's snub.] I felt at once that it had set me back twenty years, and I'm sure it did."[1] Eliot returned them all to the classroom. "Eliot had turned his back on the possibility of ever reviving my world . . . I had to watch him carry my world off with him, the fool, to the enemy . . ." This is very like the tone of Myers and du Bois about Arthur Davies and his promotion of modernism in the Show. But Williams, more talented than

they, and perhaps luckier, found a way to steer between innovation and tradition, and has consequently been credited with
freeing American poets in general from the iron chains of rhyme
and meter.[2]

There are similarities between T. S. Eliot and Duchamp: the frag-
mentation, the irony, the debt to Laforgue, the elaborate notes to
"The Waste Land" and to *The Large Glass*; one might say that the
literary equivalent to Duchamp's "extraordinary object" was Eliot's
poem. The audience of the 1920s gathered around *The Large Glass*
and "The Waste Land" in awe and curiosity, like the tribesmen round
the monolith in *2001*. These are the insignia that make both of them
modernists, and the similarity between the two can help us draw a
contrast between each one and William Carlos Williams. He felt
himself snubbed by both; in Duchamp's case it was a literal social
snub, in Eliot's it was the other man's poetics; but whereas Duchamp
retained Williams's respect and admiration, Eliot received the full
force of his resentment. Of course the issue of rivalry came up in the
first case and not in the second, since Williams was a poet and not
a painter.

"These were the years before the great catastrophe to our letters
—the appearance of T. S. Eliot's 'Waste Land.' There was heat in
us, a core and a drive that was gathering headway upon the theme
of a rediscovery of a primary impetus, the elementary principle of
art, in the local conditions. Our work staggered to a halt for a moment
under the blast of Eliot's genius which gave the poem back to the
academics. We did not know how to answer him."[3]

But if temporarily silenced, Williams eventually became a large
figure in American literature. When he died, he was praised as "the
total American writer."[4] He wrote forty-nine books in several genres,
including four long plays, four novels, fifty-two short stories, and six
hundred poems—plus the book-length poem *Paterson*. He also wrote
about the Paterson Strike in "The Wanderer" in *Al Que Quiere*.

Sometimes Williams implies a connection between his and his
friends' poetry and the New York realist painters. "We were writing
poems from the dung heap—the ashcan school. It is a fundamental
difference in the structure of our thought, which was not Eliot's."[5]
That certainly suggests one kind of parallel between Eliot's influence

and Duchamp's. But in actual artistic creed Williams allied himself not to the New York realists but to the modern American painters of Arensberg's circle or of Stieglitz's.[6]

Thus his stand in poetics was aggressively modernist and innovative. " 'The Establishment,' fixed in its commitments, has arrived at its last stand: the iambic pentameter, blank verse, the verse of Shakespeare and Marlowe which gave it its prestige. A full stop . . ."[7] He presented himself as naive, both as an American and as an individual. Chapter 1 of his autobiography begins, "I was an innocent sort of child and have remained so to this day."[8] And naivete and ordinariness, in various paradoxical combinations with sophistication and ambition, remained a key to his sense of himself. He marked himself off from his friend Ezra Pound in that Pound early displayed the flamboyant pride of an artist, while Williams claimed the humility and caution of a scientist. He was also aggressively Americanist. "The American idiom is the language we speak in the United States. It is characterized by certain differences from the language used among cultured Englishmen, being completely free from all influences which can be summed up as having to do with 'the Establishment'."[9] But his modernism made him also a formalist. What he wanted in poetry he called objectivism: a poem is an object that presents its case by its form—as a cubist painting does, or a symphony.

This was not Eliot's kind of formalism, and one crucial difference was Williams's vision of art as the means by which the religion of life values could be spread. However, Williams did not go to Taos, literally or in the spirit. His cult of life values was not so positively imprinted with the image of woman and nature, so negatively imprinted with man and adventure, as was, say, D. H. Lawrence's. *In the American Grain* gives a more adventure-dominated diagnosis of American culture than *Studies in Classic American Literature*. Williams remained in this matter a pre-1913 Americanist.

Through Sheeler, Williams got to know the precisionists, and there was a certain affinity between their pictures and his poetry. They were criticized because their pictures ignored those who worked on the machines they depicted, and Williams too depicted people struggling against illness and mental depression, not against poverty or economic depression. Both adapted modernism to native subject matter and traditional feelings in ways that make the modernism sometimes only superficial. Both lacked a political dimension, and Williams, like John Sloan, was inclined to see the artist as a spiritual entrepreneur, a type of rugged individualism. "The artist must save us—he is the only one who can," said Williams, apropos Walker Evans's photographs.[10] And when Harold Stearns attacked the exaggerated importance attributed to the artist (in *The Freeman*, in 1920) Williams replied as one personally attacked. Duchamp's blasphemies against art upset Williams, for whom *the artist* was a sacred concept, which he trusted, to redeem him from all his misdeeds.

He took important clues from French painting: "For a hundred years one of the cleanest, most alert and fecund avenues of human endeavor, a positive point of intellectual assistance from which work may depart in any direction."[11] But he also insisted on American subject matter and an Americanist and macho ideology. This was the line he took in his essays on American history, *In the American Grain*, where he talks about the eunuchs of New England. Thus he combined some of the most advanced aesthetic ideas of the Armory Show with some cultural ideas that were retrograde already in 1913.

But one thing which works powerfully to redeem him, even as an artist, is his medical practice in Rutherford. Like Chekhov, he found practical work parallel with his writing, and vice versa. "As a writer I have been a physician, and as a physician a writer."[12] This tied him to ordinary experience, and for this there was a close equivalent in the life of Dorothy Day, which makes the big city scene belong to them, and not to Duchamp at all, from most points of view. Williams says, "And my medicine was the thing which gained me entrance to these secret gardens of the self. It lay there, another world, in the self. I was permitted by my medical badge to follow the poor defeated body into those gulfs and grottoes . . ."[13] He saw one and half million patients, and delivered two thousand babies, by his count, between 1910 and 1951. I know of no count of the homeless and unemployed whom Dorothy Day cared for in the course of her career, but their presence can be felt in the columns she wrote for *The Catholic Worker*.

No such thing can be felt in Duchamp's paintings, but it would be a mistake to deny Duchamp (and Eliot in London, and Stein in Paris) all power to represent his or her city. Insofar as the cubist and futurist array of skyscrapers existed, and the forces of speed and change could be felt in those streets, Duchamp was its eye or its consciousness. If he is remote from whole ranges of human experience and values, so is it.

The most striking case of dispersal was the move of artists and intellectuals away from New York to New Mexico, either to spend their winters there or to be permanent residents. They had come to feel they could not do their work in the city and that merely to be there poisoned them.

Mabel Dodge had moved to Taos at the end of 1917, where she almost immediately began a liaison with Tony Luhan, a Pueblo Indian. According to Maurice Sterne, Tony had traveled with a Wild West Show and had appeared at, for instance, Coney Island; but Mabel found in him that other mode of being she was in search of, and this proved the most stable as well as the longest-lasting of her relationships with men. Her marriage to Sterne, always unhappy, crumbled as soon as she arrived in Taos. She invited Andrew Dasburg and Bobby Jones to join her immediately, and soon began to write letters to D. H. Lawrence saying that he too would find what he was looking for in New Mexico. John Collier came in 1920. Carl Gustav Jung came in 1925. Lawrence arrived in 1922, and put into the best words what she and others had found there. Two or three of the central Stieglitz circle artists came in time—notably Marin, O'Keeffe, and Paul Strand. And after Lawrence's death in 1930 (and his partial defection before that) she brought Robinson Jeffers out from California to replace him.

The Pueblo people she met, the Tiwa, were one of the most conservative of the twenty-two tribes who were settled from eastern New Mexico to western Arizona.[14] She says, "The singular raging lust for individuality and separateness had been impelling me all my years as it did everyone else on earth—when all of a sudden I was brought up against the Tribe . . . where virtue lay in wholeness instead of in dismemberment."[15]

Her attention was not focused exclusively on white artists or on art itself. She was concerned with the Indians of Taos (it was for her an Indian place, and its connections with Kit Carson, for instance, were of no interest to her). She herself taught knitting and sewing to the women of the Taos pueblo, and her friend John Collier became Federal Commissioner for Indian Affairs in 1933.

In his life story, *From Every Zenith*, Collier says, "The theme of this book is the community."[16] And "in 1921 a new depth of community was made known to me by the Red Indians."[17] In a poem of that year he declared:

> *Man as man has power*
> *To join in the creation of the God.*

The Indians, he says, "know the community which holds heaven on earth and beyond earth."[18] They had been his salvation, because the year 1919 had seen "the fading away of all that I, we, all of us, had put all of our being into."[19] The idea gradually came to him that the ethos and genius of the West might be the earth's doom as well as its hope.[20] The great decade after 1908, which he had known in New York, why had it failed?[21] The answer is that white culture is fatally flawed, and the sensitive individual can renew his or her life only by rerooting himself or herself elsewhere—in the Native American culture of the Southwest.

His book, *The Indians of the Americas*, begins, "They had the secret the world has lost." They have it now; and this secret is " 'Through his society, and only through his society, man experiences greatness; through it, he unites with the universe and the God, and through it, he is freed from all fear.' "[22] Collier said that the experience at Taos was paralleled only by his experience in reading Walt Whitman at the age of fifteen,[23] and he also compares it with Greek theater.[24] These references suggest how Taos could align itself with seemingly remote themes we have met before in other figures of this story—in Percy MacKaye, for instance. Western man, Collier says, has accepted the isolation of the individual as fundamental, accepted the imprisoning dichotomies of the Cartesian century, but the Indians show us a reverence and passion for the earth and its web of life and for the mysteries of personality.

It was usually the art of the Indians which aroused these newcomers' enthusiasm, but art broadly defined. John Sloan, who arrived in 1919, wrote, "The work of American Indians is a perfect demonstration that things not generally regarded as works of graphic or plastic art, are indeed the work of artists. Their pots, blankets, paintings are so evidently inspired by a consciousness of life, plus a thing we have not got—a great tradition."[25] Sloan was president of the Exposition of Indian Tribal Arts in 1931. He and Oliver la Farge wrote the catalog.

Max Weber we have described as a Taos artist in spirit; his aesthetic philosophy led him to a comparable love of primitive art. "A pot, a cup, a piece of calico, a chair, a mantel, a frame, the binding of a book, the trimming of a dress . . . these we live with."[26] D. H. Lawrence says things much like that, and Weber's ideas remind us of both Lawrence and Heidegger. "The whole race of Egypt built the Sphinx and their temples. All Greece shaped the Parthenon."[27] His stress is not on the individual artist but on the cultural tradition, which is also religious. "A form must be more than a form; it must suggest the sacred more only found in the spiritual."[28] And this is all a worship of nature. "When nature is reborn in us, it calls itself art."[29] He would rather *make* anything, than know about everything, he says in an essay called "Things"; "I would rather dig up things by the roots in a garden I have dug and sowed myself."[30] All these ideas are deeply opposite to the modernism of Duchamp.

John Marin was another Taos artist, even before he got there. The fourth of his four points of aesthetics is "The artist must from time to time renew his acquaintance with the elemental big forms which 'have everything': sky, sea, mountain, plain . . ."[31] Thus he described the sea, in September 1938: "When you are on it you are enveloped in its—BIG SMELL—To bring something of it back—I for one— hope . . . that my paint too shall smell—a little smell—as a minute equivalent to that great salty smell—out there—that it shall give forth an honest healthy stench . . ."[32] Thus in his own mind he was a realist, consistently creating paintings from the natural forms, no matter how much he experimented with form. "The sea that I paint may not be *the* sea, but it is *a* sea, not an abstraction, he says."[33] In a foreword to a book about him, Marin wrote,

I am a great believer in—Health . . .
  There's the so-called—abstractionist—the so-called—non-objective approach
    quite too often—a diseased approach
    or from another point of view—streamlined of all humanity . . .

This is what Maurice Sterne also said: "The abstractionists turned away from Nature.[34] Sterne was not a Taos artist; he left after a brief stay there—in part, no doubt, because of the domestic contretemps between him, Mabel, and Tony—but he shared the Taos artists' negative analysis of modernism. "The 'new art' is a gesture of frustration and ineptitude in carrying on from where the masters left off."[35] He blamed Picasso above all: "He is a challenger with a colossal ego, always trying to prove his superiority to himself and to the world."[36] . . . "for *la gloire* he became a monotheist, who believes in no other God but himself."[37] "The new artists were instead intent upon self-exploitation and experimentation with new forms. They denied the basic fact that the great pictorial images arise from the discovery of previously unknown aspects of nature."[38] He was fighting a losing battle; by the 1940s Sterne was unfashionable, by the fifties, forgotten, but in 1926 his exhibition had sold out, and in 1927 he turned down a commission to paint two portraits at thirty thousand dollars each, and earned sixty thousand dollars in 1930, while in 1933 the Museum of Modern Art gave him its first one-man show for an American artist. Perhaps if he had become a Taos artist he might have built a solider reputation.

The visitors to Taos were enthusiastic about the Indian serapes, jewelery, and pottery, and sent examples back to New York. (Dolly Sloan managed a Gallery of Indian Art there from 1920 to 1924.) Marsden Hartley, who moved to Santa Fe in 1918, wrote about the dances in much the way that D. H. Lawrence was to do. John Collier was won over to devote his energies to the Indians by their Dance of the Red Deer. John Marin loved the dancing—one of his favorite books was D. H. Lawrence's *Etruscan Places,*about another of these alternative cultures, again one in which dancing played an important part. In the case of Andrew Dasburg, as we know, the impact of the landscape was great, while Stuart Davis, "the most inventive and original of American cubists,"[39] found nothing to paint in Taos.

Marin was like Dasburg, and turned back from abstraction toward natural growth as the principle of painting. He called that the Great Law—what the Chinese called "the spirit's resonance."[40] If God existed, for Marin, he was the Earth (a word he always capitalized) and its Growing Things. He loved the way animals walked: the respect with which they put down their feet on the Earth. He distrusted intellectuals and critics, and hated abstract art, which he called abstractionist, because it did not come from nature.

> Go look at the bird's flight—the man's walk—
>   the sea's movement
> They have a way—to keep their motion—
>   nature's laws of motion have to be obeyed—
>   and you have to follow along . . .
> . . . the Sun's pull is just right
> Just look up—the Sun is shining
> The Earth is here and all is well—the basic law
>   is being obeyed . . .

And though his art is not explicitly sexual, his aesthetics are.

> . . . and that's the trouble with most art endeavor it is not
> sexual—
>   has no sex—that everything that lives was born of SEX.[41]

These are vitalist ideas which were popular in the Stieglitz circle, and many other places, before 1913. But they have been reborn after the war, with a new keenness of relevance, seen in the stress on Nature and Woman, sexuality and tribal cultures, and the repudiation of the city-life elements of the older, looser vitalism. One way to measure the change is to look at the difference between Stieglitz's pre-1914 photographs, like *The Hand of Man*, and the hundreds of photographs he took of Georgia O'Keeffe, and of parts of her body, after the war. The former has a good deal in common with the paintings of the New York realists, the latter belong decidedly to the erotic movement.

O'Keeffe, born in 1888, enrolled in Art Students League classes in 1907, and won prizes there, but gave up painting for four years, because it seemed that there was nothing new to be done in art, until in 1912 she found a teacher she liked, and in 1915 decided to paint only what was in her head. The following year Stieglitz saw some of her drawings and said, "Finally, a woman on paper." She lived with him from 1918 on, and both his photographs of her and her own paintings belong to the new eroticism.

O'Keeffe came to Taos for the summer in 1929 and formed a friendship with Tony Luhan. (Marin came later the same summer, and again in 1930, and produced nearly a hundred watercolors there.) After Stieglitz's death, O'Keeffe began to spend most of her time in New Mexico, and her paintings are widely interpreted as having female-erotic significance. Linda Nochlin, for instance, speaks of O'Keeffe's flowers as "analogous to the sexually awakened, intuitive heroines of D. H. Lawrence's fiction."[42] Pamela Allara extends this argument out to cover other artists in the Stieglitz circle. "Sexual symbolism was common among the painters of the Stieglitz circle, and Dove's use of it [here] is as direct and unaffected as Hartley's (in *Tinseled Flowers* 1917) and just as convincing a testimony to the generative powers of nature."[43] This article compares O'Keeffe's *Black Iris* (1926) and *Jack in the Pulpit* (1926) with Dove's *Sunrise I* (1937).

In the May 1925 issue of *Theater Arts Monthly*, Mabel Dodge published an essay called "A Bridge Between Two Cultures." She argued that any culture absolutely needs the static virtues of the Pueblo Indians. The great Indian rituals have grown out of a reverence for the soil and the wonder at fertility. It is a six-hundred-year-old culture, Apollonian in the sense Ruth Benedict gives that term—a culture which renews itself cyclically, rather than progressing lineally, which is therefore stable as opposed to explosive in the mode of white culture. (This is Lévi-Strauss's distinction between the modern thermodynamic culture, and its traditional clocklike predecessor.)

She suggested that a great outdoor theater should be built at the foot of the Sacred Mountain of Taos, and a sketch of it was drawn by Bobby Jones; Eugene O'Neill might be the theater's dramatist.

This was a scheme very like those that Rudolf von Laban was developing at that time, ideas begun in the European equivalent of Taos—the Swiss village of Ascona. For of course the forces at work in America, the set of options people had to choose between, were also to be found in Europe.

But New York became the homeland of Duchamp and his kind of modernism—the kind in which a dandified dada held the hegemony. This did not happen immediately or officially—indeed, before 1950, any such summary would have seemed absurd even to art lovers, but we can now see that in an undercover way that outcome was shaping itself through the decades.

It is, admittedly, paradoxical, to connect Duchamp with a homeland—he being so essentially and voluntarily an exile—but that is why one can talk of a general dispersal from New York even while he stayed there. At the heart of this homeland was an absence, a flickering trace, rather than a presence, a negation as powerful in its way as the Wobblies'.

Duchamp was commissioned to do a cover for *Vogue* magazine, and he made a portrait of George Washington out of a Stars and Stripes flag. We can contrast this with Bill Haywood's poster of the national flag with a scornful query on every stripe—a revolutionary icon. *Vogue*, a fashion magazine, was the appropriate place for Duchamp's irony. But the magazine did not use it, presumably because its playfulness felt too mocking and antinomian. And the two icons, or anti-icons, have in fact much in common, as conceptual-visual works of the imagination. In his infinitely remote way, Duchamp remained an ally of Haywood, secreted in the heart of the imperial capital.

Duchamp did not paint New York; indeed, he scarcely painted anything at all; but he was a presence at the heart of the city's art world which oriented other people's minds like a magnetic pole. It was a presence marked by irreverence and irresponsibility in many ways, and yet it was also felt as spiritually intense. Henri-Pierre Roché, for instance, in "Souvenirs of Marcel Duchamp," uses con-

ventional moral/religious language to praise him. He speaks of Duchamp's reducing his needs and his possessions to a minimum, in
order to remain truly free, and of the young loving him because he
lived without ambition; the young found a man's worth revealed only
in the lonely depths of his soul, and judged by this criterion, Duchamp
rated very high. Roché also wrote a novel *Victor* in the late 1950s,
which is a transparent roman à clef, about New York in 1916, and
has Duchamp as hero; he is described as *"un diable pour le bourgeois
. . . la lueur au bout du tunnel pour les autres. Il est notre prince
charmant, notre magicien, notre . . ."* One of the young women hope-
lessly in love with him realizes that he is not meant to belong to her
or any other individual; he is a missionary, sent to all, not to an
individual.[44] His mission was to free art and the imagination from
every bondage to "social" values.

He was fascinated by machines, both in their literal working and
in their cultural significance, just as he was fascinated by science—
by active, unself-conscious forms of imagination, not sleek with the
self-congratulation of art. He said that in *The Bride Stripped Bare by
Her Bachelors, Even* (*The Large Glass*) he had wanted to go back to
a completely dry drawing, and a dry conception of art, employing
exactness, precision, and chance.[45] And he damaged his eyesight by
his eight years of work on that painting, the passion which met so
many internal confusions and inhibitions in the realm of art ran pure
and strong in the realm of craft.

His friend and disciple, Man Ray, points to Duchamp's preoc-
cupation with the materials of glass and string—their connotations
being of transparency and mutability—and points also to his love for
endgames in chess.[46] Ray himself found a similar pleasure in painting
with an air-brush: "It was thrilling to paint a picture, hardly touching
the surface—a purely cerebral act, as it were."[47]

Duchamp's other friend, Picabia, preceded him in his enthusiasm
for machines, and America as the land of machines. "I have been
profoundly impressed by the vast mechanical development in America. The machine has become more than a mere adjunct of life. It is
really part of human life . . . perhaps the very soul. In seeking forms
through which to interpret ideas or by which to explore human char-

acteristics I have come at length upon the form which appears most brilliantly plastic and fraught with symbolism."[48] And Gleizes called American art "a leap head first into the impersonal."[49]

But it is Duchamp above all who haunts the art of other painters, of his generation and the next, in a strangely personal way. In one self-portrait, for instance, Charles Sheeler represents himself as a telephone, and that being a two-way communication machine, the image is thought to be an allusion also to Duchamp.[50] Indeed, Sheeler also verbally described Duchamp in such terms. "He was built with the precision and sensitiveness of an instrument for making scientific machinery." The semireflecting window in the same picture is often thought to be another Duchamp allusion, because of the symbolic importance which windows (especially shop windows) had for him. More than a frame, a window, through which and into which we look, both represents and mocks both our desire and its limitation.

Charles Demuth, who often painted Duchamp, is perhaps most famous for *My Egypt* of 1927 which showed grain elevators with lines of force (like those in *Nude Descending a Staircase*) in a pyramidlike monumentality, symmetry, and frontality. Demuth managed to stay friends with both Duchamp and Stieglitz, despite the animosity between the two, telling the latter in 1928 that the greatest picture of their times was *The Bride Stripped Bare by Her Bachelors, Even*. In 1925 Demuth was one of the Seven Americans of Stieglitz's show; they were, besides Demuth and Stieglitz himself, O'Keeffe, Marsden Hartley, John Marin, Paul Strand, and Arthur Dove; it was to the promotion of these artists that Stieglitz devoted most of his energies for the rest of his life.

When Duchamp arrived in New York he was already at work on *The Large Glass*, and that continued to occupy him up to 1923. He gave it to the Arensbergs while he was doing it, but when they moved to Los Angeles in 1921 they sold it to Katherine Dreier, so that he could continue to work on it. He did so for another two years, before he got bored. The object was displayed in 1926, and then recrated and stored, but the handlers were careless and the glass panes broke. When this was discovered in 1931, Duchamp promised to mend it, and finally took two months in 1936 to glue the fragments together, painstakingly; he found that the cracks enhanced his work—that chance had now played exactly the part in the composition which he had wanted.

He thus showed a conservative feeling about his work that has been as strong as his opposite feelings of easy boredom, reckless innovation, and refusal. Even though his works emerged from within him "unintentionally" (and by grace of hazard, not of any "unconscious") he always wanted to know where they were, and put a great deal of energy into reproducing some of them perfectly. He was in these ways a typical proud artist.

The Large Glass is a diagram, as well as a depiction, of a fantasy machine or machines. This extraordinary object is a pane of glass (actually—since the breaking—several panes glued to each other) on which diagrams ahave been drawn in oil paint, varnish, lead wire, silvering, and dust. It is divided horizontally into two regions, of which the upper one belongs to the bride, the lower to her bachelors (that is, the men who lust after her). The bride herself is an inconspicuous perpendicular figure, hanging at the top left; to her side is an enormous horizontal Milky Way, or cinematic blossoming of the bride's allure. This is a softly irregular and colored natural form. In the lower half, besides the bachelors themselves (a priest, a soldier, a mailman, etc., in their respective uniforms), there are the various machines of their lust, whose revolutions result in tiny shell bursts of desire in the upper half, aimed at but missing the bride and her beauty. (This is the briefest possible account of the work, and it should be emphasized that part of its significance lies outside itself —in the mass of interpretation and annotation which gathers about it—beginning with Duchamp's own notes.)

He invented a new physics to explain the laws of *The Large Glass*, a new mathematics for its units of measurement, and condensed language for its ideas—amusing physics, oscillating density, uncontrollable weight and emancipated metals, etc. In all this, he was following up the ideas of Picasso and his friends (and the model of Alfred Jarry). In 1910 Leon Werth wrote, apropos Picasso, "If geometry owes its certainty to the suggestions of our senses, why not reverse the process and go from geometry to nature?"[51] But as important as geometry is the idea of chance, of randomness. Duchamp's *Stoppages Etalon* are one kind of canned chance; another is his *Musical Erratum*, composed by him and his sisters, pulling musical notes out of a hat.

After stopping work on *The Large Glass*, Duchamp devoted most of his energies to chess, and in 1927 was one of the top twenty-five players in the USA. It was widely supposed that he had given up painting for good; that idea was part of his myth. After his death, however, it was found that he had been at work for years, secretly, on the construct called *Étant donnés*. This consists of a naked female mannequin outstretched in a rather elaborate landscape (it includes, for instance, a running stream); both figure and landscape are would-be naturalistic, according to an old-fashioned and naive fairground taste, and the viewer can see it only by looking through a hole which focuses his or her eye on the woman's vagina. Since the viewer is subjected to this experience inside one of the great museums of art, one of our temples of sensibility, it is clear that part of what Duchamp is mocking is our faith that our love of art (our love of Duchamp) has nothing in common with sexual voyeurism. And the secrecy and carefulness with which this work was built add again to our ambivalence—to our sense of *his* ambivalence—about art; they show his recoil from it to be both an ascetic passion and a mocking game—mocking others as much as himself.

As for the ascetic passion, when asked in an interview for "a last word for the readers of *Show*," Duchamp said to his interlocutor, "That's easy. Beware of artists. Artists are beasts . . . All artists since Courbet have been beasts. All artists should be in institutions for exaggerated egos. Courbet was the first to say, 'Take my art or leave it. I am free.' That was in 1860. Since then, every artist has felt he had to be freer than the last . . . They *call* it freedom. Drunks are put in jail. Why should artists' egos be allowed to overflow and poison the atmosphere? Can't you just smell the stench?"[52] That is passionate enough; but of course it is followed, in Duchamp's ethic and rhetoric, by something quite opposite.

Duchamp's influence is acknowledged to be strong on Tinguely, Cage, Matta, Rauschenberg, Cunningham—the postmodernists, in various arts. But he has been dear to other modernist groups. Surrealism was the French child and heir of dada, and somewhat closer to the original than the American child, so it is not surprising that its adherents admired Duchamp. André Breton, the founder, called him the most intelligent man of the twentieth century. His essay on *The Large Glass*, titled *"La Phare de la Mariée,"* appeared in the magazine *Le Minotaure* in October 1934. (The title derives from Baudelaire's reference to the great painters of the past as lighthouses of civilization; but the bride has a somewhat opposite function—to lure ships toward itself, only to wreck them—since it is a work of art that mocks art.) He spoke of Duchamp's fabulous hunt through virgin territory, at the frontiers of eroticism, of philosophical specu- lation, of the spirit of sporting competition, of the most recent doings of science, of lyricism, and of humor. At the heart of the painting Breton saw (surely rightly) *"une interprétation mécaniste, cynique, du phénomène amoureux"* ("a mechanical and cynical interpretation of the phenomena of eroticism").[53]

Breton made a hero of Duchamp, as he had before of Jacques Vaché, the surrealist who committed suicide young, and whom Breton called the archangel. (It is worth noting that Duchamp himself much admired Vaché.) Predictably enough, Duchamp evaded Breton's pur- suit of him as an ally, and Breton apparently felt rather bitter about Duchamp's coldness.[54] But it seems, less predictably, that the latter felt some guilt over this. When Breton died, Duchamp said, "I have never known a man who had a greater capacity for love, a greater power for loving the greatness of life . . . He was the lover of love in a world that believes in prostitution . . . for me, it [surrealism] was the incarnation of the most beautiful, youthful dream of a moment in the world."[55] Nearly everything in that remark is extraordinary, coming from Duchamp, and seems to indicate a sense of obligation and a regret that his own sense of the truth forbade him to respond to Breton.

His own sense of the truth was, however, quite self-contradictory. There is an implicit aesthetic idealism in his remark about surrealism, and we find the same thing, and we meet it with the same amazement in Man Ray, Duchamp's twin in skepticism most of the time. Telling how he stole paints as a child, he comments, "My conscience did not trouble me, as I felt I was doing this for a very noble cause. I considered the painting of a picture the acme of human accomplishment; even today, the conviction still persists. At least I consider all artists as privileged and sacred beings, whatever they may produce."[56] One of those privileges is within love relationships, where the artist is expected to take more than he gives; this is clear in Ray's comments on Duchamp's relationships, and seems to be clear in those relationships themselves. But as we have seen, this behavior does not impair, it rather enhances, Duchamp's claims to a spiritual, even a moral leadership among artists.

But—and this contradiction is a part of Duchamp's true interest —we find him vehemently denying all this himself. "Art has absolutely no existence as veracity, as truth. People always speak of it with this great religious reverence, but why? . . . I'm afraid I'm an agnostic in art. I just don't believe in it with all the mystical trimmings. As a drug it's probably very useful for a number of people, very sedative, but as a religion it's not even as good as God."[57] This is sometimes interpreted as Duchamp's preference for life over art; but the life he loved was essentially marginal and nonpurposeful—quite disconnected from any organized values. Art is the one thing he might have believed in—there was far less likelihood of his believing in politics or religion or erotic values, in what either the Wobblies or the artists of Taos believed in. "We are so fond of ourselves, we think we are little gods of the earth—I have my doubts about it, that's all . . . The word law is against my principles."[58] His was a deconstructed mind, joining hands on one side with Nabokov, on the other with Derrida. "I'm a pseudo all in all, that's my characteristic. I never could stand the seriousness of life, but when the seriousness is tinted with humor, it makes a nicer color."[59]

Despite his disengagement, he had a good deal of influence, quite directly, on taste in America. He worked occasionally for Katherine Dreier's Société Anonyme, making modern art known in America; Peggy Guggenheim said he taught her everything she knew; Sidney Janis sought his advice on new artists' work. An éminence grise to private collectors, he gradually but greatly affected what we see in museums and galleries.[60] He did the decor of the galleries in which the great surrealist exhibitions were held: at the 1938 Paris exhibition, he had dead leaves on the floor and twelve hundred coal sacks suspended from above; in the 1942 New York exhibition, he had a web of string, several miles long; in the 1947 Paris exhibition, the catalog had a sponge rubber breast, labeled Please touch.

Duchamp worked for the cause of modernism. He, Man Ray, and Katherine Dreier founded their Société Anonyme, for the promotion of modern art in 1920, at a time when some of the modern art galleries and little magazines were closing down. The nationalist reaction of the American Scene painters was beginning to be felt, and former pundits of modernism were falling silent; Stieglitz was confining his efforts to his own artists. By 1926 it was widely said that cubism was over.

The Société Anonyme held ten exhibitions in 1921, plus three symposia and many lectures. Nearly all the work was done by Dreier, who issued press releases, gave lunch to journalists, and offered herself as a lecturer to all sorts of groups and organizations. Her book *Western Art*, published in 1923, is a collection of such lectures.

The society had eighty-six members in its first year, but by 1924 only six or seven were coming to business meetings, and after that year she gave up the attempt to put on exhibitions in the society's own premises. She found other galleries willing to give her space, and most notably the Brooklyn Museum allowed her to put on an International Exhibition of Modern Art in 1926, which showed some three hundred works, by a hundred and six artists, of whom fewer than a quarter were French. Picasso and Braque were entirely omitted, as traitors to the cause of abstract art. Dreier's interest was especially in German painters, but it spread far beyond them.

Her ideas about art owed much to Rudolf Steiner and Madame Blavatsky, as well as Kandinsky and Mondrian. Art's function, she thought, was to free the beholder's spirit and enlarge his vision.[61] There was thus a religious color to her concepts. She wanted to call the society the Modern Ark, and her manifesto spoke of minds that are sensitive to the vibrations of a new era—its Finer Forces. She said that since 1908 we had had a new art, in harmony with our new science (Einstein had eliminated time and space, and messages were being received from Mars).[62]

Duchamp would not commit himself to the society's cause in any total way. In October 1928, when she wrote him about the danger that the society might collapse, he replied, "The more I live among artists, the more I am convinced that they are fakes from the minute that they get to be successful in the smallest way. This means also that all the dogs around the artist are crooks. If you see the combination *fakes and crooks*—how have you been able to keep some kind of faith—and in what?" Don't try to change a crook into an honest man or a fake into a fakir. "I have lost so much interest in the question that I don't suffer from it—you still do."[63] This is another way in which his aesthetic asceticism expressed itself.

Duchamp must have caused Dreier many disappointments. In 1928 she took up the cause of another young man, Ted Shawn, the dancer. She painted an abstract portrait of him in 1929, financed a performance tour of Germany for him in 1930 and 1931, and published a book about him in 1933. But Duchamp remained her main interest. In the 1930s the society in effect ceased to act, and she was more the collector and lender of pictures. In 1941 she gave her collection to Yale, though she continued to add to it up to 1950, when the Société Anonyme was formally dissolved and the catalog published. Duchamp worked on the catalog with her, and when she died he was her executor.

Nevertheless, they represent opposing ideas of art, and it is of course Duchamp's idea which is important, not Dreier's, for the history of painting as painters have read it. But when the Armory Show was reconstituted on its fiftieth anniversary, one of the sponsors was the Henry Street Settlement; and in the statement by the Settlement it is Dreier's idea which is expressed. The faith of the Settlement, we are told, is that "every individual human being, and every human community, needs the fulfillment of creative contact with the arts."[64] The social-moral function of culture is spelled out with unembarrassed didacticism. "Through these art programs . . . troubled youngsters can often be reached . . . Girls and boys who might otherwise be going home to empty apartments or to afternoons and evenings of trouble-breeding idleness and boredom, find in sculpture, dance, painting, or music, an absorbing outlet."[65] The Settlement claimed the right and the honor to sponsor this reconstitution of the Show because the latter was so important in the history of American painting, and because that painting played an organic part in the life of the Henry Street community, and in shaping its character. This is the voice of Katherine Sophie Dreier, and it is her spirit we see casting the net of culture yet again over the turbulent protests and defiant frivolity of Duchamp, Picasso, Picabia, etc., etc. But of course modernism cannot be contained by the net of culture, any more than it can escape that net.

Octavio Paz, perhaps the most comprehensive interpreter of *The Large Glass*, sees Duchamp as the opposite of Picasso, in the sense that the latter's career represents a *vertigo of acceleration*, and the former's a *vertigo of delay* (i.e., of evasion, refusal, silence). If Picasso passed through, Duchamp passed out of, the various schools and styles of modern painting, both with extraordinary virtuosity and mastery. On the other hand, "Picasso's nihilism is of a different moral and intellectual order from Duchamp's skepticism . . ."[66] Picasso, though a great artist, was "supremely incredulous, and therefore superstitious (which is why he could embrace communism at the very moment of Stalinism) . . . Duchamp was a skeptic, like Pyrrho; and therefore he was free."[67] That makes sense only if one follows Paz in his tendentious idea of freedom; which is of course to be met in other theorists of the postmodern—in literature, for instance, it is often said to be exemplified in Joyce's late work. We might perhaps align Picasso with Brecht (in his embrace of communism) and Duchamp with Joyce and Derrida (in his skepticism) and call this a contrast between modernism and postmodernism.

It is as the phenomenon of postmodernism is established as a subject of discussion that Duchamp becomes so important. To explain the difference, as well as the continuity, between the modern and the postmodern, no other career and *oeuvre* is so useful. "When the postmodern work speaks of itself, it is no longer to proclaim its autonomy, its self-sufficiency, its transcendence; rather, it is to narrate its own contingency, insufficiency, lack of transcendence."[68] Who but Duchamp has been proclaiming that so clearly for sixty years?

But from our own perspective, we are likely to see modernism and postmodernism as belonging together, in distinction from our other options. (As Duchamp himself says, "Abstract Expressionism is just a kind of second wind of Kandinsky, Mondrian, and perhaps Kupka, about 1910. And 'pop art' is just a kind of second wind of Dada.")[69] It is, at least in Brecht, a kind of political realism which makes the artist hand over his conscience to men of power, allowing them to act on his behalf, however brutally, while artists like Joyce and Duchamp refuse to deal in political realities or probabilities, serving instead a value of freedom—freedom *from* politics, as art's equivalent for freedom *in* politics. This difference does not bear on the issue of art as a spiritual project—i.e., does not let us call either strategy more spiritual.

Gertrude Stein of course belongs with Duchamp and Joyce when we divide up artists in this way. In order to enter her world and engage in her transactions, the reader must give up his or her ordinary interests and values, including political ones, or at least all ordinary control over them. In a recent article on her "Stanzas in Meditation," Stein's autobiographical poem contemporary with *The Autobiography of Alice B. Toklas*, it has been shown how completely she subordinated theme and form to certain private games with the poem. Ulla E. Dydo shows that in the manuscript of this poem the word *may*, which occurs frequently, was everywhere changed, before typing, to the word *can*, at the expense of euphony and even of meaning, because of Toklas's jealousy of Stein's youthful love for May Bookstaver.[70] (This love affair had come to Toklas's attention that year, when the long-mislaid manuscript of Stein's novel, *Q.E.D.*, was retrieved.) Apparently Stein's manuscript books, in which she wrote by night, alone, and which Toklas picked up each morning to type, were often the mechanism by which messages about their relationship passed from one woman to the other. This is not without its equivalent in the work life of Joyce and Duchamp, both of whom allow such private allusion to play the role of chance—a role to which Duchamp gave great importance in art—and to create effects of opacity in their work. However, Stein pushes this tendency further, to the point where potential readers often feel small inclination to engage in art transactions where one might say that they will do all the work themselves—or that the artist has squandered or dissipated her credit.

Calvin Tomkins associates Duchamp with postmodernist artists in various media: with John Cage, Merce Cunningham, Robert Rauschenberg, and Yves Tinguely, saying that they all tried to break down the barriers between art and life (for instance, by giving some scope to chance), and all removed the stamp or trace of self-expression from the work. Cage wants to let sounds "be themselves," and Rauschenberg says he paints "in collaboration with his materials." They all use vulgar and ready-made materials, loving the commonplace *as such.* They are sustained by humor, and by "the knowledge that their undertaking is impossible." All that is only half the story, of course. That postmodern coolness is certainly to be found in Duchamp, but it is allied to something bitterer, more agonistic, and modernist. Shallowly hidden under his gestures of play—as under theirs—are violences of repudiation.

If we turn now to the dispersal of the people involved in the Paterson Pageant, we already know that John Reed died in Moscow in 1920. We have to treat him in this section as a posthumous presence, which he became to young left-wing Americans. Julian Street (reputed author of the shingle factory epigram about Duchamp) coined a new phrase about Reed. His article in the *Saturday Evening Post* was entitled "A Soviet Saint—the Story of John Reed."

And indeed Reed became, if not a saint, then a martyr, for a large number of American intellectuals in the 1930s. The John Reed clubs for left-wing writers were quite an important part of the Communist Party network for a few years. By 1934 there were thirty of them, with about 1,200 members. Everyone read his *Ten Days That Shook the World,* which Lenin called, in the foreword he wrote for it, "A book I should like to see published in millions of copies and translated into all languages . . . what really is the Proletarian Revolution and the Dictatorship of the Proletariat . . . John Reed's book will undoubtedly help to clear this question, which is the fundamental problem of the international Labor movement." The book was immediately translated into Russian by Lenin's wife, and used as a textbook there. It was known that Reed had been charged with affiliating the Communist Party of America with the IWW on his last journey. Reed had traveled a long way from his liaison with Mabel Dodge in 1913. In Red Square he was at the heart of the world of men and politics, while she was reconstituting the world of women and art in Taos.

Editions of Reed's books, published in Berlin in the 1950s and 1960s, present him as a revolutionary hero: a young man who was born into all the privilege of capitalist wealth, but rebelled against the injustices at its source. It is not surprising that when one of those books (*The Adventures of a Young Man*) was reissued in America in 1975, the preface, by Lawrence Ferlinghetti, claimed that Reed "knew Whitman better than Lenin," and that he had "painted himself into a corner." Ferlinghetti even alleges that Reed died in Moscow, muttering "caught in a trap, caught in a trap."[71] It is a natural self-defense for American men of letters to be skeptical about anyone who claims to have burst through the limits of capitalist freedom and belles lettres. The preface quotes Rexroth's judgment on Reed, "A sentimental imitation of Jack London," and Sinclair's, "A playboy of the social revolution." One would disregard all this, except that the volume does include a late essay by Reed, entitled "Almost Thirty," which expresses a readiness to give up his political faith:

"But I am not sure any more that the working class is capable of revolution, peaceful or otherwise; the workers are so divided and bitterly hostile to each other, so blind to their class interest. The War has been a terrible shatterer of faith in economic and political idealism . . . All I know is that my happiness is built on the misery of other people, so that I eat because others go hungry, that I am clothed when other people go almost naked through frozen cities in winter; and that fact poisons me."[72] This sounds more like Tolstoy than Lenin.

"I am 29 years old, and I know that this is the end of a part of my life, the end of youth. Sometimes it seems to me the end of the world's youth too."[73] He obviously wrote this in a very depressed mood, which was sure to change, but the mechanism of change he refers to belongs to Mabel Dodge's philosophy rather than Lenin's. "I have no idea what I shall be or do one month from now. Whenever I have tried to become some one thing, I have failed; it is only by drifting with the wind that I have found myself."[74] Drifting with the wind was a motto out of the life values philosophy of Mabel Dodge and her friends (such as Frieda Lawrence, who titled her autobiography *Not I but the Wind*). If Mabel Dodge read that passage when Reed's essay was published in 1936 (sixteen years after Reed's death, six after D. H. Lawrence's) she no doubt felt again that Reed was a boy who needed someone like her to guide him. But of course this was written before the Russian Revolution took place.

We also know that Bill Haywood got himself out of America to Moscow in 1920. He was met at the station there by Mikhail Borodin, of the Comintern. He was highly honored and introduced to all the leaders of the Soviet Union. The main task they assigned him was to build an industrial colony in Kuznetsk in western Siberia. He and Dutch-born John C. Rutgers signed a contract with Lenin to receive a steel plant and coal mines plus 20,000 acres of farmland and $300,000 of venture capital, and in return to recruit 5,000 American engineers and skilled workers to run the colony.[75] In fact only 460 came, of whom, by 1923, some 50 had already gone back to America. Haywood himself found the conditions of life in Kuznetsk so severe that he could not stay there long at a time. Later he worked for an organization to raise money for the defense of radicals in the USA, collaborating therefore with Gurley Flynn at home.

He married a Russian woman, but never really learned Russian, and was by most accounts a pathetic figure in his later years in Moscow. Mary Heaton Vorse ends her autobiography with a description of meeting him in Moscow. Because of his history he remained a resonant symbol; but it was, in America in the 1920s, a resonance of pathos and defeat—he had nothing to do in Moscow. Conlin says he died disillusioned and defeated, in homesickness, idleness, and obscurity. Emma Goldman called him a pathetic harlequin in Moscow. He failed to support her in protests against the way the Bolsheviks were prosecuting the anarchists and in 1921, at the Third Comintern meeting, when Zinoviev practically told the IWW to disband itself, Haywood protested but then withdrew his protest.[76]

When he died in 1928, his official funeral was attended by the whole group of American workers in Moscow, as well as friends and delegations. Some of his ashes were buried under the Kremlin Wall and another part in the Waldheim Cemetery in Chicago. His autobiography, *Bill Haywood's Book*, was published in Moscow the following year. There were strong suspicions as to its authenticity among his former friends, suspicions which perhaps drew their force from a desire to separate the Haywood they had known from the Bolshevik he became. Ralph Chaplin (who had himself refused an invitation to join Haywood in Moscow, to become there "the poet laureate of the world revolution") refused to review the book for the *New Masses*.[77]

Chaplin was by that time, like so many others, anti-Soviet. The review was finally written by Tresca, but he too had turned away from communism and indeed socialism. He was again an anarchist, and his main energies went into preventing the rise of a fascist movement among American Italians. (When he died, murdered, in New York in 1943, both fascist and communist agents were suspected of the deed, according to Chaplin.)

If we look in this group for an equivalent to the long career of Marcel Duchamp in the world of modern art, we shall be disappointed. (Among the artists of erotic life values, Mabel Dodge's career *is* a kind of equivalent—as an organizer of art ideas and activities.) For in his negative way, not painting himself, and questioning the very activity of painting, Duchamp remained a powerful presence. If he disappeared from the general view for a decade at a time, he kept reappearing, with increased power to stimulate and challenge younger artists. He re-embodied the intellectual dandyism of Baudelaire and Mallarmé, making a powerful rhetoric out of silences, absences, gaps, refusals, doubts. This constituted a severe check to some of the eager enterprises begun by his colleagues, or coexhibitors in the Armory Show, but he undeniably developed the potential of modern art in certain other senses of that word.

The men of politics, on the other hand, were scattered. Reed and Haywood died in the 1920s, and in an exile which in some ways paralyzed their influence in America. Moreover, the idea of the IWW also had received a severe check, not from a dandyism like Duchamp's, but from the much severer systematization of bolshevik communism, in both theoretical and organizational systems, which had come to seem more authoritative and authentic. After Paterson, and after the Wobbly trials, it seemed clear that a revolutionary workers' party had to be different, to succeed; and the obvious model was the Russian Bolshevik party. The American Communist party inherited some of the keenest and ablest Wobblies, like Flynn and Foster, and the images of Lenin and Stalin or Trotsky replaced the Stetson profile of Bill Haywood.

There is then no full equivalent for Marcel Duchamp, but there is some profit in using these terms to look at the career of Gurley Flynn, who continued to work for left-wing causes; she described herself as

278

a professional agitator, and if she seems unlike Duchamp because of the impersonality and intellectual drabness of her style, that makes her all the more representative of the option of political dedication.

She established the Workers' Defense Fund in 1918 and joined the ACLU in 1920, specializing in legal defense cases for left wingers. By 1925 this was allied to the International Labor Defense, for which Haywood worked in Moscow.

She did not in fact join the Communist party until 1937, but that was because of a ten-year hiatus in her political life, 1926 to 1936, explained by ill health, but presumably related also to her break-up with Carlo Tresca in 1925. (Her sister, Bina, bore him a child in that year, and that seems to have been a climax to a career of infidelity.) She had applied for party membership in 1926, but before it could be granted, she had been diagnosed as having heart trouble, and she moved to Portland, Oregon, to be looked after by a friend, Dr. Marie Equi. (We note again how important to her were female friends and supporters.) This was the most obvious way in which her life conformed to our pattern of dispersal.

This period of invalidism—Dr. Equi herself fell ill—stretched out to ten years, and only at William Z. Foster's urging did Flynn begin again to speak and to write for the *Daily Worker* in 1937. (She wrote a feminist column for that paper.) She was therefore again in New York City, and no longer literally an exile. But she was now a citizen not so much of the city as of the Communist party; her scope of participation was narrower than it had been in 1913. As long as the party pursued its Popular Front policy, she spoke above all to liberal groups. But when Russia signed the Nazi-Soviet Pact in 1939, that policy collapsed, and communists became objects of suspicion even to liberal organizations like the ACLU, and Gurley Flynn was expelled.

In 1941 she entered the inner circles of the party leadership, its political bureau, and especially from this point on, her life can be said to represent the idea of political system. She ran for Congress as a Communist and a feminist in 1942, and won fifty thousand votes; and in 1945 she attended and helped organize a Women's Congress in Paris.

In 1951 she was indicted under the Smith Act for conspiring to overthrow the government, and got a three-year sentence after a nine-month trial. She supported Eugene Dennis's leadership of the party, and in 1961 succeeded him herself. (That year she also attended Foster's funeral, in Moscow.) She apparently decided in 1962 that Stalin must have been mad, but she never criticized Russia or the party in public. In 1964, on another visit to Russia, she fell sick of gastroenteritis, died, and was buried in Red Square. Khrushchev stood in the honor guard, and Mrs. Khrushchev helped carry the ashes to the Kremlin Wall. (Two other national leaders of communism of the Stalin period died at the same time: Maurice Thorez of France, and Palmiro Togliatti of Italy.)

However, it would be wrong to present Gurley Flynn as outside the range of American normality because of her Communist party work. Another side of her life, her whole personality, remained heartily, almost absurdly normal.

Her entry in *Notable American Women* begins, "Elizabeth Gurley Flynn, who for more than fifty years functioned as a professional revolutionary in American society . . ." This is true, but the other side of her personality is suggested by the dedication of her second volume of autobiography, *The Alderson Story*, about her years in jail.

It is dedicated to her sister, Kathie, "who made all arrangements to publish my first book while I was in prison, also wrote articles, made speeches, and helped to carry on a campaign for my release, and who by her courage, cheerfulness, understanding and great sense of humor, helped to make my time in Alderson more bearable and my whole life, at all times, easier and happier." There was in fact a bond between her and her mother and sisters which seems to have been stronger than any bond any of them had with men—with father, husband, lovers. She was usually busy organizing women when she was not addressing strikers.[78] She organized Sunday activities for strikers' families, had women explain issues to shopkeepers, explained birth control measures, arranged picketing by women, and so on. It was also an important tactic of hers to be accompanied by club women, to protect her and her cause, by preventing the police from engaging in or allowing illegal measures. Many women of prominent families, socially and politically, accompanied her to sometimes remote areas, to be her witnesses.

Though not as profoundly imaginative as Haywood, she read and wrote poetry, and had some taste for the arts. A prison poem addressed to van Gogh's self-portrait will suggest both what she had in common with the Armory Show painters, and how she differed from them.

> *Your keen and sunken eyes look down upon us,*
> *Your models were like us—the poor, the outcast, the forsaken,*
> *The old, the toil-worn, weary and discarded,*
> *In contrast to the beautiful earth, the golden fields of Arles . . .*
> *In my memory I see your pictures once again,*
> *Plain people like yourself, the Old Woman, the Potato Eaters.*
> *Miners, weavers, farmers, your fellow artists, and above all,*
> *The yellow fields, the blue rivers, the shimmering sunlight, the*
>   *green trees.*

Van Gogh was one of the Armory Show modernists, but the spirit of this poem is close to the New York realists; the passing of time had blurred those contrasts, and it was possible to treat van Gogh—but not Duchamp—as a great humanist.

The distance between Flynn's humanist idea of art and, say, Duchamp's, can be suggested, paradoxically, by the connection between them: Katherine Dreier's sister, Mary, was an old friend of Flynn's, and one of those who sent money to her in Alderson. She was president of the Women's Trade Union League, and had been arrested on a picket line in a two-month "girls" strike of 1909. Katherine Dreier herself had engaged in such work at the beginning of her life, and van Gogh was her first great experience of modern painting. Even in the second half of her life, she clearly was trying to continue to serve those values in her propaganda for Duchamp and dada—but could do so only by palpably misinterpreting his intentions.

When Flynn died, she bequeathed her belongings to Dorothy Day's House of Hospitality. This represents the continuity and parallelism between the work of both women; in the IWW, and then, by one in the American Communist party, and by the other in the Roman

Catholic Church. Both had their dealings with art, but finally invested their energies in social-political work. Both had lived in Greenwich Village and taken the sexual freedoms it offered. Day was received in the Church in 1927. (In the same year, an old radical friend, Rayna Simons, arrived in Moscow to be trained as an agent of the party. Both had found their ways to a Promised Land—Rome and Moscow.) Each bore a child without a father and brought it up with the help of friends. And both remained true to their radical beginnings. Day operated her House of Hospitality, and brought out her *Catholic Worker*, from 1933 until her death in 1980.

Thus if Flynn on the one hand represents the idea of political system and discipline, on the other she represents the idea of nurturing, especially of children. The same was true of the early Wobbly, Mother Jones, who led a children's crusade; and of Flynn's friend, Mary Heaton Vorse, who begins her autobiography by saying that she realizes, now it is written, that it has been all about children. In fact, the first scene is of the children of Lawrence arriving in New York, their journey organized by Gurley Flynn, led by Margaret Sanger, and met by Dolly Sloan at Grand Central. We find parallels to this among the women of the life values movement—as we might expect—but if we look at the women of the modern art movement, we find works of thought and imagination, but not children: women like Gertrude Stein, Marianne Moore, Mina Loy, Georgia O'Keeffe, Katherine Dreier.

There were thus several modes of dispersal—and several mitigations, by means of which those far from New York or from the mainstreams of American life, nevertheless kept in touch and participated. Indeed it can perhaps be said that those of our subjects who remained most central to New York (that is, to the New York art world) were the least American. For it was, as we know, the modernists who fell heir to New York when the other 1913 groups dispersed; and if Gurley Flynn was almost a caricature of Middle America, in all but her politics, Marcel Duchamp was almost a caricature of the sophisticated foreigner.

10

Conclusions

*Many of the city's [New York's] most impressive
structures were planned specifically as symbolic
expressions of modernity.*

—MARSHALL BERMAN,
All That Is Solid Melts into Air

■

*T*his has been a description of two events which, as well as being interesting in themselves, expressed the spirit of their times. We have called that period 1913, but of course it cannot really be limited so precisely. Floyd Dell, in *Homecoming*, talks about the years leading up to 1913, in similar terms. In 1911, he says, "Something was in the air. Something was happening, about to happen."[1] And "The year 1912 was really an extraordinary year, in America as well as in Europe. It was the year of the election of Wilson, a symptom of immense political discontent. It was a year of intense woman-suffragist activity. In the arts it marked a new era. Color was everywhere—even in neckties."[2]

The end is as hard to fix as the beginning. Henry May, in *The End of American Innocence*, calls the movement of thought that reached America in the immediate prewar years the Liberation, to distinguish it from the Progressive era. "To see the Liberation in its dazzling colors—the colors of the Russian Ballet and Matisse—one must place it for contrast against the solid true-blue background of the Progressive Era."[3] May is particularly interested in aesthetic matters and the Armory Show, which brought in the Matisse colors.[4] Jack Yeats, he reminds us, said at the time that the fiddles were tuning up all over America; this was the Liberation.[5] And John Dewey, Max Eastman's teacher, said that the chief notes of modern ethics were "unstable equilibrium, rapid fermentation, and a succession of explosive reports."[6] But this period of aestheticism was over, May insists, by 1917. That cutoff is implausibly precise and implausibly early, but that something did fall off very sharply quite soon after the peak of 1913 is a fact which we have to try to explain.

We have chosen to look at the history of modern art through the Armory Show, and at that of radical politics through the Paterson Pageant. That strategy, it is to be hoped, has proved itself useful, because these two events not only were interesting in themselves, but had their effect on other events and people. We have spoken of the effect of the Armory Show upon galleries, collectors, exhibitions, and also directly on schools of painters and individual artists. We have seen, for instance, the check it gave to the New York realists, and the encouragement it gave to abstract art. In the other case we saw the leaders' disappointment over the results of the Pageant, and the strain it put upon their collaboration, especially the hostility which developed between Bill Haywood and Gurley Flynn. So that there is some evidence that the IWW began its fatal decline after and because of the Pageant.

The memory of these events has continued to fascinate Americans of imagination. To take just one example, John Dos Passos's right-wing novel of 1960, *Mid-Century*, contains a long description of the Paterson Pageant, including portraits of Mabel Dodge and Gurley Flynn, as well as of Bill Haywood. One of that novel's central characters, Blackie Bowman, is a Wobbly. But one of the interests of this fact is that Dos Passos had used a Wobbly (Mac) as a central character in his left-wing trilogy, *U.S.A.*, published in 1930, 1932, and 1936. (While an undergraduate at Harvard, moreover, Dos Passos was dazzled by the newest fashions in art. His work as a whole shows the influence of the Paterson Pageant, as a topic, and the Armory Show, as an idea of art.)

What is perhaps most interesting in all this is the effectiveness of the form of these events as distinct from that of their content. What does it mean that they were both shows? We have some evidence that it meant a good deal. Was it not, according to Gurley Flynn, the art of the Pageant, its entertainment value, which seduced the strikers' attention away from the serious politics of the strike? Moreover, we must make a connection between the Pageant and Greenwich Village, which "produced" it, in both the literal and in a profounder sense. Was it not, according to Mabel Dodge and her friends, the art and ideas carnival of the Village which seduced Bill Haywood away from his political commitments? And is it not significant that the big shift in radical politics in the next decades was away from Wobbly adventurousness and laughter, which had failed, toward a political style marked by severe discipline, concentrated power, and analytic rigor, which had succeeded?

In the case of the Armory Show, we have to point not to a division between 1913 and what came later, but to a continuity; not to a split but to a marriage between the Show and modern art in general. Is that not one of, for instance, Marcel Duchamp's major complaints, that during his lifetime art has become a matter of advertising and publicity? And is not Duchamp's own career a proof of how even the acutest artistic conscience must nowadays proceed by a series of provocative gestures, of tricks, aimed at an audience, and aiming at success by show business standards. As Susan Sontag says, the modern artist claims to love silence, but is forever convoking an audience of art lovers, only to insult them and dismiss them. It is a corrosive bond, this marriage, because it embodies the bad conscience of bourgeois culture. Shows are, among other things, the expression of bad conscience, an overriding of scruple and doubt, in outbursts of bravura. Perhaps then, shows are bound to betray spiritual projects.

It is worth considering the popularity of shows in the period just before 1913, a period known as the Belle Epoque as well as the American renaissance and associated with overripeness. At one extreme, in the realm of high art, we have the impresario genius of Diaghilev, whose work with exhibitions of Russian paintings in Paris can remind us of the Armory Show. His career reached its climax, of course, with his creation of the Ballets Russes, which combined the modernist painters and composers with the classical tradition of the Russian ballet and the *commedia dell'arte*. We can see Diaghilev's ballets as bringing those modern paintings and music to life—i.e., turning them into a show; and in fact both Mabel Dodge and Carl Van Vechten compared the Armory Show with the Ballets Russes; that was the natural criterion for success in that kind.

The Pageant had its high art affiliations, too; it was influenced, via Robert Edmond Jones, by Gordon Craig's work in Europe. But if we think of the large numbers of participants, and their factory work, and their presentation of their own lives, we should compare it to something quite different, to for instance, the march of the mill workers of Lawrence on January 18, 1912, when ten thousand men and women, speaking and singing, it is calculated, fifty languages, paraded through the town, making their protest, making their presence felt. The Pageant put these people on stage in a very simple and direct way. We should think of Gordon Craig's temple-theater no more than of Buffalo Bill's Wild West, which put recent and indeed contemporary history on stage. Whole tribes of Indians appeared in these shows, replaying events very important to their history. (One famous example is the story of Sitting Bull, who appeared in a Wild West show with his tribe, and then took part in the Ghost Dancer revolt, and was killed—riding his show horse—while Buffalo Bill himself took part in suppressing the revolt and scalped other Indians.)

These two opposite kinds of show, Diaghilev's and Buffalo Bill's, may serve as parentheses, enclosing the antithesis or polarity we are studying. But the antithesis is not so important as the continuity between the two—that they were two of the Greatest Shows on Earth.

This popularity of shows was a mark of both the taste for display and the optimistic idealism of that moment: the message of the new journalists, for instance, that any manifestation of life (and life measured, ultimately, in show business terms) might change the very substance of history, might alter human nature and human history. It makes a very attractive spectacle, that moment; but spectacle defines its weakness as well as its strength. When we think of the great forces of history, the great facts of history, such idealism surely seems fragile? perhaps self-destructive? What happened to the virtue and solidarity of the Paterson strikers, once they had been applauded in Madison Square Garden? Were those virtues not volatilized?

These were two giant shows, and shows were in the spirit of 1913—the New Spirit, as the Armory Show program called it. We can hear that in Mabel Dodge's account of her work for the art exhibition. "*I* was going to dynamite New York and nothing would stop me . . ."[7] She told Gertrude Stein that the Show would change New York so that nothing would ever be quite the same again.

The actual organizers also used show business language about it: Walt Kuhn to Walter Pach, December 12, 1912, "You have no idea how eager everybody is about this thing and what a tremendous thing it's going to be. Everybody is electrified when we quote the names . . ."[8] Kuhn was in fact a showman; in the 1890s he raced bicycles in country fairs, later sold souvenir pictures in Georgia and Florida, and in the 1920s wrote and produced vaudeville acts. After 1913 he tried to paint in Fauve and cubist styles, without success, and found himself with a series of portraits of stage performers, rather like Max Beckmann's: tawdrily dressed figures depicted with monumental dignity, rigid and hieratic in pose, dissonant in color; the world of show business. He was not alone in his drum-beating for the Show. John Quinn, in his speech at the opening, said, "Tonight will be the red-letter night in the history not only of American but of all modern art."[9] As Milton Brown says, "The drum-beating was almost worthy of a Barnum."[10]

And the language in which the Armory Show is written about still echoes Mabel Dodge's. "In spite of ridicule and vituperation, the sweep of art history could not be impeded by either ignorance or eloquence; American art was never the same again."[11] And, describing the criticisms leveled at the Armory Show by Kenyon Cox, "The young had joyfully abandoned that tradition, opened their eyes to the world around them, found it bristling with new ideas, full of excitement and change . . . fertile torrent . . . irrepressible need to express their vitality and enthusiasm . . . The adversary is still mediocrity, complacency and smugness. Alone in the solitude of his studio, each artist must fight the battle for originality, vitality, and truth."[12] There is the same fizzy faith, that the forces of youth and enthusiasm will always carry the day if external and fossilized resistances are removed.

The Paterson Pageant does not have the extraordinary position in American labor history which the Armory Show has in the history of American art, but Wallace Stegner's remarks about the IWW express his sense of something comparable in that institution. He says there is no satisfactory history of the union because none has "the poetic understanding which should invest any history of a militant church. From 1905 to the early 20s, the IWW was just that—a church which enlisted all the enthusiasm, idealism, rebelliousness, devotion, and selfless zeal of thousands of mainly young, mainly migrant workers."[13] This too is a faith in excitement itself.

The word *show* has two senses, which we can associate with the two grammatical categories, verb and noun. As verb, show means demonstrate, communicate; as noun it means an entertainment. The second applies most obviously to the Pageant, with a stage and performers, applause, boos, hisses, cheers, and everyone dispersing late at night, tired and excited. But then the Armory Show ended with a snake dance, and there was a band playing in the gallery, and there was much laughter at, for instance, Walt Kuhn's parody of Gertrude Stein. And it scarcely needs demonstrating that both events aimed at communicating something quite serious and difficult. It was, above all, the interchange and connection between those two meanings of the word which makes *show* a key word for understanding 1913.

It has often been noted that the Progressive era (including 1913, which might more properly be called radical) was dominated by its journalists. As compared with other forms of literature, journalism is a form of showing—it reduces all the mysteries of wisdom and tradition and research to what can be shown, to everyone, every day—and it has a jauntiness which is akin to laughter and singing and dancing. We can see this in *The Masses*, the publication which best represents the Greenwich Village audience, as well as in the two institutions, the IWW (the singing and laughing union) and the AAPS or at least the Eight (as represented by Henri, Bellows, and Luks).

The historian of *The Masses* says how "immensely useful" to that magazine was Floyd Dell's "total identification" with his own time.[14] That usefulness was partly that he thereby made his readers identify with *him*. But by the same token that identification invites a later generation to turn away or to feel themselves at a distance. Such a writer lacks the permanence of the scholar or the prophet, whose truth is always theirs alone and not shared by the daily paper.

Perhaps we can both show the attractiveness of this mode of faith and knowledge, and suggest its weaknesses, by relating it to the case of H. G. Wells, taken so seriously in this same era, and neglected so soon after. As serious a socialist as Orwell acknowledged the strong formative influence on him of Wells, at more or less this moment; and yet when we now look back to what Wells said and did, we surely find him trivial, next to the real socialist heroes.

Wells was in literal fact a strong influence on these people. The editor of *The Masses*, Floyd Dell, in his intellectual autobiography, says, "Something happened to make us lose our interest in death and renew our interest in life. What happened to us was H. G. Wells."[15] Wells's effect Dell describes in these terms: "His voice was the wild west wind, from whose presence the dead leaves of old esthetic creeds and pessimistic philosophies scattered . . . a Shelleyan wind, prophetic of the Spring." He told them about grim things to come; the Great War and the famine and debacle that would follow; but he induced them to dedicate their lives to that future gaily, developing their curiosity and remaining individualists.[16] He had the high-spirited light-heartedness of 1913, so attractive at the time, and so quickly faded and foolish-looking.

He was a journalist, in the pejorative as well as the descriptive sense; a journalist, by the standards of both literature and politics, both modernism and revolution. He embodied the spirit of his times, but he did not commit himself to either of its great spiritual projects, and so he has been rejected. That judgment—on him and on the spirit of 1913—is harsh and even unfair. Such are the verdicts of history, which always deserve to be resisted. But it would be hard to reverse this one, as yet.

In all shows and in all journalism, there is likely to be felt, as in the Paterson Pageant, a contradiction between the idea of entertainment and enjoyment, and the aspiration to promote the workers' cause. We saw that contradiction expressed by Elizabeth Gurley Flynn, but we can see it put more theoretically by Susan Sontag again. She sees a fundamental incompatibility between art and radical politics—at least of a left-wing kind. "The key to understanding 'fascist aesthetics', I think, is seeing that a 'communist aesthetics' is probably a contradiction in terms. Hence, the mediocrity and staleness of the art promoted in communist countries. And when official art in the Soviet Union and China isn't resolutely old-fashioned, it is, objectively, fascist. Unlike the ideal communist society, which is totally didactic—turning every institution into a school—the fascist ideal is to mobilize everybody into a kind of national *Gesamtkunstwerk*: making the whole society into a theater . . . the moralism of *serious* communist societies not only wipes out the autonomy of the aesthetic but makes it impossible to produce art (in the modern sense) at all."[17]

The seriousness of left radicalism since 1913 thus expresses itself in part by its suspicion of art like the Pageant. And the seriousness of modern aesthetics expresses itself in Sontag's rejection of everything *not* "art in the modern sense." Thus the gay, inclusive, experimental spirit of 1913 remains attractive to us, but . . . only attractive.

Notes

1 DEFINITIONS

1. Susan Sontag, *A Susan Sontag Reader* (New York, 1982), p. 181.
2. Ibid., p. 184.
3. Mary Heaton Vorse, *A Footnote to Folly* (New York, 1935), p. 13.
4. Anne Huber Tripp, *The I.W.W. and the Paterson Silk Strike of 1913* (Urbana, Ill., 1987), p. 76.
5. Elizabeth Gurley Flynn, a speech printed in *The Industrial Worker*, February 3, 1917.
6. Michel Sanouillet, *Salt Seller* (New York, 1973), p. 133.
7. Ralph Adams Cram, *Decadence* (Boston, 1893), p. 27.

2 THE SHOW, THE PAGEANT, AND THE AUDIENCE

1. Milton W. Brown, in *The 1913 Armory Show Fiftieth Anniversary Exhibition* (New York, 1963), p. 164.
2. Henry W. Desmond, "The Work of McKim, Mead, and White," *Architectural Record* XX:3, September 1906, p. 117.
3. Leland Roth, *McKim, Mead, and White 1879–1915* (New York, 1977), p. 158.
4. Van Wyck Brooks, *The Wine of the Puritans* (New York, 1908), p. 11.
5. Ibid., pp. 14–15.
6. Ruth L. Bohan, *The Société Anonyme's Brooklyn Exhibition* (Ann Arbor, Mich., 1982), p. 8.
7. John Collier, *From Every Zenith* (Denver, Colo., 1963), p. 105.
8. Edmund Wilson, *Galahad and I Thought of Daisy* (New York, 1967), p. 161.
9. Ibid., pp. 88–89.
10. Caroline Ware, *Greenwich Village 1920–1930* (Boston, 1935), pp. 10–11.
11. Ibid., p. 17.

12. Ibid., p. 105.
13. Arthur F. Wertheim, *The New York Little Renaissance 1908–1917* (New York, 1976).
14. Ware, op. cit., p. 95.
15. Arthur and Barbara Gelb, *O'Neill* (New York, 1962), p. 284.
16. Henry F. May, *The End of American Innocence* (New York, 1959), p. 253.
17. William O'Neill, ed., *Echoes of Revolt: The Masses 1911–1917* (Chicago, 1966), p. 6.
18. Ibid., p. 5.
19. Ibid., p. 19.
20. Ibid., p. 27.
21. Floyd Dell, *Intellectual Vagabondage* (New York, 1926), p. 139.
22. Ibid., p. 161.
23. Ibid., p. 176.
24. O'Neill, op. cit., p. 23.
25. Ibid., p. 134.
26. Russell M. Horton, *Lincoln Steffens* (New York, 1974), p. 90.
27. Wertheim, op. cit., p. 65.
28. Richard Hofstadter, *The Age of Reform* (New York, 1955), p. 186.
29. Hutchins Hapgood, *The Spirit of the Ghetto*, ed. Moses Rischin (Cambridge, Mass., 1967), p. vii.
30. Ibid., p. xvi.
31. Michael D. Marcaccio, *The Hapgoods* (Charlottesville, Va., 1977), p. 561.
32. Art Young, *On My Way* (New York, 1928), p. 134.
33. Hutchins Hapgood, *A Victorian in the Modern World* (Seattle, Wash., 1972), pp. 118–19.
34. Max Eastman, *Heroes I Have Known* (New York, 1942), p. 2.
35. Ibid., p. 106.
36. Ibid., p. xiv.
37. Ibid., p. xv.
38. Margaret Sanger, *An Autobiography* (New York, 1970), p. 68.
39. Ibid., p. 69.
40. Madeline Gray, *Margaret Sanger* (New York, 1979), p. 59.
41. Ibid., p. 50.
42. Irving Howe, *The World of Our Fathers* (New York, 1976), p. 408.
43. Rischin, op. cit., p. xxxvi.
44. Marcaccio, op. cit., p. 151.
45. Ibid., p. 67.
46. Winifred L. Frazer, *Mabel Dodge Luhan* (Boston, 1984), p. 41.
47. Peter Carlson, *Roughneck* (New York, 1983), p. 26.
48. Bill Haywood, *Bill Haywood's Book* (New York, 1929), p. 43.
49. Bert Cochran, "The Achievement of Debs," in Harvey Goldberg, ed., *American Radicals* (New York, 1957), p. 167.

50. John Stuart, ed., *The Education of John Reed* (Berlin, 1955), p. 38.
51. Melvyn Dubofsky, *We Shall All Be One* (Chicago, 1955), p. 25.
52. Ibid.
53. Haywood, op. cit., p. 133.
54. Carlson, op.cit., pp. 146–47.
55. Louis Untermeyer, *From Another World* (New York, 1939), p. 38.
56. Hutchins Hapgood, *The Spirit of Labor* (New York, 1907), p. 14.
57. Louis Adamic, *Dynamite* (New York, 1931), epigraph to Part I.
58. Ibid., p. 137.
59. William H. and William N. Goetzmann, *The West of the Imagination* (New York, 1986), pp. 216, 242, 246.
60. Ibid., p. 238.
61. Ibid.
62. Ibid., pp. 254–55.
63. Ibid., p. 246.
64. Van Wyck Brooks, *John Sloan: A Painter's Life* (New York, 1955), p. 17.
65. Gertrude Stein, *Lectures in America* (New York, 1935), pp. 14–15.
66. Ibid., p. 18.
67. Ibid., p. 161.
68. Ibid., p. 166.
69. Gertrude Stein, *Geographical History of America* (New York, 1973), p. 93.
70. Gertrude Stein, *Writings and Lectures* (London, 1967), pp. 412–13.
71. Brooks, *The Wine of the Puritans*, p. 114.
72. Edward D. Fry, *Cubism* (London, 1978), p. 49.
73. Pierre Cabanne, *Dialogues with Marcel Duchamp* (New York, 1971), p. 39.
74. Dell, op. cit., pp. 196–97.
75. Brooks, *The Wine of the Puritans*, pp. 28–29.
76. Ibid., p. 32.
77. Ibid., p. 49.
78. John Marin, *Letters of John Marin*, ed. Herbert J. Seligmann (New York, 1931).
79. Daniel Aaron, *Writers on the Left* (New York, 1974), p. 7.
80. Eastman, op. cit., p. 213.
81. Eric Homberger, *American Writers and Radical Politics 1900 to 1939* (London, 1986), p. 80.
82. Gertrude Stein, *Geographical History of America*, p. 144.

3 THE SALONS

1. Lois P. Rudnick, *Mabel Dodge Luhan: New Woman, New Worlds* (Albuquerque, N.M., 1984), p. x.
2. Mabel Dodge Luhan, *European Experiences* (New York, 1935), pp. 16–17.

3. Maurice Sterne, *Shadow and Light* (New York, 1965), p. 121.
4. Luhan, *European Experiences*, p. 60.
5. Max Eastman, *The Enjoyment of Living* (New York, 1948), p. 523.
6. Ibid.
7. Ronald Steel, *Walter Lippmann and the American Century* (New York, 1980), p. 49.
8. Walter Lippmann, *Public Persons*, ed. Gilbert E. Harrison (New York, 1976), p. 126.
9. Mabel Dodge Luhan, *Movers and Shakers* (New York, 1936), p. 432.
10. Walter Lippmann, *Preface to Politics* (New York, 1913), p. 6.
11. Luhan, *Movers and Shakers*, p. 4.
12. Ibid.
13. Luhan, *Movers and Shakers*, pp. 92–93.
14. Ibid., p. 80.
15. Ibid., p. 37.
16. Eastman, *The Enjoyment of Living*, p. 525.
17. See manuscript in the Luhan collection at Beinecke Library, Yale University.
18. Luhan, *Movers and Shakers*, p. 73
19. Ibid., p. 199
20. Carl Van Vechten, *Peter Whiffle* (New York, 1922), p. 119.
21. Ibid., p. 125.
22. Ibid., p. 123.
23. Ibid., pp. 109–10.
24. Max Eastman, *Venture* (New York, 1927), p. 209.
25. Ibid., p. 210.
26. Ibid., p. 211.
27. Walter Lippmann, *Drift and Mastery* (New York, 1914), p. 25.
28. Ibid., pp. 16–17.
29. Ibid.
30. Rudnick, op. cit., p. 65.
31. Justin Kaplan, *Lincoln Steffens* (New York, 1974), p. 201.
32. Lincoln Steffens, *The Autobiography* (New York, 1931), p. 656.
33. Edmund Wilson, op. cit., p. 57.
34. Sterne, op. cit., p. 43.
35. Ibid., p. 44.
36. Dickran Tashjian, *William Carlos Williams and the American Scene* (Whitney Museum, New York, 1979), p. 50.
37. Sterne, op. cit., p. 48.
38. Janet Hobhouse, *Everybody Who Was Anybody* (New York, 1975), p. 78.
39. Alfred Werner, *Max Weber* (New York, 1975), p. 19.
40. Van Deren Coke, *Andrew Dasburg* (Albuquerque, N. M., 1979).
41. MacKinley Helm, *John Marin* (Boston, 1948), p. 22.

42. *Four Americans in Paris* (Museum of Modern Art, New York, 1970), p. 13.
43. Hobhouse, op. cit., p. 76.
44. Marsden Hartley, *Adventures in the Arts* (New York, 1921), p. 194.
45. Luhan, *European Experiences*, p. 324.
46. Ibid., p. 327.
47. Ibid., p. 326.
48. Leo Stein, *Journey into the Self* (New York, 1950), p. 218.
49. Luhan, *European Experiences*, p. 326.
50. Leo Stein, op. cit., p. 52.
51. Ibid., p. xii.
52. Ernest Crosby, *Edward Carpenter: Poet and Prophet* (Philadelphia, 1901), p. 50.
53. Leo Stein, op. cit., p. 119.
54. Luhan, *European Experiences*, pp. 321–22.
55. Bruce St. John, *John Sloan's New York Scene* (New York, 1965), p. 75.
56. Fry, op. cit., p. 14.
57. Ibid., p. 15.
58. Gertrude Stein, *Lectures in America* (New York, 1935), p. 66.
59. Ibid., p. 67.
60. Rudnick, op. cit., pp. 45–46.
61. Gertrude Stein, *The Autobiography of Alice B. Toklas* (New York, 1933), p. 39.
62. Ibid., p. 259.
63. Ibid., p. 111.
64. Gertrude Stein, *Everybody's Autobiography* (New York, 1937), p. 21.
65. Gertrude Stein, *The Autobiography of Alice B. Toklas*, p. 259.
66. John Golding, *Cubism: A History and an Analysis 1907–14* (Philadelphia, 1968), p. 37.
67. Mark Roskill, *The Interpretation of Cubism* (Philadelphia, 1985), p. 37.
68. Ibid., p. 55
69. Ibid., p. 82.
70. Ibid., p. 188.
71. Fry, op. cit., p. 9.
72. Ibid., p. 10.
73. Ibid., pp. 76–77.
74. Richard Bridgman, *Gertrude Stein in Pieces* (New York, 1970), p. 118.
75. Roskill, op. cit., p. 169.
76. Fry, op. cit., p. 69.
77. Philip S. Foner, *The I.W.W. 1905–17* (New York, 1965), p. 151.
78. Ralph Chaplin, *Wobbly* (Chicago, 1948), p. 79.
79. Ibid., p. 11.
80. Ibid., p. 89.

81. Elizabeth Gurley Flynn, "Memories of the I.W.W.," *American Marxist Society Occasional Papers* 24 (New York, 1977), p. 4.
82. Ibid., p. 18.
83. Joyce Kornbluh, ed., *Rebel Voices: An I.W.W. Anthology* (Ann Arbor, Mich., 1964), p. 67.
84. Mark Twain, *Roughing It* (New York, 1962), p. 309.
85. Kornbluh, op. cit., p. 80.
86. Ibid., p. 82.
87. Ibid., p. 71.
88. Foner, op. cit., p. 318.
89. Kornbluh, op. cit., p. 160.
90. Foner, op. cit., p. 316.
91. Ibid., p. 317.
92. Margaret Gerteis, *Coming of Age in the I.W.W.*, Tufts University M.A. thesis, 1975.
93. Elizabeth Gurley Flynn, *Rebel Girl* (New York, 1973), p. 154.
94. Haywood, op. cit., p. 260.
95. Philip Scranton, ed., *Silk City* (New Jersey Historical Society, 1965), introduction.
96. Steve Golin, "Bimson's Mistake; or, How the Paterson Police Helped to Spread the 1913 Strike," *New Jersey History*, vol. 100 (Spring/Summer, 1982), pp. 57–86.
97. Ibid., p. 64
98. Ibid., p. 71.
99. Ibid., p. 74.
100. Scranton, ibid.
101. Tripp, op. cit., 236–37.
102. Ibid., p. 76.
103. Ibid., p. 90.
104. Haywood, op. cit., p. 269.
105. Ibid.

4 THE LEADERS

1. Robert A. Rosenstone, *Romantic Revolutionary* (New York, 1975), p. 9.
2. Granville Hicks, *John Reed: The Making of a Revolutionary* (New York, 1936), p. 5.
3. Rosenstone, op. cit., p. 10.
4. Ibid.
5. Mabel Dodge Luhan, *Intimate Memories* (New York, 1933), p. 27.
6. Ibid., p. 45.

7. Ibid., p. 122.
8. Homberger, op. cit., p. 62. See also the Appendix.
9. Luhan, *Intimate Memories*, p. 145.
10. Rosenstone, op. cit., p. 5.
11. Young, *On My Way*, p. 111.
12. Eastman, *Heroes I Have Known*, p. 219.
13. Young, op. cit., p. 112.
14. O'Neill, op. cit., p. 117.
15. Ibid., p. 122.
16. Ibid., p. 117.
17. Ibid.
18. Rosenstone, op. cit., p. 4.
19. Ibid., p. 14.
20. Ibid., p. 3.
21. Harry Kemp, *More Miles* (New York, 1926), p. 104.
22. Rosenstone, op. cit., p. 150.
23. John Stuart, ed., *The Education of John Reed* (Berlin, 1955), p. 17.
24. Quoted in Brooks, *John Sloan*, p. 55.
25. Rosenstone, op. cit., p. 98.
26. Ibid., p. 110.
27. Ibid., p. 113.
28. Ibid., p. 112.
29. Luhan, *European Experiences*, p. 47.
30. Quoted in Rudnick, op. cit., p. 35.
31. Luhan, *European Experiences*, p. 349.
32. Rudnick, op. cit., p. x.
33. Rosenstone, op. cit., p. 119.
34. Hapgood, *A Victorian in the Modern World*, p. 353.
35. Rosenstone, op. cit., p. 3.
36. Ibid., p. 131.
37. Ibid., p. 5.
38. Luhan, *Movers and Shakers*, p. 80.
39. Ibid., p. 218.
40. Rosenstone, op. cit., pp.154–56.
41. Ibid., p. 141.
42. Gertrude Stein, *The Autobiography of Alice B. Toklas*, p. 19.
43. Luhan, *Movers and Shakers*, p. 35.
44. John Malcolm Brinnin, *The Third Rose* (Boston, 1959), p. xiv.
45. Bridgman, op. cit., p. 13.
46. Hobhouse, op. cit., p. 3.
47. Bridgman, op. cit., p. 7.
48. *Four Americans in Paris*, p. 16.

49. Hobhouse, op. cit., p. 3.
50. Linda Simon, ed., *Gertrude Stein: A Composite Portrait* (New York, 1974), p. 111.
51. Gertrude Stein, *Geographical History of America* (New York, 1973).
52. *Four Americans in Paris*, p. 52.
53. Kynaston McShine, *Marcel Duchamp* (New York, 1973), p. 48.
54. Robert Lebel, *Marcel Duchamp* (London, 1959), p. 2.
55. Pierre Cabanne, *The Brothers Duchamp* (Boston, 1976), p. 18.
56. Lebel, op. cit., p. 91.
57. Cabanne, op. cit., p. 73.
58. Lebel, op. cit, p. 27.
59. Cabanne, *The Brothers Duchamp*, p. 29.
60. Cabanne, *Dialogues with Marcel Duchamp*, p. 15.
61. Man Ray, *Self-Portrait* (London, 1963), pp. 85, 241.
62. Cabanne, *Dialogues with Marcel Duchamp*, p. 10.
63. Calvin Tomkins, *The Bride and the Bachelors* (New York, 1965), p. 67.
64. Joseph Mashek, ed., *Marcel Duchamp in Perspective* (Englewood Cliffs, N. J., 1975), p. 3.
65. Ibid., p. 43.
66. Ibid., p. 91.
67. Cabanne, *Dialogues with Marcel Duchamp*, p. 32.
68. Ibid., p. 24.
69. *Four Americans in Paris*, p. 59.
70. Simon, op. cit., p. 106.
71. *Four Americans in Paris*, p. 54.
72. Brinnin, op. cit., p. 180.
73. *Four Americans in Paris*, p. 51.
74. Ibid., p. 52.
75. Gertrude Stein, *Geographical History of America*, p. 6.
76. *Four Americans in Paris*, p. 62.
77. Luhan, *Movers and Shakers*, p. 27.
78. Gertrude Stein, *The Autobiography of Alice B. Toklas*, p. 94.
79. Hobhouse, op. cit., p. 98.
80. *Four Americans in Paris*, p. 29.
81. Sterne, op. cit., p. 251.
82. Cabanne, *The Brothers Duchamp*, p. 7.
83. Sanouillet, op. cit., p. 4.
84. Cabanne, *Dialogues with Marcel Duchamp*, p. 19.
85. Ibid., p. 89.
86. Ibid., p. 16.
87. Ibid., p. 17.
88. McShine, op. cit., p. 34.

89. Haywood, op. cit., p. 28.
90. Ibid., p. 29.
91. Ibid., p. 73.
92. Joseph R. Conlin, *Big Bill Haywood and the Radical Union Movement* (Syracuse, N.Y., 1969), p. 10.
93. Ibid., p. 15.
94. Carlson, op. cit., p. 48.
95. Haywood, op. cit., p. 208.
96. Flynn, *Rebel Girl*, p. 63.
97. *Notable American Women* entry on Flynn, p. 243.
98. Flynn, *Rebel Girl*, p. 58.
99. Ibid., p. 53.
100. Flynn, "Memories of the I.W.W.," p. 3.
101. Flynn, *Rebel Girl*, p. 88.
102. Ibid., p. 85.
103. Ibid., p. 95.
104. Ibid., p. 81.
105. Ibid., p. 82.
106. Ibid., p. 90.
107. Ibid., p. 94.
108. Haywood, op. cit., p. 145.
109. Ibid., p. 160.
110. Adamic, op. cit., p. 155.
111. Haywood, op. cit., p. 219.
112. Flynn, *Rebel Girl*, p. 86.
113. Ibid., p. 113.
114. Ibid., p. 114.
115. Conlin, op. cit., p. 115.
116. Tripp, op. cit., p. 132.
117. Conlin, op. cit., p. 130.
118. Eastman, *Heroes I Have Known*, p. 18.
119. H. C. Camp, *Gurley*, Columbia University Ph. D. thesis, 1980, p. 109.
120. Ibid., p. 83
121. Eastman, *Heroes I Have Known*, p. 26
122. Camp, op. cit., p. 46.
123. Flynn, *Rebel Girl*, p. 62.
124. Vorse, op. cit., p. 8.
125. Flynn, "Memories of the I.W.W.," p. 10.
126. Flynn, *Rebel Girl*, p. 120.
127. Ibid., p. 121.
128. Hapgood, *A Victorian in the Modern World*, p. 295.
129. Ibid., p. 293.

5 THE ORGANIZATIONS

1. Milton W. Brown, *The Story of the Armory Show* (Hirschhorn Museum, Washington, D.C., 1963), p. 207.
2. Milton W. Brown, *American Painting from the Armory Show to the Depression* (Princeton, N.J., 1955), p. vi.
3. W.I. Homer, *Alfred Stieglitz and the American Avant-Garde* (New York, 1977), p. 82.
4. Young, *On My Way*, p. 200.
5. Brooks, *John Sloan*, p. 49.
6. Brooks, *The Wine of the Puritans*, p. 122.
7. Brooks, *John Sloan*, p. 191.
8. Brooks, *The Wine of the Puritans*, p. 124.
9. Walter Pach, *Queer Thing, Painting* (Freeport, N. Y., 1971), p. 25.
10. Brown, *American Painting from the Armory Show to the Depression*, p. 5.
11. Pach, op. cit., p. 30.
12. Hartley, op. cit., pp. 42–43.
13. Brown, *American Painting from the Armory Show to the Depression*, pp. 13, 15.
14. Ibid., p. vi.
15. Ibid., p. 6.
16. Pach, op. cit., p. 45.
17. Brown, *American Painting from the Armory Show to the Depression*, p. 10.
18. Hapgood, *A Victorian in the Modern World*, p. 295.
19. Guy Pène du Bois, *Artists Say the Silliest Things* (New York, 1940), p. 81.
20. Ibid., p. 82.
21. Ibid., p. 85.
22. Floyd Dell, *Homecoming* (New York, 1933), p. 251.
23. St. John, op. cit., p. 434.
24. John Sloan, *Gist of Art* (New York, 1977), p. 41.
25. St. John, op. cit., p. xx.
26. Ibid., p. 607.
27. Sloan, op. cit., p. 10.
28. Ibid., p. xvii.
29. Exhibition catalog, Moore College of Art, *John Sloan/Robert Henri: Their Philadelphia Years 1886–1904* (Philadelphia, 1976), p. 9.
30. Brown, *American Painting from the Armory Show to the Depression*, p. 12.
31. Brooks, *John Sloan*, p. 20.
32. Hapgood, *The Spirit of Labor*, p. 398.
33. May, op. cit., p. 306.
34. Eastman, *The Enjoyment of Living*, p. 400.
35. Nathanael Poussette-Dart, *Robert Henri* (New York, 1922), p. viii.
36. Ibid., p. ix.

37. Brown, *American Painting from the Armory Show to the Depression*, p. 9.
38. May, op. cit., p. 287.
39. Eastman, *Heroes I Have Known*, p. 71.
40. Ibid., p. 72.
41. Brown, *The Story of the Armory Show*, p. 39.
42. Hartley, op. cit., p. 53.
43. Ellen Berezin, *Arthur B. Davies* (Worcester Art Museum Bulletin, Worcester, Mass., 1976), p. 1.
44. *Camera Work* 41 (April/June, 1913), p. 47.
45. Homer, op. cit., p. 69.
46. Brown, *American Painting from the Armory Show to the Depression*, p. 42.
47. Homer, op. cit., p. 72.
48. *Camera Work*, p. 16.
49. Brown, *American Painting from the Armory Show to the Depression*, p. 39.
50. Ibid., p. 42.
51. Linda Dalrymple Henderson, "Mabel Dodge, Gertrude Stein, and Max Weber: A Fourth Dimensional Trio," *Arts* (September 1982), p. 108.
52. Werner, op. cit., pp.18, 23.
53. Homberger, op. cit., p. 163.
54. Foner, op. cit., p. 21.
55. Ibid., p. 147.
56. Charles Ashleigh, *Rambling Kid* (London, 1930), p. 92.
57. Ibid., p. 123.
58. Ibid., p. 109.
59. Dubofsky, op. cit., pp. 5–6.
60. Ibid., p. 13.
61. Patrick Renshaw, *The Wobblies* (New York, 1967), p. 50.
62. Ibid., p. 60.
63. *Survey* XXX (April/September 1913), p. 355.
64. Ibid., pp.358–59.
65. James B. Gilbert, *Writers and Partisans* (New York, 1968), p. 11.
66. Foner, op. cit., p. 162.
67. Ibid., p. 164.
68. Ibid., p. 148.
69. Conlin, op. cit., p. 109.
70. Ibid., p. 113.
71. Kornbluh, op. cit., p. 1.
72. *Survey* XXVII, p. 1633.
73. Chaplin, op. cit., p. 194.
74. Ibid., p. 188.
75. Kornbluh, op. cit., p. 202.
76. Conlin, op. cit., p. 25.
77. Ibid., p. 23.

78. Renshaw, op. cit., p. 47.
79. Ibid., p. 29.
80. Gerteis, op. cit., p. 43.
81. Steve Golin, "The Unity and Strategy of the Paterson Silk Manufacturers in the Great Strike," in *Silk City*, ed. Philip Scranton (New Jersey Historical Society, 1985).
82. Kornbluh, op. cit., p. 27.
83. Hapgood, *The Spirit of Labor*, p. 12.
84. Ibid., p. 17.
85. Ibid., p. 103.
86. Ibid., p. 402.
87. Nels Anderson, *The Milk and Honey Route* (New York, 1931), p. 16.
88. Hapgood, *The Spirit of Labor*, p. 42.
89. Haywood, op. cit., p. 127.
90. Ibid., p. 84.
91. Chaplin, op. cit., p. 182.
92. Ibid., p. 88.
93. Linda Nochlin, "The Paterson Pageant," *Art in America* (May/June, 1974), pp. 64–68.
94. Percy MacKaye, *Caliban* (New York, 1916), p. xvi.
95. *Percy MacKaye on His 50th Birthday: A Symposium* (Dartmouth, Mass., 1928), p. 21.
96. Ibid., p. 31.
97. Ibid., p. 48.
98. Hapgood, *A Victorian in the Modern World*, p. 294.
99. Ibid.
100. Ibid.

6 THE SHOW

1. Brown, *The Story of the Armory Show*, passim.
2. Ibid., p. 68.
3. *Camera Work*, p. 16.
4. Pach, op. cit., p. 207.
5. Brown, *The 1913 Armory Show Fiftieth Anniversary Exhibition*, p. 157.
6. Arthur J. Eddy, *Cubists and Post-Impressionists* (Chicago, 1914), p. 112.
7. Sterne, op. cit., p. xxx.
8. Brown, *The Story of the Armory Show*, p. 136.
9. Jerome Myers, *Artist in Manhattan* (New York, 1940), p. 36.
10. Ibid., p. 32.
11. Ibid., p. 41.
12. Du Bois, op. cit., pp. 86–87.

13. Ibid.
14. Brown, *The Story of the Armory Show*, p. 139.
15. Ibid.
16. Brown, *The 1913 Armory Show Fiftieth Anniversary Exhibition*, p. 36.
17. Ibid., p. 164.
18. Ibid., p. 5.
19. Ibid., p. 165.
20. Ibid., p. 168.
21. Brown, *American Painting from the Armory Show to the Depression*, p. 54.
22. *The New Review*, December 1913, pp. 964–70.
23. Aaron, op. cit., p. 15.
24. Brown, *The Story of the Armory Show*, p. 152.
25. Ibid., pp. 155–56.
26. Hapgood, *A Victorian in the Modern World*, pp. 340–41.
27. Rudnick, op. cit., p. 87.
28. Hapgood, *A Victorian in the Modern World*, pp. 341–42.
29. May, op. cit., pp. 17–18.
30. Pach, op. cit., p. 200.
31. Brown, *The 1913 Armory Show Fiftieth Anniversary Exhibition*, pp. 160–61.
32. Du Bois, op. cit., p. 88.
33. Ibid., p. 91.
34. Sloan, *Gist of Art*, p. xliii.
35. Myers, op. cit., pp. 36–37.
36. Du Bois, op. cit., p. 83.
37. William A. Camfield, *Francis Picabia* (Princeton, N. J., 1979), p. 44.
38. Aaron Sheon, "1913: Forgotten Cubist Exhibitions in America," *Art in America* (March 1983), pp. 93–107.
39. Brown, *The Story of the Armory Show*, p. 97.
40. Sloan, *Gist of Art*, p. vi.
41. Ibid.
42. Exhibition catalog, *John Sloan/Robert Henri*, p. 28.
43. St. John, op. cit., p. 382.
44. Pach, op. cit., p. 158.
45. Brown, *The Modern Spirit: American Painting 1908–1935* (Arts Council, London, 1977), p. 22.

7 THE PAGEANT

1. *The Independent*, June 19, 1913, p. 1306.
2. Steve Golin, "Defeat Becomes Disaster: The Paterson Strike of 1913 and the Decline of the I.W.W.," *Labor History* 24/2 (Spring 1983), pp. 223–48, p. 235.

3. Steve Golin, "The Paterson Pageant: Success or Failure?" *Socialist Review* 69 (1983), pp. 45–71, p. 52.

4. Foner, op. cit., p. 365.

5. This letter is among the John Reed papers at Houghton Library at Harvard University.

6. Robert A. M. Stern, *New York 1900* (New York, 1983), p. 151.

7. Luhan, *Movers and Shakers*, p. 205.

8. *The New York Times*, June 9, 1913.

9. *The Call*, June 9, 1913, p. 57.

10. Ibid.

11. Hicks, op. cit., p. 101.

12. Stuart, op. cit., p. 52.

13. Reed, *The Adventures of a Young Man* (San Francisco, 1975), p. 141.

14. Hapgood, *A Victorian in the Modern World*, pp. 351–52.

15. See "The Pageant as a Form of Propaganda," *Current Opinion* (August 1913).

16. Ibid., p. 80.

17. Ibid.

18. *Survey*, June 28, 1913, p. 428.

19. Susan Glaspell, *The Road to the Temple* (New York, 1927), pp. 250, 258.

20. Ibid., pp. 252–53.

21. Ibid.

22. Flynn, *Rebel Girl*, p. 168.

23. Gerteis, op. cit., p. 113.

24. Vorse, op. cit., p. 53.

25. Golin, "The Paterson Pageant," p. 65.

26. Luhan, *Movers and Shakers*, p. 59.

27. Ibid., p. 89.

28. Ibid., p. 116.

29. Ibid., p. 187.

30. Reed, *The Adventures of a Young Man*, p. 142.

31. Luhan, *Movers and Shakers*, p. 210.

32. Tripp., op. cit., p. 151.

33. Golin, "Defeat Becomes Disaster," pp. 224–25.

34. Ibid., p. 225.

35. Sanger, *An Autobiography*, p. 84.

36. Golin, "Defeat Becomes Disaster," p. 236.

37. Golin, "The Paterson Pageant," pp. 45–46.

38. Chaplin, op. cit., p. 140.

39. Golin, "The Paterson Pageant," p. 45.

40. Golin, "Defeat Becomes Disaster," p. 223.

41. Golin, "The Paterson Pageant," p. 65.

42. Ibid., p. 67.

8 THE CHECK:1913–1920

1. Rosenstone, op. cit., p. 151.
2. Ibid., p. 154.
3. Reed, *The Adventures of a Young Man*, p. 143.
4. Hapgood, *A Victorian in the Modern World*, p. 407.
5. Ibid., p. 400.
6. Stuart, op. cit., p. 191.
7. Brooks, *John Sloan*, p. 123.
8. Ibid., p. 98.
9. Werner, op. cit., p. 29.
10. Max Weber, *Essays on Art* (New York, 1916), p. 28.
11. Ibid., p. 27.
12. Ibid., p. 37.
13. Cabanne, *Dialogues with Marcel Duchamp*, p. 54.
14. Homer, op. cit., p. 185.
15. Dickran Tashjian, *Skyscraper Primitives* (Middletown, Conn., 1975), p. 49.
16. Le Corbusier, *Toward a New Architecture* (New York, 1960), p. 33.
17. Patrick L. Stewart, "The European Art Invasion: American Art and the Arensberg Circle, 1914–18," *Arts* LI/9 (May 1977), pp. 108–12.
18. Brown, *The Modern Spirit: American Painting 1908–1935*, p. 24.
19. Lewis Mumford, *Technics and Civilization* (New York, 1934), p. 334.
20. A.C. Ritchie, *Charles Demuth* (New York, 1950).
21. Hapgood, *A Victorian in the Modern World*, p. 219.
22. Ibid., p. 331.
23. Eastman, *Heroes I Have Known*, p. 220.
24. Ibid., p. 234.
25. Mel Piehl, *Breaking Bread* (Philadelphia, 1982), p. 11.
26. William Miller, *Dorothy Day* (New York, 1982), p. 62.
27. Young, *On My Way*, p. 126.
28. William Carlos Williams, *The Autobiography of William Carlos Williams* (New York, 1951), p. 134.
29. William Carlos Williams, *Collected Poems*, Vol. I (New York, 1986), p. 112.
30. Williams, *The Autobiography of William Carlos Williams*, p. 137.
31. Bram Dijkstra, ed., *A Recognizable Image* (New York, 1978), p. 12.
32. Tashjian, op. cit., p. 73.
33. Haywood, op. cit., p. 280.
34. Renshaw, op. cit., p. 216.
35. Harrison, op. cit., p. 42.
36. Young, *On My Way*, p. 158.

37. "The Secret of War," in the Luhan papers at Beinecke Library, Yale University.
38. Quoted by Sterne in *Shadow and Light*, p. 112.
39. Ibid., p. 126.
40. Ibid., p. 56.
41. Ibid., p. 90.
42. Ibid., p. 111.
43. Luhan, *Movers and Shakers*, p. 352.
44. Sterne, op. cit., p. 136.
45. Coke, op. cit., p. 53.
46. Eastman, *Heroes I Have Known*, p. 58.
47. Tomkins, *The Bride and the Bachelors*, p. 36.
48. Cabanne, *The Brothers Duchamp*, p. 139.
49. Calvin Tomkins, *The World of Marcel Duchamp* (New York, 1966), p. 36.
50. Moira Roth, "Marcel Duchamp in America: A Self Ready-Made," *Arts*, pp. 92–96.
51. Ibid., p. 94.
52. Ruth L. Bohan, "Katherine Sophie Dreier and New York Dada," *Arts* LI/9 (May 1977), pp. 97–101.
53. Ruth L. Bohan, *The Société Anonyme's Brooklyn Exhibition*, p. xviii.
54. Ibid., p. 12.
55. Ibid., p. 11.
56. Robert L. Herbert, Eleanor S. Apter, and Elise H. Kenney, *Société Anonyme Catalog* (New Haven, Conn., 1984), p. 12.
57. Ibid., p. 14.
58. Stuart, op. cit., p. 211.
59. Chaplin, op. cit., p. 245.
60. Haywood, op. cit., p. 361.
61. Luhan, *Movers and Shakers*, p. 421.
62. Eastman, *Heroes I Have Known*, p. 222.
63. Rosenstone, op. cit., p. 328.
64. P.F. Palermo, *Lincoln Steffens* (Boston, 1978), p. 119.
65. Collier, op. cit., p. 101.
66. Tomkins, *The World of Marcel Duchamp*, p. 56.
67. Ibid., p. 57.
68. Ibid., p. 58.
69. Ibid., p. 65.
70. Homer, op. cit., p. 182.
71. Tomkins, *The Bride and the Bachelors*, p. 26.
72. Ibid.
73. Jean Clair, *Marcel Duchamp ou le grand fictif* (Paris, 1975), p. 9.
74. Ibid., p. 45.
75. Michel Carrouges, *Les Machines Célibataires* (Paris, 1954), p. 8.

76. Ibid., p. 59.
77. Ruth L. Bohan, "Katherine Sophie Dreier and New York Dada," pp. 97–101.
78. Cabanne, *Dialogues with Marcel Duchamp*, p. 48.
79. Hartley, op. cit., p. 247.
80. Ibid., p. 248.
81. Ibid., p. 249.
82. Ibid., p. 251.

9 THE DISPERSAL

1. Williams, *The Autobiography of William Carlos Williams*, p. 174.
2. William Carlos Williams, *Imaginations*, ed. Webster Schott (New York, 1970), introduction, p. x.
3. Williams, *The Autobiography of William Carlos Williams*, p. 146.
4. Williams, *Imaginations*, p. x.
5. Linda Wagner, *Interviews with William Carlos Williams* (New York, 1976), p. 64.
6. Williams, *The Autobiography of William Carlos Williams*, p. 148.
7. Wagner, *Interviews with William Carlos Williams*, p. 102.
8. Williams, *The Autobiography of William Carlos Williams*, p. 3.
9. Wagner, *Interviews with William Carlos Williams*, p. 101.
10. Djikstra, ed., *A Recognizable Image*, p. 15.
11. Tashjian, *William Carlos Williams and the American Scene*, p. 30.
12. Williams, *The Autobiography of William Carlos Williams*, p. xii.
13. Ibid., p. 288.
14. Rudnick, op. cit., p. 149.
15. Luhan, *On the Edge of the Taos Desert* (London, 1937), p. 63.
16. Collier, op. cit., p. 10.
17. Ibid., p. 11.
18. Ibid., p. 10.
19. Ibid., p. 115.
20. Ibid., p. 68.
21. Ibid., p. 92.
22. John Collier, *The Indians of the Americas* (New York, 1947), p. 28.
23. Ibid., p. 19.
24. Ibid., p. 20.
25. Sloan, *Gist of Art*, p. 21.
26. Weber, *Essays on Art*, p. 47.
27. Ibid., p. 20.
28. Ibid., p. 26.
29. Ibid., p. 47.
30. Ibid., p. 32.

31. Helm, op. cit., p. 63.
32. Ibid., p. 80.
33. Ibid., p. 103.
34. Sterne, op. cit., p. 250.
35. Ibid., p. 248.
36. Ibid., p. 250.
37. Ibid., p. 251.
38. Ibid., p. 61.
39. Brown, *The Modern Spirit: American Painting 1908–1935*, p. 23.
40. Cleve Gray, ed., *John Marin* (New York, n.d.), p. 12.
41. Ibid., pp. 47, 54.
42. A.S. Harris and Linda Nochlin, *Women Artists 1550–1950* (New York, 1976), p. 67.
43. Pamela Allara, "The Lane Collection," *ART News* 82 (October 1983), p. 116.
44. Henri-Pierre Roché, *Victor*, in *Plan pour écrire une vie de Marcel Duchamp* (Pompidou Centre, Paris, 1977), pp. 19–20.
45. Sanouillet, op. cit., p. 130.
46. Ray, op. cit., p. 239.
47. Ibid., p. 73.
48. Barbara Zabel, "The Machine as Metaphor, Model, and Microcosm: Technology in American Art," *Arts* LVII/4 (December 1982), pp. 100–5.
49. Susan Fillin Yeh, "Charles Sheeler's 1923 'Self-Portrait'," *Arts* LII/5 (January 1978), pp. 106–9.
50. Ibid., p. 109.
51. Fry, op. cit., p. 57.
52. Francis Steegmuller, *Stories and True Stories* (Boston, 1972), p. 194.
53. Clair, op. cit., p. 18.
54. McShine, op. cit., p. 140.
55. Ibid.
56. Ray, op. cit., p. 5–6.
57. Tomkins, *The Bride and the Bachelors*, p. 18.
58. Ibid., p. 34.
59. Ibid.
60. McShine, op. cit., p. 42.
61. Bohan, *The Société Anonyme's Brooklyn Exhibition*, p. 19.
62. *The Société Anonyme Catalog*, p. 3.
63. Ibid., p. 13.
64. Brown, *The 1913 Armory Show Fiftieth Anniversary Exhibition*, p. 13.
65. Ibid.
66. Octavio Paz, *Marcel Duchamp* (New York, 1978), p. 174.
67. Ibid.

68. Craig Owens, "The Allegorical Impulse," Part 2 (*October 13, 1980*), p. 80.
69. Steegmuller, op. cit., p. 194.
70. Ulla E. Dydo, "Stanzas in Meditation: The Other Autobiography," *Chicago Review*, 35/2 (1986), pp.4–20.
71. Reed, *The Adventures of a Young Man*, p. 8.
72. Ibid., p. 141–42.
73. Ibid., p. 125.
74. Ibid., p. 126.
75. Carlson, op. cit., p. 318.
76. Conlin, op. cit., p. 207.
77. Chaplin, op. cit., p. 348.
78. Gerteis, op. cit., p. 194.

10 CONCLUSIONS

1. Dell, *Homecoming*, p. 217.
2. Ibid., p. 218.
3. May, op. cit., p. 219.
4. Ibid., p. 245.
5. Ibid., p. 221.
6. Ibid.
7. Luhan, *Movers and Shakers*, p. 36.
8. Brown, *The 1913 Armory Show Fiftieth Anniversary Exhibition*, p. 159.
9. Brown, *The Story of the Armory Show*, p. 26.
10. Ibid., p. 68.
11. Ibid., p. 27.
12. Brown, *The 1913 Armory Show Fiftieth Anniversary Exhibition*, p. 6.
13. Wallace Stegner, *The Preacher and the Slave* (Boston, 1950), p. 11.
14. O'Neill, op. cit., p. 54.
15. Dell, *Intellectual Vagabondage*, p. 221–22.
16. Ibid., pp. 225–26.
17. Sontag, op. cit., p. 331.

Index